Computer Forensics
FOR
DUMMIES®

Computer Forensics FOR DUMMIES®

by Linda Volonino
(Ph.D., MBA, CISSP, ACFE)

**and
Reynaldo Anzaldua**

(MBA, CISSP, EnCE, CHFI, IBM I-Series)

John Wiley & Sons, Inc.

Computer Forensics For Dummies®

Published by
John Wiley & Sons, Inc.
111 River Street
Hoboken, NJ 07030-5774
www.wiley.com

Copyright © 2008 by John Wiley & Sons, Inc., Hoboken, New Jersey

Published by John Wiley & Sons, Inc., Hoboken, New Jersey

Published simultaneously in Canada

For general information on our other products and services, please contact our Customer Care Department within the U.S. at 877-762-2974, outside the U.S. at 317-572-3993, or fax 317-572-4002.

For technical support, please visit www.wiley.com/techsupport.

Wiley publishes in a variety of print and electronic formats and by print-on-demand. Some material included with standard print versions of this book may not be included in e-books or in print-on-demand. If this book refers to media such as a CD or DVD that is not included in the version you purchased, you may download this material at http://booksupport.wiley.com. For more information about Wiley products, visit www.wiley.com.

Library of Congress Control Number: 2008935815

ISBN 978-0-470-37191-6 (pbk); ISBN 978-0-470-43478-9 (ebk); ISBN 978-0-470-43495-6 (ebk); ISBN 978-0-470-45783-2 (ebk)

10 9 8 7 6 5 4

WILEY

About the Authors

Linda Volonino (Ph.D., MBA, CISSP, ACFE) entered the field of computer forensics in 1998 with a Ph.D. and MBA in Information Systems. She's taught computer forensics at the State University of New York at Buffalo School of Law, and to attorneys and state Supreme Court Justices as part of Continuing Legal Education (CLE) programs, and to the FBI. In 2003, Linda was the computer forensics adviser to Michael Battle, then-U.S. Attorney for the Western District of New York. She's a computer forensics investigator and expert witness with Robson Forensic, Inc. working for plaintiff and defense lawyers in civil and criminal cases.

Linda's given many entertaining/frightening seminars, including several in Las Vegas entitled "What Goes On in Vegas, Stays." She has co-authored four textbooks; two on information technology, one on information security, and one on computer forensics — the latter with Rey Anzaldua and Jana Godwin. She's a member of InfraGard and Program Chair for the Conference on Digital Forensics, Security and Law (CDFSL 2009). She can be reached via her blog at http://computerforensicsonline.wordpress.com/.

Reynaldo Anzaldua (MBA, CISSP, EnCE, CHFI, IBM I-Series) has been doing computer forensics since 1987 when it was only thought of as data recovery and considered an arcane geek skill. He has worked the computer field spectrum from computer repair technician to Information Technology director for various firms domestic and international as well as founding several computer related firms. In his current capacity at South Texas College, Rey created a new degree in Information Security and currently instructs in a wide range of computer security subjects. As part of the community mission of South Texas College, he is also working with the State Bar of Texas to offer Continuing Legal Education (CLE) programs to help attorneys understand computer forensic issues.

Rey is often asked to comment on television, radio, and newspaper regarding topics such as computer forensics, computer security, Internet privacy issues, and identity theft. In addition to regular media, he also gives seminars and guest speaks for various civic organizations.

He is currently helping to advise members of the Texas Legislature on issues regarding computer forensics and security in addition to keeping busy with a small consulting business specializing in computer, crime scene, and DNA forensics. He has worked with clients at the local, State, Federal, and International level over the years on a wide array of forensic cases as well as co-authoring a previous book on computer forensics.

He can be reached via r.anzaldua@csi-worldwide.com, rey@southtexas college.edu, or http://computerforensicsonline.wordpress.com/.

Dedication

To my parents and children: Each one encourages me in their unique way to keep reaching higher.

— Reynaldo Anzaldua

Authors' Acknowledgments

We were most fortunate to have the world's best team working with us. Great thanks to Amy Fandrei, Acquisitions Editor, and Rebecca Senninger, Project Editor.

And very special thanks to our copy editor Becky Whitney and technical editor Brian Koerner. We're grateful to Mary Bednarek, Executive Acquisitions Director of Dummies Tech, for launching the project and Melody Layne, Business Development Account Manager, for putting us into motion. Sincere thanks.

Publisher's Acknowledgments

We're proud of this book; please send us your comments through our online registration form located at www.dummies.com/register/.

Some of the people who helped bring this book to market include the following:

Acquisitions and Editorial

Project Editor: Rebecca Senninger

Acquisitions Editor: Amy Fandrei

Copy Editor: Rebecca Whitney

Technical Editor: Brian Koerner

Editorial Manager: Leah Cameron

Editorial Assistant: Amanda Foxworth

Sr. Editorial Assistant: Cherie Case

Cartoons: Rich Tennant
(www.the5thwave.com)

Composition Services

Project Coordinator: Erin Smith

Layout and Graphics: Reuben W. Davis, Melanee Habig, Melissa K. Jester, Christine Swinford, Christine Williams

Proofreader: Broccoli Information Management

Indexer: Broccoli Information Management

Publishing and Editorial for Technology Dummies

> **Richard Swadley,** Vice President and Executive Group Publisher
>
> **Andy Cummings,** Vice President and Publisher
>
> **Mary Bednarek,** Executive Acquisitions Director
>
> **Mary C. Corder,** Editorial Director

Publishing for Consumer Dummies

> **Kathleen Nebenhaus,** Vice President and Executive Publisher

Composition Services

> **Debbie Stailey,** Director of Composition Services

Contents at a Glance

Table of Contents

Introduction

Who cares about digital footprints? Who cares about invisible trails of unshreddable electronic evidence *(e-evidence)* left by PCs and cellphones, PDAs and iPods, e-mail and social networks, visited Web sites and instant messaging, and every wireless and online activity? The sweeping answer is that you — and the many other people reading this book — care, and for good reasons. Investigators, attorneys, suspicious spouses, and the news media are *legitimately* interested in finding out what was sent over the Internet or private networks, what's stored on backup tapes or logs, and who wrote what in corporate e-mail or the blogosphere.

People concerned with what's happening to personal privacy certainly care. Anyone involved in litigation, criminal investigation, network intrusion, fraud or financial audit, marital or contract dispute, employment claim, or background check will care — sooner or later. Hardly a case goes to court — or avoids going to court — these days without the help of electronic gumshoes.

Digging up data to expose who did what and when, with whom, where, why, and how is a primary purpose of computer forensics. Computer forensics falls within the broader legal concept of *electronic discovery,* or *e-discovery,* the process of gathering data, documents, or e-mail in preparation for legal action that may lead to trial. Both these topics are serious stuff, as you soon find out in this book.

Searches for evildoers or illegal doings are now done megabyte by megabyte. But computers, network logs, and cell devices aren't only breeding grounds for proof of guilt. E-evidence can be your best alibi if you're wrongly accused. We've lightheartedly dubbed that type of evidence the *e-alibi.*

Who Should Read This Book?

Computer Forensics For Dummies was written for hands-on and armchair investigators. It's designed to give you more than just a basic understanding of digital detective work, e-discovery, computer forensics, and e-evidence. Assume that we're looking over your shoulder to guide you to do what's right and to avoid doing irreversible wrongs.

This book is for individuals concerned about how their personal information becomes digitally recorded — investigators looking for a smoking gun or smoldering e-mail held in all types of electronic media; professionals required by lawsuit or audit to turn over their e-mail or business records; information technologists facing a subpoena or discovery request for electronic documents; lawyers wanting to know how to identify and use electronically stored information (ESI) to either win or not lose a case; and members of the court who want to know how to evaluate arguments about e-discovery (costs and burdens), the admissibility of paperless evidence, and the truth that it reveals.

Anyone who needs a quick read to understand e-evidence and computer forensics will benefit from this book too. From our experience, those folks are the accused, crime victims, anyone facing discovery requests, and their lawyers.

About This Book

Computer Forensics For Dummies is an introduction to the exploding field of computer forensics and e-discovery. Computer forensics and e-evidence are important because the crime scene is where the evidence is — which makes computers and handheld devices qualify as crime scenes. So, more and more cases hinge on e-evidence.

We explain how your data gets recorded, how to find and recover data; and how lawyers try to use or refute that evidence to win their cases.

We explain — from the forensic point of view — what's important and why it's important. This nuts-and-bolts how-to guide shows you how to

- ✔ Prepare for and conduct computer forensic investigations in actual practice.

- ✔ Find out the current state of computer forensic methods, software, tools, and equipment that are generally accepted by law enforcement, the FBI, the courts, and regulatory agencies, such as the Securities and Exchange Commission (SEC).

- ✔ Conduct investigations according to generally accepted methods and avoid the risks of ignoring best practices.

- ✔ View e-evidence and computer forensics from the trenches — from the up-close perspective of investigators who work with people, companies, agencies, and their lawyers on cases involving e-evidence.

How to Use This Book

Although all topics in *Computer Forensics For Dummies* are related, they're distinct enough to fit into a modular format. You can use this book as a reference by going directly to the section related to your investigation or defense.

If you're new to crime scenes and evidentiary issues, you should understand them before tackling the technical issues. Keep in mind that you get no do-overs with evidence. Mess with evidence and you no longer have any!

If you're new to technical intricacies, you can explore how cybertrails are created and how to find them. Then move on to more advanced topics, such as identifying key search terms to locate relevant messages in response to an e-discovery request. You can find out how to dig up e-mail and documents that seemingly have been deleted, determine which Web sites a user visited, and find which key words were used to get there.

What You Don't Need to Read

Depending on your background in law, criminal justice, investigative methods, or technology, you can skip the stuff you already know. If you're the victim, the accused, the plaintiff, or the defendant, feel free to skip sections that don't relate directly to your case or predicament.

Foolish Assumptions

We make a few assumptions about your interests, motives, and job requirements. As investigators, we're hardwired to avoid preconceived notions about the crime and evidence. But, in this book, we assume that you fit one or several of these characteristics:

- ✔ You understand basic computer concepts and terms, such as *cookie* and *hard drive*.
- ✔ You use e-mail, the Internet, and other digital devices.
- ✔ You have an interest in justice. (Or should we call it e-*justice*?)
- ✔ You like detective work and solving mysteries.
- ✔ You're considering a career in computer forensics.
- ✔ You're concerned about your privacy and other civil rights.

How This Book Is Organized

This book is organized into five parts. They're modular so that you can zero in on any issues of immediate concern. The more you discover, the more you want to discover, so we're sure that you'll return to read other sections. (Don't worry: The order in which you read this book doesn't leave a trace — unless you send an e-mail or blog about it.)

Part I: Digging Out and Documenting Electronic Evidence

The book starts by introducing you to life in a digitally recorded world. You find out how digital devices create indelible records of what happened — and how logs of Internet activities accumulate into a sort of digital underworld. The focus in Part I is on how to dig out those records for use as evidence in a lawsuit or criminal investigation — to either prove guilt or defend against it. We help you understand relevant rules — rules of evidence, discovery, and civil and criminal procedure. You read about computer forensics tactics, documenting crime scenes, and getting authorization to search and seize.

Part II: Preparing to Crack the Case

This part details the legal loopholes to avoid to keep a tight forensic defense or that you should look for in your opponent's methods to your advantage. We tell you how to pick cases to get involved in and those to walk away from. You see the technical side of forensics, including how to create a forensically sound image of a hard drive. Then you jump into the art of searching to find the e-evidence you need in order to prove the case or defend against it. To break through attempts to hide evidence from you, Part II also details password cracking.

Part III: Doing Computer Forensic Investigations

To find out how to start investigating e-mail and instant messages, data storage systems, documents, mobiles, networks, and unusual hiding places, ranging in size from pockets to homes, read Part II. You see how to re-create the past from the perspective of almost anything with digital pockets.

Part IV: Succeeding in Court

Your job as a computer forensic investigator doesn't end when the e-evidence has been dug out, documented, and dissected. You memorized the laws of evidence and the rules of computer forensics to score a touchdown at trial. Now you need to survive Daubert (not to be confused with the cartoon character *Dilbert*) and defend your methods in court. Find out how to keep your cool in the court's hot seat.

Part V: The Part of Tens

Every *For Dummies* book has The Part of Tens, and we give you three top-ten lists of items that everyone interested in computer forensics should know, do, and build. Find out how to qualify for a career in computer forensics, what to do to be an excellent investigator and expert witness, and how to build a forensic lab or toolkit.

Glossary

We include a complete minidictionary of technical and legal terms used throughout this book.

About the Web Site and Blog

We're providing a place to blog with us for readers who are personally or professionally interested in technical and legal information about e-evidence and computer forensics. You can check out our blog at

```
http://cf4dummies.wordpress.com
```

You can find links to forensic software demos, documents, videos, and other digital goodies online. You can check out the Web site for this book at

```
www.dummies.com/go/computerforensics
```

Icons Used in This Book

Useful clues represented by icons highlight especially significant issues in this book. The following paragraphs (with their representative icons) give you an idea of what to expect when you see these icons.

Save yourself time and effort, and save somebody else money or grief. Computer forensics often involves high-stakes issues pitting determined adversaries against each other — ranging from megadollar civil cases to criminal cases of the worst kind. These icons flag paragraphs that can be goldmines of information.

Take an in-depth look at real-world cases and issues — both good and bad.

Computer forensic investigations can involve one booby trap after another — you're never out of the woods. And, the land mines can explode your efforts. We flag the land mines with this icon to draw your attention to killer mistakes.

We use this heads-up icon to flag certain concepts that you should keep in mind.

Technology addicts may savor the technical details of digging into the depths of the unseen digital universe, but if you don't like excruciating detail, move on.

Where to Go from Here

How many digital devices do you own that you didn't own five years ago? Two years ago? How many features do your cell devices have now that they didn't have five or two years ago? Do you wonder which devices you can't live without that haven't been developed yet? Your answers point to the inevitable growing scope of computer forensics. Certainly, computer forensics and all its specialty offshoots form an exciting field that this book helps you discover. Use it as a reference you turn to for advice, methods, and tactics about computers or the courts.

Part I
Digging Out and Documenting Electronic Evidence

The 5th Wave — By Rich Tennant

"Finding data in here is tougher than we thought."

In this part . . .

This part covers the basic component of computer forensic investigations: finding electronic data, documents, or
dirt to use as evidence. And we tell you in Chapter 1 not only
how to find it but also how to ensure that it can be used to
win or prevail in a legal action. Let's face it: If you're involved
in a computer forensic mission, it's not because you want to
recover your lost vacation photos. For less money than you
would pay for an investigation, you could redo the vacation
and retake those photos. Computer forensics is more like
the art of war — strategies and tactics to successfully navigate a tough environment, as you find out in Chapter 2.

In the first two chapters, you start to understand the number of ways in which your data and digital content get "out
there," how investigators find and recover e-evidence, and
how lawyers use the evidence to win their cases. You'll find
out about technical issues and the dumb mistakes made by
users trying to erase their tracks. Big Mistake #1 is thinking
that the Delete key is the cyberequivalent of a paper
shredder.

Mistakes stemming from delusions of grandeur can harm an
investigation, as you read in Chapter 3. If you're about to
start an examination, you have to avoid Big Mistake #2 —
jumping into an investigation without appreciating how fragile electronic data, and your posterior, are. Either one might
get damaged if you don't have the authority to proceed.
Then in Chapter 4 you see strategies from the trenches for
documenting and managing the scene of a crime.

*The thousands of criminals I have seen in 40 years of
law enforcement have had one thing in common:
Every single one was a liar.*

— J. Edgar Hoover, FBI director (1924–1972)

Chapter 1

Knowing What Your Digital Devices Create, Capture, and Pack Away — Until Revelation Day

Think of computers, cell phones, PDAs, iPods, and other handheld devices as items with durable digital brains. Imagine that a detailed copy of every e-mail, text message, document, Internet upload or download, Google search, Facebook personal chat and posting, iPhone webChatter conversation, photo, financial transaction, and address book gets packed into electronic closets.

The amount of information left in each of these places is the basic reason that criminals are caught and found guilty and lawsuits are won or lost. When you use computer forensics tools to pick these digital brains or find skeletons in electronic closets, your case takes shape with e-evidence that's tough to refute. *Electronic evidence (e-evidence,* for short) can play a starring role in the civil, criminal, matrimonial, or workplace cases you investigate. It's as though people who use digital devices and social networks missed every *CSI* episode where incriminating e-mail, cell calls, and online activity became courtroom exhibits.

In this chapter, you become familiar with the locations and staying power of the all-too-accurate electronic records of actions, decisions, and indiscretions. You want to be smarter — or at least up to speed — with your opposition. For first responders to a crime scene and people planning litigation strategy, you learn how to answer your new call of duty. Methods used to hunt through hard drives and perform digital autopsies must be generally accepted by the legal system so that your results hold up. You need to be familiar, therefore, with rules of evidence, some legal-speak, and the concept of loopholes. And, you need good report-writing skills to explain the results of your cybersleuthing in simplified detail. If the case goes to trial, so do you as an expert witness. Testifying in court is about as much fun as one person can stand.

Living and Working in a Recorded World

Ever since the World Wide Web (WWW — _the big one_) dropped into our lives in 1991, rabid growth has taken place in the personal, professional, and criminal use of computers, the Internet, e-mail, wireless tech toys, and social networks. These devices create and capture greater amounts of "digital details" that are stored in more places than most people realize. You have less chance of destroying detail-trails perfectly than of committing the perfect crime. Like the fingerprint left on the seat adjustment of a car used in a crime, a rogue digital fingerprint always lives on to tell the tale.

Once in electronic form, almost all data, documents, and other file types can be analyzed offline of the application that produced it. Computer forensics software makes this process possible by converting an entire hard drive into a single searchable file — called an _image_ — that has no hiding places.

Deleting is a misnomer

A hard drive is a big place, and data or other digital content from prior years may be retrievable in pristine condition even if someone has deleted it. In this section, we discuss how a computer operating system (OS) helps a file — and your investigation — survive.

Imagine that you compose a Word document and save it on your laptop with the filename Sand.doc. The process of saving a file on your hard disk involves three basic events:

- An entry is made into the File Allocation Table (FAT) to indicate the space where Sand.doc is stored in the Data Region. Like all files, Sand.doc is assigned (allocated) space on the hard drive. Those spaces are _clusters_. The FAT file system is supported by virtually all existing operating systems for personal computers.

- A directory entry is made to indicate Sand.doc as the filename, its size, link to the FAT, and some other information.

- Sand.doc is written to the data region. That is, it's saved to a cluster on the hard drive. (Of course, files may occupy more than one cluster, but we're keeping it simple.)

But when you decide to delete Sand.doc, only two events happen:

✔ The FAT entry for the file is *zeroed out*. That's geek-speak for "the cluster that's storing Sand.doc is declared digitally vacant and available to store another file."

✔ The first character of the directory entry filename is changed to a special character so that the operating system knows to ignore it. In effect, it's only pretending that the file isn't there.

Like many deleted files, Sand.doc remains intact because nothing has been done to it. For Sand.doc to be totally overwritten and (almost) unrecoverable requires two events:

✔ The operating system must save another file (such as Water.doc) in the exact same cluster.

✔ Water.doc must be at least as large as Sand.doc.

A computer system never truly deletes files.

If, for example, Sand.doc filled an entire cluster and Water.doc file data took up less space, remnants of Sand.doc remain and are recoverable. The unused portion of the cluster is the *slack space*. More precisely, it's the portion of the cluster not used by the new file. Figure 1-1 shows how the Sand file wasn't dissolved (so to speak) by the Water file. Slack space cannot be seen without the specialized tools you find out about in Chapter 6.

Figure 1-1:
Slack space
holds the
content of
the former
file.

When it comes to operating systems, remember these two concepts:

✔ You have no control over where the operating system saves files.

✔ The bigger the hard drive, the lower the probability that an existing deleted file will be overwritten.

Semisavvy criminals may try to outsmart the operating system by deleting the text, replacing it with non-incriminating content, and saving it with the same filename. But if they forget to account for the file size issue and compose a shorter file, remnants of the original file remain for recovery.

Online dragnet

If you're thinking that guilty parties would take action to avoid detection, follow any high-profile or murder case on CNN. Also consider the computer genius David L. Smith, who was charged with creating and unleashing the Melissa e-mail virus. Smith's claim to fame is that he was the first person prosecuted for spreading a computer virus. His Melissa creation inflicted more than $80 million in damages in 1999. He was sentenced to 20 months in the federal pen.

Smith either didn't know or didn't care that he could be identified by serial numbers in the software he created. Antivirus researchers, who tracked the activities of known virus writers, connected Smith to the online identity VicodinES. The digital fingerprints of Melissa's document serial number matched other documents on VicodinES's Web site. And, the timing of his postings gave away the region where he lived. Smith had posted the virus using a stolen America Online member's account. AOL keeps records of who calls in, and can track a person by using his Internet address.

Nothing that's digitally stored gets vaporized. Not being able to find a file that you saved just yesterday only means that you lost it. Losing a file is simply your computer's silicon sense of humor. The file is there.

Getting backed up

Workplaces have disaster-recovery and business-continuity systems that perform automatic backups. Companies are required to retain business records for audit or litigation purposes. Even if you never saved a particular file to the networked server, it might still be retained on multiple backup media somewhere. Instant, text, and voice messages exist in digital format and, therefore, are stored on the servers of your Internet service provider (ISP), cell provider, or phone company. Although text messages are more transient than e-mail, messages are stored and backed up the same way. Recipients have copies that may also be stored and backed up.

You can envision the explosion in the number of servers and hard drives that retain a copy of an e-mail message that has been CC'ed to a lot of people who then forward it on and on. Like a computer virus, e-mail evidence spreads far and wide. Your job is to find it.

E-mail is the richest source of evidence. E-mail is used as evidence of white-collar crime, fraud, trade theft, harassment, negligence, and infidelity. It is also used in violent crime cases.

Delusions of privacy danced in their headsets

You can find information relevant to almost any case on cell phones, iPods, personal digital assistants (PDAs), global positioning systems (GPS), transcripts of every word — or the letters used in place of words — in personal chats or any other forum that stores or transmit messages. Why? Because people have delusions of privacy when they're communicating with their buddies or partners in crime or friendship. E-mail and other messages share three characteristics that make them rich sources for revealing evidence. They are candid, casual, and careless.

When faced with other supporting evidence, jurors tend to believe that what is said on those devices is the honest truth.

In an IRS investigation into illegal tax shelters, eighteen accountants were indicted for tax fraud, among other charges. Exhibits that became the center-piece of evidence in taxpayer lawsuits against their firm were e-mail messages. The case depended not on how flimsy the tax shelters were, but rather on a series of incriminating e-mails in which the accountants snickered about misleading the IRS. You can guess who got the last laugh.

Giving the Third Degree to Computers, Electronics, and the Internet

E-evidence is like a vampire lurking out of sight who can be neither destroyed nor intimidated. But this seemingly indestructible evidence can be tampered with, planted, or compromised accidentally. You don't want to be the one who accidentally compromises good evidence.

Before starting your investigation, here are a few general concepts to know:

- ✔ You must use specialized computer forensics software and toolkits according to generally accepted procedures. See Chapter 6.

- ✔ As with other types of evidence, you have to carefully handle the evidence so that it isn't compromised, and you have to keep the evidence under control at all times to be able to verify that no one has tampered with it. See Chapter 4.

- ✔ You don't get a do-over after you compromise e-evidence by mishandling it. See Chapter 5.

✔ Computer forensics isn't a magic or dark art. You can't make things appear that never existed. Your objective is to find what's there. See Chapter 7.

This last point is deceivingly important. Picture this: ACME Company is facing a wrongful-termination lawsuit for firing someone wrongfully. ACME management knows that they're guilty, so they need a defense (read: cover-up). An epiphany! They think, "Let's find something incriminating on his computer that we can use to whitewash our actions. To make it believable, we'll hire a computer forensics investigator and tell her we suspect that the former employee engaged in [fill-in any deviant behavior]." It's possible that the former employee had engaged in that activity, but the investigator would clearly and correctly date her activities in the report. The scheme could work. Ethical issues crop up all the time.

Be afraid — very afraid — of do-it-yourselfers. A do-it-yourselfer may try to recover lost files or find evidence of wrongdoing that he wants to use against his nemesis. A small-business owner can download a free trial version of RecoverThatFile or NoDeal, for example, and probe through the hard drive looking for proof that an employee copied and stole customer files. When that method fails, you might be called in. You cannot magically undo the damage done by the self-search so that it's usable in a legal action.

What lurks on the computer is not only content created or downloaded by the user. Computer software, like bookies who record and track gambling bets, is also making book (for example, creating logs, temporary files, and metadata) on what's going on. You need to investigate and analyze these details thoroughly for several reasons:

✔ To collect potentially valuable data that can support or refute other e-evidence

✔ To check for signs of tampering

✔ To avoid having to explain to the court why you didn't and then suffering the consequences

You're dealing with potential evidence. Your job is to do an intensive interrogation to learn the truth about what did or did not happen. But *Dirty Harry*-style investigative methods — however justifiable in your mind — will cause you much frustration later when the e-evidence is tossed out.

Answering the Big Questions

You need to understand the two dimensions of the digital underworld and what they hold as potential evidence. The contents of both the visible and invisible dimensions can be recovered with forensics tools. General examples of each type are shown in this list:

- ✔ **Visible**

    - Documents, spreadsheets, image files, e-mail messages

    - Files and folders

    - Programs and applications

    - Link files

    - Log files

- ✔ **Invisible**

    - Deleted documents, spreadsheets, image files, e-mail messages

    - Files and folders deliberately made invisible (hidden)

    - File system artifacts

    - Internet history

    - Print jobs

    - Random Access Memory (RAM)

    - Protected storage areas (where credit card numbers entered on Web browsers are held)

    - Storage areas outside the operating system's file system (areas that aren't readable by the operating system and that make good hiding places for files, even though computer forensics software can still find them)

    - System log files

Several of these items are created not by the user but, rather, because of what the user *does*. Visible contents can be created by either the user or the machine, and so can invisible contents. In Part III, you find out more about these sources of e-evidence.

Whereas only 1 percent of crimes involve DNA evidence, more than 50 percent of cases involve some sort of e-evidence.

What is my computer doing behind my back?

The short answer to what your computer does behind your back is "plenty." When files and messages are saved or sent, computer software (that no one ever sees) automatically generates artifacts, or *metadata*. Metadata exists in virtually every electronic document. It includes information about who created the document, the date it was created, when it was last modified, and more. Figure 1-2 shows the general metadata for a .doc file. Look at the

Attributes section, near the bottom of the figure. You see that the file itself isn't hidden. Even hidden files have metadata.

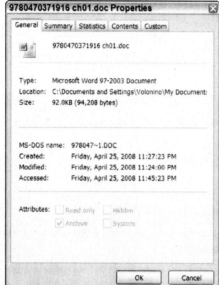

Figure 1-2:
Metadata created automatically by Word software.

Unlike other forms of evidence, e-evidence tends to be more complete, can show intent or behavior patterns, and is harder to refute or deny. For example, metadata can be as revealing as a fingerprint or ballistic print. It can reveal the names of everyone who has worked on or viewed a specific document, text and comments that have been deleted, and different drafts of the document.

Can you hear me now?

Cell phones are another revealing source of data. Think about what you have stored and saved on your cell — and what you would feel if someone stole your phone. When you watch the TV show *Law and Order,* you hear a detective tell someone to "dump the phone." That person is referring to finding evidence — not to dumping Verizon for Vonage.

The 2004 Kobe Bryant case was the first high-profile U.S. criminal case involving cell phone text messages. A judge granted Bryant's attorneys access to cell phone text messages sent among three people — including the accuser — in the hours after the alleged attack. The judge ordered AT&T to produce the records of one of the accuser's friends to whom she sent text messages.

Digital communications seem anonymous, but quite the opposite is true.

Surfers Non-Anonymous

You can find out a lot about a person from the fertile trail left by her Internet activities. As e-evidence, social networks and blogs are almost too good to be true. Law enforcement can obtain text messages that were sent and received just about anywhere. People hurl information about themselves from Facebook and MySpace *and* chat about their illegal activities. A subpoena, rather than special forensics tools, might be needed to obtain this information. E-mail or chats from social networks, like other e-mail and chats, may be admissible as evidence.

Although some posting and content may not be admissible, you can use it to develop a profile of a suspect.

The unblinking eyes of search engines

In some circumstances, search engines such as Google and Yahoo! can identify the search terms used by a specific user. Internet searches have helped put many murderers in jail. The list that Google can produce shows IP addresses or cookies, not an actual list of people, unless they have provided their names when they registered. But IP addresses can be all that's needed to pick up the trail.

An IP address is like a cell phone number for your computer. Your computer, like your cell phone, is connected to a network. To communicate with the network (the Internet, for example) and devices on it (millions of computers attached to the Internet), your computer uses its unique IP address. An IP address can be private for use on a private network, or public for use on the Internet or other public network. Figure 1-3 shows the standard format of an IP address.

An IP address is made up of four bytes (think of them as four numbers) of information. Each of the four numbers in the IP address uses 8 bits of storage. Each of the four numbers, therefore, can represent any of the 256 numbers in the range between 0 (binary 00000000) and 255 (binary 11111111). A quick calculation in your head should tell you that more than 4 billion possible different IP addresses are possible — or more precisely, $256 \times 256 \times 256 \times 256 = 4,294,967,296$.

Find the IP address of your computer and read much more about IP addresses by visiting `http://whatismyipaddress.com`.

A *cookie* is a simple text file that can collect and store data about you on the hard drive of your own computer, such as which Web pages you've visited. Many sites use cookies as a way to track visitor information or to customize information for you.

In a long, complex case, investigators backtracked through an ISP to a hotel in the U.S. and from that were able to look at travel records and figure out which person was at the hotel at the time.

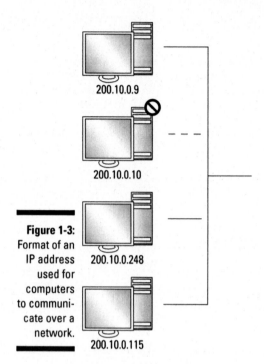

Figure 1-3:
Format of an
IP address
used for
computers
to communi-
cate over a
network.

How does my data get out there?

Google, YouTube, Yahoo!, MySpace, and their competitors aren't humanitarian efforts. These profit-driven empires deal in digital currency — personal information. Their basic business model is simple: Collect it and sell it. The more they collect, the more they have to sell. Getting the picture?

People who register with almost every social network, sign up with frequent-buyer programs (Coke and Pepsi programs, for example), fill in profiles with AOL or Gmail, use chat and text messaging, play online games while sipping lattés at Internet cafés with unsecured hot spots — their data is out there. Gullible users reveal alarming amounts of information for a chance to win an i-anything.

Think about what you do that leaves a trace. You pay for every convenience with your privacy. For example, in an E-ZPass system, both car and driver are imaged with precise times, locations, and driving speeds.

Web servers contain *logs* (these are simply text files) that record visitors' activities. Server logs act like an automatic visitor sign-in sheet.

When you gain access to those logs, some of the information you can find out is

- **The Internet Protocol (IP) address of the visitor's computer:** Every computer attached to a network has a unique address, or Internet Protocol, so that the network can interact with it. An IP address is similar to a temporary phone number. A computer can be traced by its IP address. It's even possible to identify the person at the keyboard by his unique username.

- **The information in the cache:** Users may not think to clear the cache in their computers or digital devices. A cache is similar to a closet of a computer or handheld device that stores recent data. Web pages that a user visits are stored in the computer's cache. The purpose of the cache is to speed up the computer by holding on to visited Web pages to redisplay them without having to go back through the Internet to retrieve them. Even if a user wants to clear the cache, she might not know how. It's possible to find which pages were viewed, the date and time the visitor accessed each page, and images from the *referring URL* (the Web site the user came from).

Why can data be discovered and recovered easily?

Full-feature digital devices have brains and memories. Computers do too. Despite all their capabilities, computers are unable to *truly* delete a file so that that it no longer exists. Military-strength software to eradicate digital content can be applied to a hard drive, but it can't eradicate the files that were backed up or sent out to another computer.

Many computer forensics hardware and software tools have the power to acquire the contents of a hard drive or SIM card of a cell phone. Encrypted or password-protected files do not stop the tools from accomplishing their mission — at least not all of the time. Crime-supporting tools make it more difficult to recover e-evidence. But with the proper investigative tools and methods, that evidence may still be recoverable.

Aside from the technology factor, people don't expect to get caught. Consider sunbathers at the beach who rely on the fallible method of hiding keys by ingeniously stuffing them deep into the toe of a sneaker. And don't forget all those drivers caught speeding by radar. The human factor makes it easier for the technology to recover data.

Examining Investigative Methods

Your job as a computer forensics investigator involves a series of processes to find, analyze, and preserve the relevant digital files or data for use as e-evidence. You perform those functions as part of a case. Each computer forensic case has a life cycle that starts with getting permission to invade someone else's private property. You might enter into the case at a later stage in the life cycle. Taken to completion, the case ends in court where a correct verdict is made, unless something causes the case to terminate earlier.

Getting permission

Police can't arrest people without reading them their rights. And investigators can't just show up and check or confiscate a person's computer without a search warrant — usually.

When law enforcement needs to gather evidence in a criminal case, it tends to be immediate. Generally, the FBI has the power to seize information and bank accounts, issue subpoenas or search warrants, or even break down doors in exigent circumstances.

Civil cases do not include that type of authority. In civil cases, parties need to show proof that they're entitled to evidence. Meanwhile, relevant evidence can be destroyed, lost, or deleted.

Don't touch anything until you see or receive confirmation to proceed. See Chapter 3 for more on this issue.

Choosing your forensic tools

Evidence verification depends on the use of the proper software and hardware tools, equipment, and environment. A Swiss army knife for forensics hasn't been invented. No single methodology or set of tools or crystal ball exists for conducting a computer forensics investigation. Some of the many factors affecting the choice of tools are

- Type of device
- Operating system
- Software applications
- Hardware platforms

✔ State of the data

✔ Domestic and international laws that apply

Knowing what to look for and where

This area is where the deductive art of computer forensics comes into play. The importance of this thinking stage cannot be overstated. You have to think about both sides of the situation. That is, your objective is to look for the truth about what did or did not happen. But you're restricted because you don't have unlimited time or money. Strategies for focusing and refining your search are covered in Chapter 7.

In the days of paper-only discovery, lawyers asked for and received truckloads of paper documents, sometimes brought in from distant warehouses. Their strategy involved finding the "smoking gun" document that would win the case and a huge jury verdict. Trial strategies didn't change — the nature of documents did. E-evidence for a case might fill supertankers if it were in hard copy.

Gathering evidence properly

Your goal is to have e-evidence that is admissible in court. Consider evidence as the football, and court as the goal line. Keep your eye on the evidence. Preserving e-evidence and maintaining good documentation of the steps taken during the evidence processing are essential for success.

People may lie, but the e-evidence rarely does. Prepare your e-evidence with care so that it's allowed to tell the truth.

Revealing Investigation Results

Every investigative step, from acquisition to examination of the e-evidence, may someday need to be explained in court on direct examination — and then defended on cross-examination (or *cross*). During cross, the less-than-friendly opposing lawyer tries to impeach or discredit your testimony. Mistakes create loopholes that can devastate a case.

Preparing bulletproof findings

Working in the legal system carries a huge responsibility for you to perform your work with diligence, competence, honesty, and good judgment. Those qualities are your best defense in preparing your findings.

You need to admit to any possible problems and explain why they didn't compromise the evidence. Above all, always tell the truth.

Making it through trial

Most cases don't involve eyewitnesses. Even you can't see what happened without a lot of equipment. Without the benefit of direct testimony by an eyewitness, juries and judges rely on you to "connect the dots" of the circumstantial evidence. (This topic alone warrants an entire *For Dummies* book.)

Your ability to successfully make it through trial depends on your degree of preparation — and eating a good breakfast. Fortunately, the common challenges of giving testimony in open court and the stages of a trial are covered in Part IV.

Chapter 2

Suiting Up for a Lawsuit or Criminal Investigation

*I*nvestigators routinely deal with fingerprints, skid marks, bloodstains, bullets, burned buildings, and other traces left by criminals that connect them to the crime scene. What these types of physical evidence may have in common with electronic evidence is that they have no eyewitnesses. When no one has seen or heard a crime in progress to give direct evidence about what they saw or heard, the evidence speaks for itself — so to speak — with the help of experts. It can carry more weight and credibility in a case than direct, eyewitness testimony.

E-evidence is also powerful because it has perfect memory and no reason to lie, and it can't be eliminated or intimidated by a Smith & Wesson weapon. The Achilles heel of e-evidence is that the lawyers, judges, and juries who are involved in the case may not understand the technological details and, as a result, not appreciate the relevance of the e-evidence — at least not until you fluently translate between technology and legal terms so that they can understand.

In this chapter, you find out how rules of evidence, legal procedures, and e-discovery processes converge to create admissible e-evidence — or why it fails to do so.

Deciphering the Legal Codes

Laws of evidence play a big role in the career of every type of investigator. The concept of relevancy is the foundation of evidence law. Relevancy is always the first issue regarding evidence because it's the primary basis for admitting evidence.

Here are the first two rules of evidence:

✔ Only relevant evidence is admissible.

✔ All relevant evidence is admissible unless some other rule says that it isn't admissible.

When you think about the logic of the second rule, you quickly realize that the word *unless* puts a mysterious spin on what admissible evidence is. If you think that the rule is saying, in effect, "Evidence is admissible unless it isn't admissible" — you're right! With these few basic concepts in mind, you can make sense of evidence rules.

Learning about relevancy and admissibility

With amazing power, the first rule of evidence law splits all facts in a legal action into binary parts: relevant and irrelevant. That sounds simple. It's not, though, because many "buts" are factors on the path from *relevant* to *admissible.* "Buts" fall into two categories:

✔ **Exclusions:** Rules that act like anti-rules. Evidence tagged as an exclusion reverses the rule. For example, one rule says that an e-mail message may be used as evidence. Any exclusion to that rule reverses it. Then that e-mail message isn't allowed as evidence.

✔ **Exceptions:** Rules that act like anti-exclusions. If an exception to the exclusion is found, the exclusion is ignored. In our example, the e-mail message would become admissible again.

Figure 2-1 illustrates the basic steps in determining whether e-evidence is admissible. Judges have the authority to decide whether evidence is admissible in a trial.

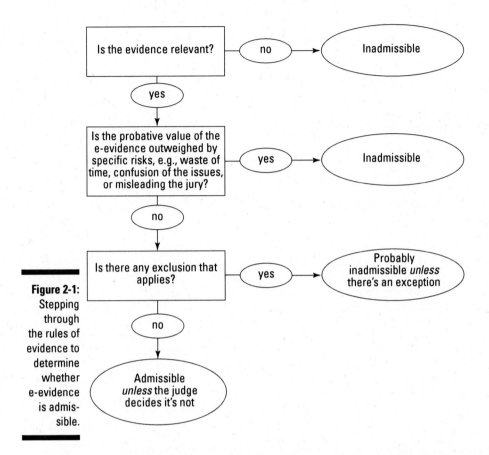

Figure 2-1:
Stepping
through
the rules of
evidence to
determine
whether
e-evidence
is admis-
sible.

Exclusions and exceptions are discussed in the later section "Playing by the rules." Legal-speak is confusing because it's so often spoken in the negative, or double negative, or worse. Expect to hear a lot of discussion in the negative or double negative; for example, the e-evidence is not inadmissible.

Exploring evidence rules in detail can cause what seems like a temporary loss of consciousness. Mercifully, some rules are obvious or apply only in obscure situations. We condense the rest into an overview of essential rules that you need to know to investigate and prepare cases.

Clutter is the nemesis of clarity — and your career. Being able to condense material and delete clutter serves you well with judges and juries.

Getting started with electronic discovery

You first deal with evidence and the rules of evidence early in a case, during *discovery,* the investigative phase of the litigation process. When you deal with e-evidence, this process is cleverly referred to as electronic discovery, or *e-discovery*. Each side has to give (or *produce*) to the other side what they need in order to prepare a case.

Discovery rules are designed to eliminate surprises. Unlike in TV dramas, surprising your opponent with information, witnesses, or experts doesn't happen. If you think about it, without rules against surprises, trials might never end! Each side would keep adding surprises.

You can think of discovery as a multistage process, most often a painful one, of identifying, collecting, searching, filtering, reviewing, and producing information for the opposing side in preparation for trial or legal action. For e-discovery, you as a computer forensic expert play a starring role, as do the software and toolset you use. Many cases settle on the basis of information that surfaces during discovery and negotiations.

E-discovery demands can become a weapon in many cases. Parties have even been forced to settle winnable cases to avoid staggering e-discovery costs. E-discovery rules try to prevent the risk of *extortion by e-discovery*. Suppose that a company estimates that defending itself in a lawsuit would cost $1.3 million for e-discovery plus other legal fees. If the company were being sued for less than e-discovery costs, the case wouldn't get to court. The company would be predisposed to settle the lawsuit to avoid the cost of the e-discovery process.

Deciding what's in and what's not

Legally, *evidence* is material used to persuade a judge or jury of the truth or falsity of a disputed fact. Rules of evidence that control which material the judge and jury can consider (what's in) and which they cannot consider (what's out) vary depending on the type of case and court. (We cover only federal court.) Three primary rules determine this in-out split:

- **Federal Rules of Evidence, or Fed. R. Evid.:** Used by federal courts to determine which evidence is relevant in civil or criminal cases. To be admissible, information must be relevant and material (useful) to a disputed issue.

- **Federal Rules of Civil Procedure, or Fed. R. Civ. P.:** Control discovery and e-discovery during civil litigation in federal court. In 2006, amendments to the Fed. R. Civ. P. specifically addressed electronically stored information, or ESI, to make e-discovery less of a guessing game. The rules were completely rewritten to make them simpler, clearer, and more specific about ESI. Now, all ESI that's relevant to a legal action, no matter how glaringly incriminating, must be made available for discovery. The jury is still out (an irresistible pun) on how helpful the new rules are. They may have made life easier for investigators by "motivating" organizations to preserve ESI and by handing out harsh penalties when it isn't preserved. You find out about these rules in greater detail in the "Managing E-Discovery" section, later in this chapter.

✔ **Federal Rules of Criminal Procedure:** Control the conduct of all criminal proceedings brought in federal courts to ensure that a defendant's rights are protected.

In ruling on the appropriateness of producing ESI in a criminal matter, Judge John M. Facciola said that it would be "foolish" to disregard Fed. R. Civ. P. because the problems associated with the production of electronic documents are the same whether the matter is civil or criminal (*United States v. O'Keefe*, Feb. 2008).

Playing by the rules

Computer forensics often deals with circumstantial *(indirect)* evidence. Circumstantial evidence in every case is divided into two categories: relevant and irrelevant. Anything that a Federal Rule or judge says is irrelevant is excluded. Relevant material remains in play, but is whittled away until all that remains is the evidence that the judge or jury uses to decide the outcome.

The judge decides which evidence is admissible. The jury decides the weight and credibility of the admissible evidence.

Common exclusionary rules and some of their exceptions are

✔ **Hearsay evidence:** This unreliable, secondhand evidence isn't allowed. But the hearsay rule has 30 exceptions. For instance, electronic and paper business records are hearsay, but business records created in the ordinary course of doing business are an exception. Therefore, e-mail and other electronic records are admissible as business records as long as their reliability can be proved.

✔ **Privilege:** Certain communications, such as between an attorney and client, are confidential and protected by law. Documents created as part of the legal preparation for a client are work product and are also privileged. Work products include documents and reports from or to a client, witness, or computer forensic investigator. Privilege applies to electronic communications and work product. You always need to be careful with your communications during a case.

✔ **Waste of time:** Evidence must have *probative value* — it must relate to an element of the case and be capable of proving something worthwhile. If it can't, the court doesn't waste its time. Evidence that needlessly delays a trial because it has no reasonable connection to the disputed issues is excluded.

✔ **Confusion of the issues or misleading the jury:** Even if the e-evidence isn't knocked out of court because of an exclusion, you must still overcome another hurdle — most jurors don't understand computers beyond the basic familiarity needed to operate them (such as sending e-mail and searching the Internet). And, the education level of the typical juror is roughly eighth grade. Not confusing or misleading this group may be your greatest challenge and triumph.

Most of the battles and decisions about what's relevant evidence and what's not takes place during e-discovery. You can see how critical this stage is. Lawyers who lose the e-discovery battle can safely expect to lose the case, unless they're saved by a technicality or other loophole. Anyone who violates the rules of discovery, either deliberately or from negligence, can also expect to feel the fury of the court. Failure to comply with electronic production obligations can lead to serious sanctions, sometimes to the tune of millions of dollars. For example, in *Best Buy v. Developers Diversified Realty* (2007), the responding parties argued that e-mails that they were ordered to produce were stored on backup media, and therefore, weren't reasonably accessible. The judge wasn't swayed by the problem and ordered that the ESI be produced within 28 days.

Lawyers can use any of these rules to influence which evidence is excluded by raising an objection based on one of them. If the judge sustains a lawyer's objection, that evidence is excluded. If the objection is overruled, the evidence remains.

In the 2007 patent infringement case over video compression patents that Qualcomm brought against Broadcom Corp., it was learned during trial that Qualcomm failed to produce relevant e-mail. It produced 1.2 million pages of marginally relevant documents while hiding 46,000 critically important ones. Qualcomm argued that its attorneys failed to produce the evidence. The 19 attorneys argued that they had been hoodwinked by their client. The judge didn't believe either side and sanctioned them both.

Managing E-Discovery

E-discovery is a brawl between two opposing sides: the requesting party and the responding (or producing) party. This brawl is hostile, ugly, and subject to the Federal Rules (see the previous section).

Here's how e-discovery works:

1. The requesting party submits questions to the opposing party to learn the lay of the opposing party's digital landscape.

2. The responding party (the *respondent*) provides answers. The answers also identify information that the responding party needs to preserve.

3. The requesting party formulates the request for the production of ESI.

4. The responding party can agree with or dispute the request. Disputes that parties can't settle are decided by the court.

In the following sections, we take a look at difficulties you have to overcome with e-discovery.

Understanding that timing is everything

In the area of e-discovery, timing is critical and you must follow the deadlines. Fed. R. Civ. P. Rule 26(f) imposes deadlines regarding e-discovery:

✔ **Rule 16, Pretrial conferences:** Requires opposing parties to meet and discuss a discovery plan and evaluate the protection and production of ESI within 99 days of the filing of a lawsuit.

✔ **Rule 26(a), initial disclosure of sources of discoverable information:** Parties must identify all sources and types of ESI to the opposing side according to a time schedule imposed by the court.

During the trial of *Z4 Technologies v. Microsoft* (2006), it came to light that certain e-mail evidence hadn't been produced during discovery and that the existence of a database wasn't disclosed. The judge ordered Microsoft to pay additional damages of $25 million plus $2 million in lawyer's fees for litigation misconduct.

When a lawsuit is filed, rules trigger and a clock starts ticking toward several deadlines. The total elapsed time from a lawsuit filing to an e-discovery plan being presented to the court is 120 days:

✔ **Day 1:** The lawsuit is filed and served on the defendant.

✔ **By Day 99:** Opposing parties must meet and confer for a planning session. From this negotiation comes an e-discovery plan. Discussion topics and questions to be settled include the ones in this list:

- What ESI is available?

- Where does the ESI reside?

- What steps will be taken to preserve ESI?

- In what forms will ESI be produced?

- What's the difficulty and cost of producing the ESI?

- What is the schedule of production?

- What are the agreements about privilege or work-product protection?

- What ESI will not be produced because it is not reasonably accessible or is an undue burden?

✔ **By Day 120:** The e-discovery plan is due to the court by the representing attorney's office, which is usually a paralegal.

If you're not armed with all details and the expert help necessary to negotiate the scope of discovery at the planning meeting, you can't possibly set up a favorable plan. The next section goes into detail about why it's so important to have a favorable plan.

Grasping ESI discovery problems

To understand how to negotiate an e-discovery plan, you have to take time to appreciate the causes of the conflict. ESI differs from paper-based information in ways that add to the complexity of e-discovery and disputes about it. This list describes several of those differences:

✔ **An exponentially greater volume of ESI exists.**

Consider all the electronic gadgets that people carry, the number of people addicted to social networking and blogging (rather than working) while at work, and the volume of texting and e-mail. Then factor in backups and the fact that nothing is deleted. Now you have a picture of why the volume of ESI far exceeds that of paper.

✔ **ESI is located in multiple places and on multiple devices.**

Portable data devices are standard equipment for many people. Imagine trying to round up handheld device and portable storage devices that might contain discoverable e-content, as well as servers and massive data warehouses.

✔ **ESI has final versions and intermediary draft versions.**

Backup systems catch draft versions and rarely does anyone even think about it — until e-discovery.

✔ **ESI has invisible but relevant metadata and embedded data.**

Most often, ESI must be produced in its native format and not be printed and submitted. The requesting party wants access to the metadata that could support its side of the case.

✔ **ESI is dependent on the system or device that created it.**

After a company's data is backed up to tape, it usually doesn't create new backups when upgrading its system. When those tapes must be restored, the company probably doesn't have the equipment to do it. The same concept applies to new accounting or financial systems. A company may need to produce 4-year-old financial records in a fraud investigation. If it has switched accounting systems, though, it can't retrieve the records.

Finding relevant and responsive data in every possible location, filtering it to remove content that is not requested or that is privileged, de-duping the data to delete duplicates, and further processing the data to produce the smallest volume can easily cost a million dollars. It costs roughly $1,000 to restore and search one tape. If a company has 20,000 backup tapes containing millions of messages, the tally for that electronic search is $20 million.

Avoiding overbroad requests

The volume and intractable sources of ESI can cause disputes about the scope of discovery. Lawyers are looking for "dirty laundry" or "smoking guns" or fighting other lawyers' attempts to uncover them. The requesting lawyer takes anything that you hand over. Your job is to limit the amount the opposing side receives.

If the requesting party demands all e-mail messages and documents contained on the defendant's laptop and Blackberry or similar device, and the passwords needed to inspect them, there's going to be a fight.

Such a broad request (all documents and e-mail messages) will fail. The reason is that courts try to limit production to material and necessary e-evidence only to protect responding parties from the unfair burden of excessive costs and overbroad requests. In reviewing specific requests for ESI, the court *rejects* requests that, in its opinion:

✔ Ask for irrelevant information

✔ Are not proper in scope

✔ Are unduly burdensome

✔ Lack a compelling reason for access to the requested information

✔ Violate privilege

✔ Have unsupported allegations

In plain English, wildly speculative requests are rejected. To succeed, your requests need to be specific (give dates and names) and tailored (state specific subject matter or keywords) and give a reason for each ESI demand. (No buckshot approaches are allowed here.) Limit requests to ESI that's both material and necessary to the prosecution of the case or action.

An overbroad request puts the whole request in jeopardy. The judge can reject (or *vacate*, in legal-speak) the request entirely, and you would forfeit your chance to get hold of ESI that was relevant.

Shaping the request

There are no easy ESI requests: Requesting ESI is tedious, specialized work. You can't just say "Turn over your e-mail and spreadsheets." That's too broad. Shaping a request requires knowing the opponent's computer systems, including operating systems, networks, databases, e-mail system, backup procedures, and application software. It requires understanding what ESI is relevant and where it is, such as metadata and hidden files.

Because you're an expert at recovering data, you can play a vital role by helping frame and shape requests and formulate the e-discovery strategy. From our experiences, computer forensic experts acting as consultants help the legal team by identifying data sources they had not thought to request.

You can help demonstrate the reasonableness of a producing party's efforts in the following ways:

- ✔ Identify the custodians of the ESI, who has it, and who knows how and where it was created and stored.

- ✔ Specify types and locations of the ESI, date ranges, and keywords to use in the searches to limit the scope of responsive documents, data, and e-mail.

Except for unusually small cases, responding to e-discovery requests cannot be done without the use of an e-discovery or computer forensic toolset (toolkit). Forensic toolkits are discussed in Chapter 6. Several toolsets and experts may be necessary because of volume and a variety of data sources.

Stepping through the response

When you receive a request for e-discovery, you have to respond to it. Here's how:

1. **Identify the types, sources, and locations of the ESI being asked for.**

   This is a good time to identify which information might be privileged and, therefore, protected against disclosure.

2. **Preserve the ESI.**

   You must protect the ESI from destruction and alteration. Forensic data capture is quite important at this stage. If files or e-mail have been deleted, creating forensic copies of the ESI is essential. Inform all owners and holders of the identified ESI not to delete it and explain why. The forensic copies of backups can save the day when people react to a preservation order by deleting them instead. A *preservation order* is a legal notice that ESI must be preserved for a lawsuit that will be filed or has been filed. In 2004, Philip Morris was sanctioned $2.75 million for failing to preserve electronic information.

3. **Start collecting from all applicable sources and devices.**

   Potential e-evidence must be accounted for from collection until admittance at trial to prove its authenticity. Documenting the chain of custody of potential, relevant evidence to disprove tampering or alteration is critical to admissibility at trial. *Chain of custody* is the process by which computer forensic specialists or other investigators preserve the ESI or crime scene. It documents that the e-evidence was handled and preserved properly and was never at risk of being compromised. The documentation must include

   - Where the evidence was stored

   - Who had access to the evidence

   - What was done to the evidence

   You must carefully document each step so that if the case reaches court, lawyers can show that the ESI wasn't altered as the investigation progressed. Without a documented chain of custody, it's impossible to prove after the fact that evidence has not been altered. Computer forensic toolkits perform that necessary recordkeeping and documentation of proper handling. A big complication is restoring backup tapes so that ESI can be collected from them.

4. **Process and filter the ESI.**

   The collection process resembles a huge fishing net that catches too much. The ESI-catch needs to be filtered to remove files that are outside the scope, duplicates (also called *de-duping*), confidential, or privileged. Record what happens, and why, in a report that will accompany the produced ESI. Again, you can complete this step with forensic software. With computer forensic tools, a complete search for deleted documents and e-mails can be done in a much shorter period in order to identify items of privilege.

5. **Review the ESI.**

   Whatever remains at this stage needs to be reviewed. That is, someone has to read it and decide what to do with it. Inarguably, now is the time to flag any *hot files* that are incriminating or embarrassing. (You want to get out in front of that possible train wreck.)

6. **Analyze the ESI a final time.**

   This final review is usually done by people who would be preparing this case for trial, which include the lawyers, paralegals, assistants, and law school students.

7. **Deliver the ESI and reports to the lawyer you work for.**

   Remember to include reports that authenticate the e-evidence and verify that the chain of custody was preserved. A copy of your reports must reach the lawyer in time to be delivered to the opposing lawyer before the deadline.

Figure 2-2 shows the steps in this process.

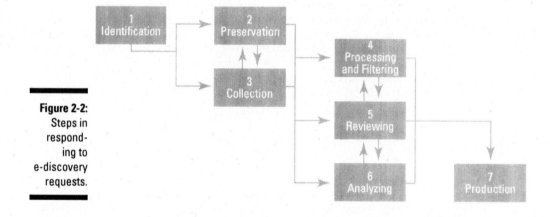

Figure 2-2:
Steps in responding to e-discovery requests.

Tampering with e-discovery can cost more than failing to comply with requests to produce ESI. For overwriting files and concealing e-evidence, the court punished Morgan Stanley with a $1.6 billion fine in 2005.

Conducting the Investigation in Good Faith

The Fed. R. Civ. P. require parties to respond to e-discovery in good faith. To act in *good faith* means to be fair and honest. A party acts in good faith by not taking an unfair advantage over another party. Acting in good faith isn't optional in legal cases — it's a legal obligation. When either party finds e-evidence that will bury its case, that faith becomes severely strained.

This statement may be tough to believe, but it's better to try to explain a smoking gun at trial than to explain why it's missing. The latter puts you at the mercilessness of the court.

When you don't conduct good faith, you may damage, or spoil, the case. *Spoliation* includes not only deliberate destruction of evidence but also any change or alteration from neglect, accident, or mistake. Put another way, spoliation is a powerful tool for the opposing side. Your opponent can use it to persuade the judge or jury that it would have proven their case.

Acting in good faith is a duty and is never optional.

E-discovery is an obligation on all litigating parties: the litigants, their computer staff, legal team, and investigative team. The legal team is obligated to perform a *reasonable* investigation (or good faith effort) to determine whether its client and investigative team have complied with its e-discovery obligations in good faith. Managing the e-discovery process and parties involved in it is similar to herding cats: They're not easily controlled or motivated.

What if, for example, the company (the responding party) involved in analyzing and producing ESI deliberately or unintentionally fails to turn over incriminating files? Does the legal team have a duty to send in the equivalent of Imperial storm troopers to verify the loyalty and obedience of their clients to the e-discovery rules? The answer is not No (another example of double negatives).

Courts cut no slack to anyone who violates e-discovery. Only lawyers or clients with a death wish or serious ego problem hide evidence from the court.

Sloppiness in checking for ESI has the same result as hiding it. When ESI isn't produced, trial courts don't care who is at fault or why. The consequences for people who trifle with the court usually aren't pretty, and reach well into the millions of dollars.

The *safe harbor* rule says that, except for exceptional circumstances, a court may not impose sanctions on a party for failing to provide ESI that's lost as a result of the routine, good-faith operation of an electronic information system.

Deciding Who's Paying the Bill

The debate surrounding e-discovery involves not only what types of electronic data can be discovered during litigation but also who should have to pay for producing the ESI. Traditionally, the producing party had to pay the costs of reviewing, copying, and producing documents. The need to hire computer forensic experts and consultants to perform the search to respond to e-discovery requests greatly increases the costs.

In the 2003 landmark case of *Zubulake v. USB Warburg*, U.S. District Judge Shira A. Scheindlin warned that "discovery is not just about uncovering the truth, but also about how much of the truth the parties can afford to disinter."

To decide which party should pay for e-discovery costs, Judge Scheindlin looked at five criteria of the data:

- ✔ **Active, online data:** Data that is in an "active" stage in its life and is available for access as it is created and processed. Storage examples include hard drives or active network servers.

- ✔ **Near-line data:** Data that's typically housed on removable media, with multiple read/write devices used to store and retrieve records. Storage examples include optical discs and magnetic tape.

- ✔ **Offline storage and archives:** Data on removable media that have been placed in storage. Offline storage of electronic records is traditionally used for disaster recovery or for records considered "archival" in that their likelihood of retrieval is minimal.

- ✔ **Backup tapes:** Data that isn't organized for retrieval of individual documents or files because the organization of the data mirrors the computer's structure, not the human records-management structure. Data stored on backup tapes is also typically compressed, allowing storage of greater volumes of data, but also making restoration more time consuming and expensive.

- ✔ **Erased, fragmented, or damaged data:** Data that has been tagged for deletion by a computer user, but may still exist somewhere on the free space of the computer until it's overwritten by new data. Significant efforts are required to access this data.

The first three types of data are considered accessible, and the last two types are considered inaccessible. For data in accessible format, the usual rules of discovery apply: The responding party pays for production. When inaccessible data is at issue, the judge can consider shifting costs to the requesting party. If the requesting party wants it, it has to pay for it. This burden limits overbroad and irrelevant requests.

The Zubulake test examines seven burden factors, listed in decreasing order of importance; the first two are the most important:

- ✔ The extent to which the request is specifically tailored to discover relevant information

- ✔ The availability of such information from other sources

- ✔ The total cost of production, compared to the amount in dispute

- ✔ The total cost of production, compared to the resources available to each party

✔ The relative ability of each party to control costs and its incentive to do so

✔ The importance of the issues at stake in the litigation

✔ The relative benefits to the parties of obtaining the information

The last two factors rarely come into play. Consideration of these seven factors helps the court decide whether the e-discovery process is burdensome and, if so, whether the responding or requesting party, or both, should pay for its production. Zubulake ultimately concluded that the requesting party should pay 25 percent of the cost of e-discovery.

Chapter 3

Getting Authorized to Search and Seize

*Y*ou can get yourself into serious trouble or mess up an investigation if you bulldoze over the rules for search and seizure of e-evidence. You've seen crime movies where the dedicated detective — such as Dirty Harry or Andy Sipowicz from *NYPD Blue* — finds convincing incriminating evidence, only to have it tossed out because he didn't have the authority to make the search in the first place. That news is painful. You want to avoid the frustration of letting criminals go free because of a technicality surrounding your search. Worse, you can get into legal hot water if you throw away the rulebook and are found guilty of misconduct. Wrongdoers know how to manipulate the justice system, but you don't get that option.

Standing between you and the devices or information you want to search and seize is the Fourth Amendment to the U.S. Constitution. It states that people have the right to "be secure in their persons, houses, papers, and effects, against unreasonable searches and seizures."

The Fourth also says that search warrants must be approved by judges. A judge's approval depends on probable cause, which means that you're not on a fishing expedition for evidence. However, exceptions to the warrant requirement exist, such as consent to search, the plain view doctrine, and exigent circumstances.

In this chapter, you find out the rules about authority, their purpose in privacy protection, when they're in play, and exceptions to the rules. You're figuring out how to do things by the book — the law side of computer forensics — and will get a good feel for what Harry and Andy faced.

Getting Authority: Never Start Without It

Understanding the technical side of computer forensic investigation is a commendable and daunting accomplishment, but you still have to learn the law. Legal requirements *always* come first. Don't touch that device unless you understand the law and its lingo so that you can investigate ethically and without putting yourself in harm's way.

Acknowledging who's the boss (not you!)

Investigations are a team sport, so to speak. Even the legendary fighter of injustices, the Lone Ranger, got help from his partner, Tonto. In many cases, being the computer forensic professional means that you're the technical expert but not necessarily the lead investigator in charge. You may be and should be working with a legal expert who guides the team through the intricacies of legal traps.

Depending on the range and type of case — criminal or civil — you may need to get permission from more than one authority. You'll know the basics of subpoenas and search warrants if you read this entire book, but don't try to be a hero out in the field. Let law enforcement or legal counsel be the boss, depending on the type of case:

- ✔ **Criminal cases:** The authority is exclusively the domain of government and is subject to a stringent set of rules.

- ✔ **Civil cases:** The authority can be either the government (the attorney general, or AG, for example) or a private party, such as a corporation, and subject to lower standards for authorizing searches and seizures.

Putting together your team

Using the team approach in civil and criminal cases increases the odds that procedures and reports withstand the scrutiny of the court and cross-examination by opposing counsel. If the opposing counsel is well prepared, it can be a tough audience and a capable opponent.

In a common criminal computer forensic case, you find three types of investigative team members:

✔ **Prosecutor:** This attorney ensures that the team complies with all applicable laws and legal procedures before and during a search or seizure. Because the prosecutor appears before a court to litigate the case, he has a vested interest in making sure that the investigative team leaves no legal loophole that the defense team can walk through. Chapter 5 is dedicated to minding and finding loopholes (although loopholes are beneficial if you're the one finding and using them to your advantage).

✔ **Lead investigator:** This person manages and coordinates investigation procedures and ensures that they're performed correctly. The person might not have technical expertise with electronic devices, but knows which information is useful and which is beyond the scope of the case. (You're working without a net if you go beyond the scope of the case!)

✔ **Technical expert:** This computer forensics expert knows how to acquire, analyze, examine, and interpret electronic content so that it's incontestable in court — or at least as resistant as possible to being contested. This person is crucial to the lead investigator and prosecutor. *You* are likely this person.

Computer forensic teams in civil cases share the same basic structure as their criminal counterparts, but a more varied set of professions may be involved. In civil cases, bear in mind that although the standards may be lower, sloppy work always comes back to damage your case!

Civil case teams consist of these three people:

✔ **Attorney:** Deciphers legal jargon and knows which policies, procedures, and laws apply to a specific case. In practice, expect to advise attorneys on more than just the technical aspects of the case. This area of law is relatively new, and you may have to point the attorney in the right direction regarding case law in this area. You depend on them to understand what must be done or not done to minimize liability. The attorney should know local rules and advise your team accordingly.

✔ **Case manager:** Manages the case. The person filling this role varies by circumstance or according to who has requested the investigation. In all instances, this person is responsible for how the investigation is conducted. The case manager for a corporation may be a department head; for a college, a human resource representative; and, for a small company, its owner.

✔ **Technical expert:** This person is the same as in criminal cases.

You want to have a bulletproof case with incontestable e-evidence. Your goal is to complete the forensics analysis, pass your report across the table to an opposing counsel who realizes that your results are so irrefutable that your opponent must settle out of court or drop the lawsuit. No more time and money than are necessary are spent on pointless court trials.

Involving external sources

The authority to conduct an investigation comes from different external sources depending on — you guessed it — whether you're working on a civil case or a criminal case:

✔ **Judges and magistrates:** Given the high stakes of a criminal case, the authority to conduct searches usually comes from judges or magistrates. We talk more about requesting this authority in the section "Criminal Cases: Papering Your Behind (CYA)," later in this chapter.

Exigent circumstances are the rare exception. When law enforcement officials have a "reasonable" expectation that evidence will be destroyed or altered in some form, they have the authority to seize the evidence without a search warrant. But you had better be able to back up your actions to a judge or jury when asked why you seized the evidence without a search warrant.

✔ **Owners, managers, and supervisors:** In U.S. companies, employees cannot claim an expectation of privacy as easily as their counterparts in Europe can. Managers, supervisors, or owners can give you the authority to search a computer. In some cases, co-worker authorization can provide access to data. An example is when management hires you because they suspect accounting irregularities and want you to find out what's happening. Because the search is private, the Fourth Amendment doesn't apply and you can proceed without a search warrant. We talk more about this kind of authorization in the section "Civil Cases: Verifying Company Policies," later in this chapter.

Don't rely solely on a co-worker who gives you authorization unless you already had the go-ahead from an owner or a senior executive to search and analyze evidence unless you have no other options. The co-worker may be trying to be helpful, but he may not have authority to give authority.

✔ **Licensing bureaus:** Only rarely would you as a forensic investigator work as your own authority. Many states are now adopting rules putting computer forensic or data recovery services under new licensing guidelines. Some states are making it illegal to perform computer forensic investigations unless you have a private investigation license. States might allow exceptions if you're working under the authority of an attorney on a case specifically authorized by that attorney. This development is still new and changing rapidly because computer forensic professionals are questioning the need to be licensed as private investigators when other disciplines, such as DNA and crime scene forensic investigators, aren't required to be licensed private investigators.

No warrant, no problem (if it's done legally)

A search warrant may not be necessary to conduct a search in any of these situations, but be sure to verify first, anyway:

- ✔ **Consent search:** If an individual voluntarily agrees to a search, no warrant is needed. The key question is what legally qualifies as a voluntary agreement. For the search to be legal, an individual must be in control of the area or equipment to be searched and must not have been pressured or tricked into agreeing to the search.

- ✔ **Plain view search:** An investigator spotting an object in plain view doesn't need a search warrant to seize it. To make the search legal, the investigator must have a right to be at the location, and the object he seizes must be plainly visible there.

- ✔ **Search incident to arrest:** In situations when a suspect has been legally arrested, law enforcement officials may search the defendant and the area within the defendant's immediate control. For the search to be legal, a spatial relationship must exist between the defendant and the object.

- ✔ **Protective-sweep search:** This situation is a series of two events. After an arrest, law enforcement officials may sweep the area if they reasonably believe that a dangerous accomplice may be hiding nearby. For example, police are allowed to walk through a residence and make a visual inspection without having to obtain a warrant. If evidence of, or related to, a criminal activity is in plain view during the search, the evidence can be legally seized.

Criminal Cases: Papering Your Behind (CYA)

Suppose that you want to convince the external authority in charge of a case that *you* should work on the case. In the case of criminal search warrants, the process is fairly formal and dependent on how you present yourself. Just saying to a judge, "I think they did something wrong" only irritates the judge.

The process is straightforward in that you present your reasons by way of an affidavit to the judge, and a search warrant is issued, which gives you permission to search.

You're the technical expert, but it's a legal game and you're not the referee. You have a certain amount of responsibility to ensure that your legal point person is doing the job correctly so that all your hard work doesn't end up being tossed out of court. If you're truly unlucky, you can end up in court defending your reasons for performing an illegal search.

To help you avoid that situation, we discuss in the following sections each of the steps you take to get that approval from a judge.

Learning about the case and the target

At the beginning of every investigation, verify that you're constructing a solid foundation of proper legal procedure. Without this defensive strategy, you

✔ Waste your time

✔ Allow someone to get away with a crime

✔ Risk your reputation and financial well-being

Take these steps to learn about your case:

1. **To make everyone's jobs smoother, ask questions about the type of information you're looking for.**

   The answers determine where you look, which tools you need, and which information you're *not* looking for. Make sure to get answers and write them down. If you're searching and seizing computers at a local bank, for example, here's a list of possible crucial questions:

   • Are you looking for financial or bank data or accounting ledgers? Or child pornography? Or a simple chat session?

   • Which operating system will you work with — Linux, Mac, or Windows?

   • Is a network involved? If yes, which type? Is it wireless or wired? Windows or Unix based?

   • Do you have numerous CDs to handle, or does the computer system have external flash drives?

   • Are passwords or encryption involved?

2. **Identify the specific sources of e-evidence.**

   Consider whether the data is located on the network, computers, digital devices, or — in the worst case — on the Internet. (This is where your fun starts, depending on your sense of humor.) Each of these considerations affects your search warrant strategy.

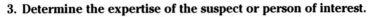
3. Determine the expertise of the suspect or person of interest.

Don't overlook this step because you think that computer criminals aren't technically adept. Trust us when we say that certain users can run circles around some technical geniuses. Never underestimate the human factor. If the person of interest has some expertise, look at the investigation from "outside the box." Instead of just relying on the computer forensic software, you may need to either look at the evidence in a more technical way or even study the suspect's behavior to understand how they might have hidden evidence.

Drafting an affidavit for a search warrant

After you have in hand the information you gathered about the case, you're ready to begin drafting an affidavit to obtain a search warrant. An example of an affidavit is shown in Figure 3-1. You can find many examples of search warrants and affidavits at the Web sites of the FBI at www.fbi.gov; CNN's *CourtTV* at www.cnn.com/CRIME and The Smoking Gun at www.thesmokinggun.com.

An affidavit accomplishes these three objectives:

✔ Identifies and describes *which* items to be searched and possibly seized

✔ Describes your search strategy — how you plan to conduct the search and possible seizure

✔ Explains the probable cause as defined by the legal advisor

Probable cause is the reasonable belief that a crime has been committed or that evidence of a crime exists at the site being searched. You can see that reasonable belief is a gel-like concept: It's tough to nail down. Determining whether probable cause exists depends on a magistrate's common sense in looking at the total picture of the circumstances.

The more information you give the judge in an affidavit, the more comfortable the judge is in issuing you a search warrant. Without that warrant, you're done. To stay on the case, you need to consider these four basic guidelines for drafting an affidavit:

✔ **Explain all technical terms.**

Put them at the beginning of your affidavit. Don't be shy — spell out the technical information.

✔ **Be clear about what you want to search.**

State whether the computer or other device you want to search is itself the evidence of a crime or is merely the container holding the evidence you seek.

	Original warrant - Return
	1st copy - Prosecutor
Original affidavit - Court	2nd copy - Serve
1st copy - Prosecutor	3rd copy - Issuing judge
Approved, SCAO	2nd copy - Serve

STATE OF MICHIGAN JUDICIAL DISTRICT	AFFIDAVIT FOR SEARCH WARRANT	CASE NO.

Please type or press hard   *See other side for instuctions*   Police Agency
Report Number: _____

_____ , affiant(s), state that:

1. The person, place, or thing to be searched is described as and is located at:

2. The PROPERTY to be searched for and seized, if found, is specifically described as:

3. The FACTS establishing probable cause or the grounds for search are:

This affidavit consists of _____ pages.

_____
Affiant

Review on _____	Subscribed and sworn to be before me on _____
Date	Date
by _____	_____
Prosecuting official	Judge/Magistrate

DC 231   (6/94)   **AFFIDAVIT FOR SEARCH WARRANT**

Original warrant - Return
1st copy - Prosecutor
2nd copy - Serve
3rd copy - Issuing judge

Original affidavit - Court
1st copy - Prosecutor
2nd copy - Serve

Approved, SCAO

STATE OF MICHIGAN **JUDICIAL DISTRICT**	**SEARCH WARRANT**	**CASE NO.**

TO THE SHERIFF OR ANY PEACE OFFICER:

Police Agency
Report Number: _____

_____ , has sworn to the attached affidavit regarding the following:

1. The person, place, or thing to be searched is described as and is located at:

2. The PROPERTY to be searched for and seized, if found, is specifically described as:

IN THE NAME OF THE PEOPLE OF THE STATE OF MICHIGAN: I have found that probable cause exists and you are commanded to make the search and seize the described property. Leave a copy of this warrant with affidavit attached and a tabulation (a written inventory) of all property taken with the person from whom the property was taken or at the premises. You are further commanded to promptly return this warrant and tabulation to the court.

Issued:_____   _____
　　　　　Date   Judge/Magistrate   Bar no.

RETURN AND TABULATION

Search was made _____ and the following property was seized:
　　　　　　　　　　　Date

☐ Continued on reverse side

_____
Officer
Copy of affidavit, warrant, and tabulation served on: _____
　　　　　　　　　　　　　　　　　　　　　　　　　　　Name
Tabulation filed: _____
　　　　　　　　　　Date

DC 231   (6/94)   **AFFIDAVIT FOR SEARCH WARRANT**

Figure 3-1:
This example of an affidavit for a warrant to search identifies the reasons and scope of a search warrant.

✔ **Explain your processes.**

Be sure that the judge understands the process of creating forensic images or other means of making a forensic copy on-site and why you think this process is necessary.

✔ **Add an explanation.**

Explain why you need to seize the computer and conduct an off-site search, if that's what you think is necessary.

While drafting the affidavit for the judge, you're developing the plan for your team to follow after the search warrant is issued. The plan should include the type of forensic equipment you need in order to execute the search warrant, how the evidence is to be preserved or extracted, and how you plan to move the evidence from the scene back to your lab. But life happens, and your plan may get blown to bits by some unforeseen event. Be flexible and have a backup plan ready.

We're giving you basic guidelines — not legal advice. Always check with your local legal representative to make sure that you know how local rules apply in your case.

Presenting an affidavit for judicial processing

Suppose that you collected the necessary information on your case and target and you fully explained your reasoning in an affidavit. The next phase is to present your affidavit to a judge or magistrate so that she can authorize you to search and seize via a search warrant. Here are the steps in this process:

1. **Present the judge or magistrate with the affidavit for review.**

   Typically, the investigative agent or prosecutor has the honor to present.

2. **Answer the judge's questions clearly, completely, and honestly.**

   Judges usually have a few questions about the affidavit that you need to be prepared to answer. If you didn't learn about your case or target from the outset, this questioning session is painful. A judge may deny a search warrant if you lack the proper knowledge about a case.

3. **Wait while the judge confirms that the affidavit is complete and the investigator isn't violating the Fourth Amendment or relevant case law.**

   Begging may not be effective.

4. **Be happy if the judge issues the search warrant and move on to the next step.**

   If the judge declines to issue a subpoena, address the grounds for the decision, and after you satisfy the judge's concerns, resubmit the affidavit.

5. **Review the affidavit and search warrant.**

   See Figure 3-2 for an example of a search warrant. See the nearby side-bar, "Keystone Cops," to understand why this step is important.

   Go to `www.usdoj.gov/usao/eousa/foia_reading_room/usam/ title9/crm00265.htm` to print a search warrant.

Attorney Search Warrant Form

To: Policy and Statutory Enforcement Unit   From:
     Office of Enforcement Operations   [AUSA or Department
     Criminal Division   Attorney]
     1301 New York Ave., N.W., 10th   [Address]
     Floor   [District or Division]
     Washington, D.C. 20005

     Phone: (202) 514-5541   Phone:
     Fax: (202) 514-1468   Fax:

Anticipated Search Date:
   1. (a) Attorney/Firm Name:
       (b) Violations (cite statutes):
       (c) Brief factual summary:
   2. Premises to be searched:
       ___ Law Firm ___ Residence ___ Law Office
       ___ Business or Corporation
       ___ Other:_____
   3. Records, information, and/or objects of the search:
       ___ Client Files ___ Attorney Business Records
       ___ Computer Files
       ___ Client Financial or Business Records
       ___ Audio or Video tapes ___ Physical Objects
       ____ Other:_____
   4. Reasons why less intrusive means (e.g., subpoena) cannot be used and information cannot be obtained from other sources:
   5. Procedure to be followed to protect privilege and to ensure that the prosecution team is not tainted:
   6. If you anticipate that computers may be searched or seized, please describe how you propose to conduct the search and what procedures will be followed to minimize intrusion into computerized attorney-client files:
   7. Please attach copies of the draft affidavit, search warrant, and instructions to agents executing the warrant.

   _____
   United States Attorney or AAG

Figure 3-2:
The attorney search warrant form to get permission to search and seize computers or other personal property.

Keystone Cops

Agents of a federal agency entered a suspect's office late one morning to execute a search warrant that had been signed by a judge.

To obtain the warrant, the government had presented evidence that convinced a judge that there was probable cause that criminal activity was afoot. Attached to the application for the warrant was an affidavit listing items to be seized.

After entering the suspect's office, the agents noticed a problem with the warrant: No list of items to be seized was included in, or attached to, the search warrant. The suspect, quick of mind and aware of his rights, objected to the omission, thereby grounding the search-and-seizure effort. After consulting with a supervisory IRS agent, the agents repeated the steps to obtain a new search warrant. The agents took action to secure the office, but didn't perform

a search. They didn't want to lose their case, so they videotaped and diagrammed the offices and labeled items such as file cabinets while they were waiting.

The second warrant arrived. It contained an attachment listing items to be seized, but the agents saw, in a Keystone Cops moment, that the list referred to items to be seized in a related search at a different location. After consulting with a supervisory IRS agent, the determined agents repeated their steps to obtain a valid search warrant before proceeding.

The third time was the charm: The agents obtained the warrant, and their search of the premises began early that evening. The warrant called for the search of the entire business premises this time and was used to the fullest extent of the law. The good guys prevailed.

6. **Execute the search warrant as soon as possible and complete your case.**

   Take the search warrant with you to the scene with as many copies as you think you will need for everyone involved.

Civil Cases: Verifying Company Policy

Searches of company or organizational computer assets under direct control of that company or organization don't require a search warrant. Whether government agents or agents of the company perform the search, it can usually be done without a warrant if a person in a position of authority of that organization authorizes it.

When you're asked to conduct a search by an organization or an asset it controls, keep these principles in mind:

✔ **Get authorization to search in writing from someone who is authorized to give it.**

In large organizations, issues of overlapping responsibility can create a problem for you. The last thing you need is another manager showing up and angrily demanding that you stop what you're doing. Your response should be to present the signed authorization.

If you're not sure who can give you authority, check the organization's policies and procedures. You might find out whom to ask. Or, the person using the computer of interest can grant this authority.

✔ **Adopt a trust-but-verify mantra.**

This strategy works for the military and also serves you well!

✔ **Review any privacy policies.**

Most organizations have policies that employees must sign as a condition of their employment. Just to double-check that everyone understands why you have the authority to conduct your search, pay close attention to the part about any expectations of privacy on company-owned computer equipment. U.S. courts have generally ruled in favor of the organization as long as employees are made aware that any activities they perform on company computers aren't considered private and are, in fact, subject to company monitoring.

If no such policy exists, you generally need formal written permission as a backup to the verbal permission you received to conduct the search.

Always have some form of authorization for whatever you do.

Searching with verbal permission (without a warrant)

The first thing to know about verbal permission to search a computer is that it's a bad idea. But you may face an urgent circumstance where it is impossible to receive formal or written authority in a timely manner. Here are two examples of valid reasons:

✔ **Digital evidence is easily destroyed or changed by something as simple as a keystroke.**

In cases where a suspect may destroy evidence, a verbal authorization is all you may have time for. Under exigent circumstances, the law provides for discretion on the part of law enforcement officials to search or seize evidence to preserve it.

✔ **Digital evidence is extremely mobile and volatile.**

With the advent of e-mail or other network software, digital evidence can speed across the globe in the blink of an eye, so waiting for a search warrant in circumstances where the data may no longer exist in five minutes usually calls for verbal permission.

For non-law enforcement and law enforcement, receiving verbal permission and only verbal permission is essentially playing Russian roulette because without written authority, it's your word against theirs.

Obtaining a subpoena

In civil cases, subpoenas are used to gain access to and collect evidence for trial. The word *subpoena* translates as "under punishment." Figure 3-3 shows an application for a subpoena.

APPLICATION FOR SUBPOENA
(Complete this form in ink and type or print all information)

CASE NAME: _____

DOCKET NUMBER: _____

DATE HEARING SCHEDULED: _____

PERSON REQUESTING SUBPOENA: _____

ADDRESS: _____

_____

PHONE NUMBER: _____

PERSON TO BE SUBPOENAED: _____

ADDRESS: _____

_____

IS THIS PERSON NEEDED:

    TO TESTIFY AT TRIAL?   YES _____   NO _____

    TO BRING RECORDS/PAPERWORK/FILES? YES _____   NO _____

SPECIFY REASONS: _____

_____

_____

_____

_____

DATE OF REQUEST: _____ SIGNATURE: _____

You must also complete the attached SUBPOENA and submit with this application. Be sure to print legibly in ink or type.

****

If the Court grants your request for subpoena, **you** are responsible for arranging timely service of the subpoena.

REQUEST: DENIED _____ GRANTED: _____

JUDGE: _____

DATED: _____

STATE OF NEW YORK : COUNTY OF _____
CITY OF _____ : CITY COURT
IN THE MATTER OF:

_____
PLAINTIFF/PETITIONER

              VS.

DOCKET NUMBER: _____
(   ) CIVIL SUBPOENA
(   ) CRIMINAL SUBPOENA
(   ) SUBPOENA DUCES TECUM

DEFENDANT/RESPONDENT
_____
          TO: _____
                 _____
                 _____

YOU ARE HEREBY COMMANDED THAT, ALL BUSINESS AND EXCUSES BEING LAID ASIDE,

(   ) TO APPEAR BEFORE THE CITY COURT JUDGE OF THE CITY OF _____ LOCATED AT
_____ ON _____ AT _____ TO TESTIFY AND
GIVE EVIDENCE IN THE ACTION OR PROCEEDING THERE PENDING AND BRING WITH YOU AND PRODUCE
AT THE TIME AND PLACE AFORESAID, THE FOLLOWING:
_____
_____
_____

(   ) SUBPOENA DUCES TECUM: TO PRODUCE AT THE _____ CITY COURT LOCATED AT
_____ ON OR BEFORE _____ AT
_____THE FOLLOWING RECORDS; NO PERSONAL APPEARANCE NECESSARY:
_____
_____
_____
_____

FAILURE TO COMPLY WITH THIS SUBPOENA SHALL DEEM YOU GUILTY OF CONTEMPT OF COURT.

DATED:

_____   _____
    CLERK OF THE COURT   CITY COURT JUDGE

Figure 3-3: An application for a subpoena demanding that a witness appear in court.

In law, a subpoena is a command to do something. Two types of subpoenas of interest to you are described in this list:

✔ ***Subpoena ad testificandum:*** This type of subpoena is the one you typically think of when you hear the word *subpoena.* This type of court summons compels the witness to appear in court or another specified location to give oral testimony at a hearing or trial.

✔ ***Subpoena duces tecum:*** This Latin phrase translates to "bring with you under penalty of punishment." This type of court summons compels the witness to do three things:

- Appear in court or another specified location.

- Provide oral testimony for use at a hearing or trial.

- Bring evidence in person and produce to the court any documents, files, books, or papers that can help clarify the matter at issue.

The clerk of the court usually issues subpoenas on behalf of the judge and, in most cases, also issues blank subpoenas to attorneys practicing in the court. This arrangement makes sense because clerks are considered *officers of the court.* To you as the technical expert, the attorney on your team therefore has the power to issue subpoenas commanding the other party to turn over evidence or preserve evidence or give you access to the evidence.

Just because you don't have to ask a judge for subpoenas, don't consider it a free pass to do sloppy work.

Chapter 4

Documenting and Managing the Crime Scene

*1*n many police TV dramas, the crime scene is marked off with yellow tape to preserve the evidence and prevent contamination by rubberneckers and bystanders. For those who can't grasp the meaning of the phrase "Do not cross" printed on the tape, a burly police officer physically directs them away, saying "Nothing to see — move along." When the crime scene is electronic, however, there truly may not be anything to see, but your duty to preserve and protect is just as great. (For simplicity throughout this chapter, *crime scene* means one that involves the e-evidence you're charged with safeguarding.)

Viewed within the context of a TV crime drama, your role during this stage is that of a supporting cast member. As the computer forensic specialist, you support the principal investigator, the *investigator-in-charge* (IIC), by identifying and collecting e-evidence. Your role and responsibilities are crucial and require the utmost in professionalism. Your compass — that which gives you the sense of direction — is the set of tried-and-true forensic methodologies. Using those methods, you can dodge the sting of an examination gone wrong. To paraphrase a cautionary Yogi-ism (from the famed Yankees catcher Yogi Berra): You've got to be very careful if you don't know what you're doing because you might not do it."

Keep in mind that there's no such thing as a small investigation — only one that's just getting started. When processing a crime scene, expect the starting location to sprout into a multiregional crime scene affair! Be prepared for the worst. This chapter explains how to document, control, and manage crime scene sites, including those whose scope takes you to evidence *outside* the initial application of yellow tape.

Obsessing over Documentation

E-evidence must be preserved and authenticated. When you handle e-evidence, always follow the three *C*s of evidence: care, control, and chain of custody. When you follow these guidelines, you ensure that the e-evidence you present is the same as that which you seized. This process requires that you document the evidence in its original state and every step in the preparation for civil or criminal proceedings. Following these guidelines can be brutal. For example, to prove that an e-mail hasn't been tainted, you might have to establish the origin of the message, the integrity of the system in which the message was transmitted, and the chain of custody of the message.

We recommend that you maintain three types of records:

- ✔ Chain of custody
- ✔ Documentation of the crime scene
- ✔ Documentation of your action, such as recording a diary or reporting your procedures on a blog

Documenting your actions isn't mandatory, but you'll be thankful later if you maintain that type of record. You need a permanent record of events and e-evidence for a review that might not take place until years later.

Document everything! There's no such thing as overdocumenting a crime scene in either criminal or civil cases.

In the following sections, we outline the reasons why it's important for you to document everything.

Keeping the chain complete

You absolutely need to maintain chain-of-custody documentation of e-evidence. That chain extends from the initial crime scene through the final disposition at the end of a trial, and possibly the appeal. The chain of custody requires that the e-evidence be accounted for at every step of the investigation, including who has handled the e-evidence, when it was handled, and why it was handled.

You must be prepared to answer the killer question from opposing counsel or the judge: "How do we know that you didn't taint the evidence?"

Every investigation has something unique or weird or new about it. And, each computer forensic investigator has a slightly different way of approaching the task of documentation. But the underlying compass is the same. Known best practices exist, such as using the proper chain of custody forms and using technology to document your investigation, depending on circumstances.

Dealing with carbon memories

What did you have for lunch 12 days ago? What color is the shirt you wore two Mondays ago? If you can answer those questions correctly and confidently, you're not a normal person! Most people have difficulty remembering what they did last week, much less remembering the exact details of a crime scene from a year ago.

With a crammed caseload, you can't risk forgetting the details needed in high-stakes criminal cases. On the civil side, the stakes often come in the form of multimillion-dollar fines or judgments. Documenting a crime scene in an impartial, fact-based manner is essential to the integrity of your case.

Even highly trained professionals can have different views of the same crime scene because of biases or different levels of experience. A common example is one investigator remembering that the suspect's computer mouse was on the right side of computer, and another analyst remembering that the mouse was on the left side. If the suspect is right-handed and the analyst makes the mistake of "remembering" the mouse on the left, a smart defense attorney can point out that his client couldn't be the person who used the computer because the computer was set up for a left-handed person.

To err is human. Digital cameras and videos don't err the way humans do. That's why you should record everything.

Deciding who gets the evidence first

Throughout the life cycle of an investigation, a variety of people analyze the e-evidence to extract facts for investigative or court use. Analysts check a computer for DNA evidence that can physically link it to a suspect. A computer forensic analyst checks the e-evidence to possibly link it digitally to the suspect and to the suspect's computer.

If the agency or organization you work with is large enough to cover multiple forensic disciplines, you face the issue of which type of analysis goes first, whether it's computer forensics, DNA, ballistics, bloodstain, or any other of the dozens of physical forensic disciplines. The determining factor is whether any analysis will harm the evidence or interfere with any later analysis by another forensic discipline.

DNA tests may use chemicals that ruin efforts to gather digital forensic evidence, for example. In a typical scenario, a compact disc (CD) found at a crime scene has both physical and digital latent evidence. The computer analysis might compromise the physical DNA evidence. The DNA analysis might damage the CD enough that digital data cannot be extracted. (And you probably thought that chain of custody was a simple issue!)

Getting to the truth

What separates amateurs from true professionals is the degree of commitment to their jobs — that is, pride and professionalism. Just as in any profession, the work effort of people in the investigative field ranges from minimalist to going the extra digital mile to find the whole truth. Results of incomplete analysis cannot be trusted.

Make sure that the truth comes out in an incontestable way. Psychic visions and hunches add drama to Hollywood movies, but they don't play well in court. When you're on the witness stand and the judge asks you on what evidence or analysis of evidence you based your conclusions, you don't want to be caught short.

As a computer forensic scientist, you're stating what you believe happened based on the evidence you have found. Documentation is an integral part of this process because it provides an unbiased platform to begin forming your conclusions. You can prove cases without good supporting documentation; eventually, though, someone will challenge a case based not on the conclusion you reached, but rather on *how* you reached this conclusion if your documentation isn't thorough or even present.

Using scientific methods

You can find the truth by using forensic science. Forensic science is *scientific.* Here's the general sequence of steps in the scientific method:

1. Raise a question or an issue.

2. Observe and collect data.

3. Develop multiple working *hypotheses,* which are ideas to explain the observations.

4. Test the hypotheses based on analysis of the evidence, and do one of the following:

    a. Accept the hypothesis.

    b. Reject the hypothesis.

    c. Modify the hypothesis.

5. When a hypothesis has considerable observational support, it's accepted and others are rejected, and it may become a theory.

You're using testing and e-evidence to support your hypothesis and develop a theory about what you believe happened.

Recognizing Occam's razor

Sometimes it's hard to reach the truth when you're buried in analysis. Here to help is the principle of *Occam's razor,* named after the medieval philosopher William of Occam. His principle underlies good scientific theory building:

> All other things being equal, the simplest solution is the best.

According to this principle, you shouldn't make more assumptions than the minimum number needed to explain a concept.

In other words, when faced with multiple competing but equal theories, select the theory that introduces the fewest assumptions.

Occam's razor helps you shave off information that isn't truly needed to explain what happened. Think of the advantages: By following this principle in developing a theory that explains what happened, you reduce the chance of introducing inconsistencies, ambiguities, and redundancies

Directing the Scene

How do you begin to document a case? Every case is unique, so you have to make judgment calls on what your jurisdictional policies and procedures call for. This section gives you basic guidelines to follow.

Papering the trail

Most people hate to do paperwork. Most types of paperwork have a purpose, though. The computer forensic investigative world is no different: Paper trails are essential to document the what, why, where, and how of a case. Although forms and reports vary among organizations, here are the basic types:

- ✔ **Chain of custody:** This form shows where the evidence has been and who has been responsible for it.

- ✔ **Intake form:** Detail on this inventory list the equipment you have accepted into your custody. This type of form is related to the chain-of-custody form, but is used as a reference for you or your department.

- ✔ **Case journal:** On this running list, record what analysis you've done and its results. Most forensic software toolsets have this function built in. Keep a case journal if you're not using a tool.

✔ **Investigative report:** After your analysis is complete, a report contains your conclusions and describes how you arrived at them.

A forensic toolset has a built-in report function, but you may also want to use a standard form in case your department requires a customized report format.

✔ **Case file index:** Eventually, someone will request an old case report and you will draw a blank. After you complete the case analysis, develop an organized way to store it and retrieve it later.

The purpose of these forms is to build a case that stands up in court and to give the opposing party no room to wiggle or opening to exploit.

Recording the scene: Video

Digital video and images can be collected with great speed, ease, and efficiency. You can photograph evidence at the scene, review the results, and, if the picture is unsatisfactory, immediately reshoot before the setting is disturbed.

Using video exhibits in court helps jurors understand the e-evidence and the crime scene. Jurors have better recall of evidence that they both see and hear.

One of the best ways to document a crime scene is to use digital video documentation, which ranges from still photographs to full-motion videos of the crime scene.

When you're getting your equipment ready, follow these guidelines:

✔ **Use date/time stamps.**

Many digital cameras put a date-and-time stamp directly on a digital image. The use of the time and date stamps allows you to create a timeline.

✔ **Bring extra lights.**

Not all crime scenes have camera-ready lighting. Take extra lights, and large one, to ensure that nothing is hidden by shadows.

✔ **Carry spare batteries.**

Murphy's law has special relevance to batteries. To prevent your battery from dying at a critical time, *always carry at least one fully charged spare.* Carrying two is an even better strategy.

✔ **Carry extra memory.**

Always carry extra memory storage devices for your camera. You want enough to record everything you need.

✔ **Use a computer with a viewer.**

Carry a computer or another device that allows you to download and inspect images on the scene.

✔ **Use a microphone.**

If your camera system has audio capability, use it.

After a perimeter has been set up around the crime scene, you can begin to shoot and document. You can choose from several methods of documenting a scene:

✔ **360 degrees and 3D:** Document *everything* within a 360-degree field of view. Your first pass should take in as much of your view as possible *before* you start your investigation.

You're working in a three-dimensional space and not in a two-dimensional space. Look at the ceiling to find items of interest. If you're working with a false ceiling, pop a tile and video *above* the ceiling. If you're working with a false floor, do the same. It's amazing what you can find in those two places.

✔ **Zoom:** Zoom in to bring an object up close and personal, by capturing details that aren't apparent or that need to be emphasized. Examples of items to zoom in on, and where to zoom, are books on a shelf, peripheral devices, external media devices, tools, the back of a computer showing where the location of each cable is, and an on-screen list of programs that are running.

✔ **You:** This one doesn't often make the list, but some investigators record on video all the work they do. They document how they processed a crime scene to show what was done to safeguard the evidence. The video also documents tasks that weren't done that could have contaminated the evidence.

You're documenting the scene for future reference and showing the opposing side that you did a professionally competent and thorough job.

When you have all the video you believe is necessary, save it. Some investigators take laptops or small desktop computers to the scene to process evidence and download video. Others wait until they're back in the lab to start downloading. Technologically savvy investigators have set up systems to wirelessly transmit video to servers in the lab for real-time data archival. Whichever manner you use, make sure that the data is transferred in an organized and safe manner. Some investigators even *hash* their video documentation: The hash mark proves that the video hasn't been tampered with or altered in any way.

Recording the sounds: Audio

Don't overlook audio as a source of documentation. Granted, during audio documentation, you look like you're talking to yourself, but that image is now commonplace in our wireless Bluetooth world! Audio documentation is comparable to medical doctors' use of dictation. You're recording your findings for future use in a report.

Many investigators have ditched their pads and pencils in favor of digital recorders because it's easier and faster to "speak" notes than to write them. Dictating is an efficient way to store large amounts of notes in an organized way. Here's a short list of things to document on audio:

- ✔ **Your arrival information:** Include the time and date that you arrived, the general condition of the crime scene, the names of the lead investigator and the first responder, and related information.

- ✔ **A detailed explanation of your findings:** In addition to recording on video, you can keep a detailed running commentary on your findings. You can also record your preliminary perceptions of the evidence.

- ✔ **Your departure information:** Include the time and date that you finish your crime scene work. This information is also good to have when you debrief the lead investigator to document the topics discussed during this debriefing.

You may look eccentric while recording audio documentation, but it has a place in every computer forensic analyst's toolbox. Just as with video files, you want to upload and save audio files (to avoid losing or damaging information) and hash them (to be able to verify their integrity).

Getting the lead out

Maybe you're into the classic detective look: fedora, trench coat, and pencil. There's nothing wrong with this setup. It reflects your tried-and-true method of documenting. The nontechnical pencil-and-paper method has some advantages, however: It uses no batteries, it's versatile, and many investigators use it to *sketch* the crime scene!

Have you ever noticed that home builders use sketches and plans, rather than video or audio plans, to build houses? The same concept applies when documenting a crime scene: You're looking for an overhead view that has enough detail to reconstruct the crime scene. You can videotape a crime scene and describe it on an audio recording, but a good overview sketch gives the "50,000 foot" view. Toss the Fedora and trench coat if you must, but don't lose the pencil!

Managing Evidence Behind the Yellow Tape

Basic techniques to complete a field forensic recovery are the same for civilian and law enforcement analysts, but the frameworks differ in a couple of key areas. Searches by law enforcement are bound by the Fourth Amendment; searches by civilian investigators aren't. Another difference is that law enforcement evidence is held to a higher standard of proof than civilian evidence.

Differences in how the camps work are obvious in the way crime scenes are treated:

- **Law enforcement:** Officials set up a perimeter around a crime scene with the intention of keeping out anyone who could contaminate the scene. They can arrest anyone who doesn't obey.

- **Civilian:** Usually, a "crime scene" is handled by someone in charge of the equipment or location, such as a manager or supervisor. Because that person is in charge, if you interfere with the investigation, you're fired or charged with trespassing.

In the following sections, we discuss how to complete your investigation at the crime scene without disturbing those in charge.

Arriving ready to roll: Bringing the right tools

As with any expert, the tools you use determine how well you can perform your job.

Make this statement your mantra: "Use the right tool for the right job." Chapter 20 lists tools used in computer forensics that include write blockers, forensic software, and password crackers.

Here are the tools and equipment that you use on the scene. Using some of these items involves common sense, but using others may surprise you:

- **Mechanical or hardware tools:** You need tools to disassemble computers and equipment. A comprehensive collection of screwdrivers, Torx bits, hex nut drivers, regular and needle-nose pliers, wire cutters, and tweezers are *basic* items. Macs require special tools, so your toolkit needs to include specialized hardware as well.

✔ **Supplementary forensic field supplies:** Some items you would never think of until you need them. You need a good set of latex gloves (no garden gloves!). Latex gloves help preserve latent forensic evidence for DNA or fingerprint analysis. Depending on the type of crime scene, paper or cloth "booties" over your shoes may be needed. Other items you need are felt tip pens, tags for cables, labels, a flashlight, a magnifying glass, spare media (floppy disk, CD/DVD disc, and USB flash drive), spare batteries, cable ties, rubber bands, a spare power strip, and a ream of printer paper.

✔ **Seizure supplies:** You can't just back up the police van to the suspect's door and start throwing in evidence to take back to the lab! You need to catalogue, organize, and protect the items from the crime scene all the way back to your lab. The single most important shipping item is a set of clear, antistatic plastic bags. Putting small media, books, magazines, printouts, paper scraps, photographs, and any other small, easily lost items in those bags saves headaches and time if they're properly labeled and catalogued. Other items you need are boxes of different sizes, packing tape, packing material (bubble wrap is useful), and a sturdy dolly or hand truck. For transport, have bungee tie-downs, antistatic mats, a climate-controlled vehicle, and a vehicle that has easy access for loading heavy, bulky boxes.

✔ **Specialized wireless equipment:** As the world transitions to wireless mode, forensic technology has to keep up. The seizure of wireless devices requires that you consider the volatility of wireless devices. The data you're seeking could possibly be lost as soon as your battery loses all power. To be prepared, make equipment such as Faraday bags, mobile device chargers, and mobile device vehicle chargers part of your tool bag. Bear in mind that many different types of devices are out there, so find a universal power system that works with most models.

Magnets and computer forensics don't mix! Never use a magnetic tool of any kind, even if you're working on optical media. You may just forget one day and use it on magnetic media by accident.

Your jurisdiction and unique circumstances determine what type of equipment you need in the field for your particular case. Just remember that it's a horrible feeling to know you're unprepared.

Minimizing your presence

A universal rule of computer forensics is "Don't change anything." The goal of *all* computer forensic analysis is to recognize, collect, analyze, and generate a report based on evidence that hasn't been altered or changed in any way. Because e-evidence can be *extremely* fragile, you can accidentally alter it in many ways while you're collecting it.

You have to minimize any trace of you at a crime scene. A classic story to illustrate is that of a detective who found a latent fingerprint on a crime scene computer. He couldn't match it to any criminal database. The detective was adamant that this fingerprint could break open the case, so he expanded his database search. Within minutes, the search came back with a positive match: his own fingerprint.

Even a professional can often contaminate a scene without knowing it. Several in-the-field guidelines can help computer forensic professionals handle equipment so as not to change or contaminate the evidence. Use a fair dose of common sense when following these guidelines.

Here's how to deal with any equipment you find at a crime scene:

✔ **If the computer is turned off, leave it off.**

Never, never, never (never) turn on a computer that's off in the field. The number of changes that can occur when you start a computer is astounding! Literally hundreds of files are changed on a computer system on startup. If you must start a computer in the field, see Chapter 6, where we provide a much more detailed explanation of how to accomplish a field analysis.

✔ **If the computer is on, you have options.**

The first thing to do when you see a computer is figure out whether it is in fact on. Don't punch the keyboard or move the mouse to accomplish this! Look for these signs that a computer is on:

- The Num Lock light on the keyboard is on.

- You can hear a fan running in back of the computer.

- The monitor is warm to the touch.

All these subtle signs indicate that the computer is on and that you should move carefully near the computer.

If the computer is on, you have two options to ensure that you preserve as much evidence as possible: Unplug or shut down. The rule that most computer forensic investigators use is to unplug nonserver computers and shut down server computers. Policies in your jurisdiction may vary, which is where your common sense comes into play.

After you turn off a computer of any type, the contents of RAM disappear completely. Programs such as Winhex can extract this data from RAM, but you run the risk of contaminating the evidence! Chapter 10 covers RAM evidence in more detail.

✔ **Keep power supplied to volatile data devices.**

Mobile phones, PDAs (personal digital assistants), pagers, and many other devices lose their evidentiary value if power is lost and the devices lose the contents retained in memory. Do everything possible to keep the power supplied to these types of devices. At the same time, keep any new data from being sent to these devices, especially wireless devices by using a Faraday bag or other types of devices that do not allow wireless signals to reach the device.

✔ **Preserve information on networked computers.**

When you're dealing with networked computers, remember that e-evidence is now *outside* the lone computer in front of you. Data files might be stored on the Internet or on remote computers, e-mail can be stored on distant servers, and hackers can control a computer from an entirely different time zone. Networked computer data trails tend to go stale quite quickly, and following them may require help from outside agencies or organizations.

A consideration that more and more organizations are dealing with is the increased use of wireless routers in both home and commercial environments. Within a known radius, wireless routers can communicate with any other device set up to communicate wirelessly, and you may be looking at a crime scene perimeter within the wireless range of the wireless access point. You need to preserve information that points to other places where evidence may be found, and to follow up and find those systems as quickly as possible before the cybertrails go cold.

A computer forensic investigator played the key role in identifying Lisa Montgomery, who was later arrested and charged with strangling pregnant Bobbie Jo Stinnett and kidnapping her 8-month-old fetus. Using the Kansas City Regional Computer Forensics Lab, police investigating the murder and kidnapping zeroed in on Montgomery by searching the victim's computer records and tracing an IP address to a computer at Montgomery's home. An *IP address* is the unique number given to every Internet-connected computer. E-evidence showed that just before the slaying, Montgomery had corresponded over the Internet with the victim about buying a dog from her. If the case hadn't been cracked within hours, the outcome could have been even worse.

Stepping Through the Scene

Most of this chapter describes how to process a computer forensic field analysis without having a logical progression to follow. Earlier, we give you the pieces to the puzzle; in this section, we show you how the puzzle pieces fit together. This section shows you how a standard computer forensic field case works and describes some common actions to take. Figure 4-1 shows you what to watch out for.

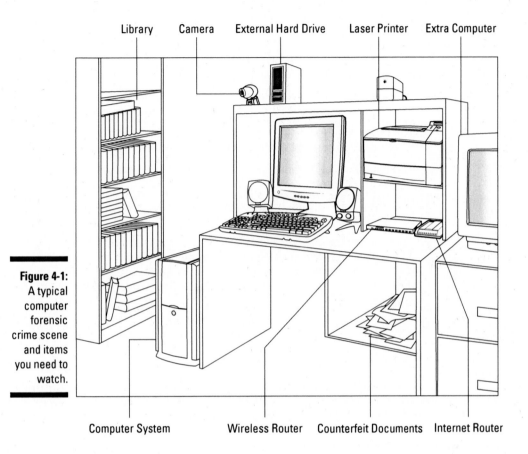

Library Camera External Hard Drive Laser Printer Extra Computer

Computer System Wireless Router Counterfeit Documents Internet Router

Figure 4-1:
A typical
computer
forensic
crime scene
and items
you need to
watch.

Securing the area

As the computer forensic analyst, you're usually not one of the first responders. Rarely are you called on to secure a crime scene. Regardless, you still need to know how this part of the process works so that you don't inadvertently compromise the perimeter or crime scene:

1. A first responder always assumes that a crime is still in progress until they can secure the scene.

   Safety for themselves and others is paramount at this point. If anyone requires medical assistance, it occurs now.

2. After a first responder verifies that the crime scene is no longer a danger or threat, evidence preservation becomes the priority.

   Perimeters are set up, and all suspects, witnesses, and bystanders are separated and questioned.

3. After perimeters are set up, access is controlled, and documentation begins, first responders prepare to hand over the crime scene to the lead investigator or investigator in charge (IIC) depending on what term is used in your jurisdiction.

   Handing off the responsibility to the lead investigator requires a briefing to exchange as much detailed information as time permits.

4. The lead investigator does a scene walk-through to figure out exactly what needs to be done to process the crime scene.

5. You receive a call to pick up your toolkit and start making your way to the crime scene.

6. When you arrive at the crime scene, you contact the lead investigator to receive a full briefing.

   Your documentation should now be in motion. During the briefing, ask which protocols are in place for the crime scene, such as access, suspect locations, witness locations, types of equipment that investigators think they have, and, most importantly, which evidence you need to look for.

Surveying the scene

You have the lay of the land and have been briefed by the person in charge. Now what? The next step you take is documenting the scene, or *surveying the scene*. In this step, you're essentially recording in some form the scene as you came upon it and quite possibly your actions at the scene up to when you leave.

Always consult the policies and procedures in your local area before starting your survey.

When you begin your survey, follow these steps:

1. **Interview owners and users before stepping foot in the crime scene.**

   You interview the owners or users of the system to begin building an idea of what environment you're walking into. Questions you typically ask involve the purpose of the computer, any passwords, any encryption, destructive devices, and whether any off-premise storage devices are used. Make sure to interview people separately and in the presence of another member of your team.

2. **Videotape the crime scene.**

   Your first step into the crime scene should stop right there. Take a 360-degree look around to get your bearings. At this point, you should be knee-deep in the documentation process to show what the scene looked like *before* you walked in.

3. **Do a walk-through.**

   Walk through the crime scene to look at items that give you insight into which type of computer system you're dealing with. Are books or magazines close by? Does the system have a scanner or camera attached to it? All these items build a profile and a scenario to guide your hypotheses. If you find advanced data encryption books, you know that it will be a long day.

4. **Check the suspect's computer and devices.**

   It's time for your documentation and analysis of the suspect's computer and devices.

5. **Decide where to do the analysis.**

   Decide whether to do a field analysis or pack everything and take it to your lab. Most of the time, you pack up.

   If you head to the forensic lab for further analysis, document where everything was placed as you start to tear down the crime scene for analysis in your lab. Extra effort in this step saves you time and aggravation later when trying to reconstruct the scene.

The order in which these steps occur is also based on circumstances, but use common sense and good judgment at all times.

Transporting the e-evidence

After you have everything in your vehicle and ready to go, head straight to the lab. Don't make any side trips or take longer than is necessary, because you're dealing with fragile evidence. Letting computer equipment and media sit in a hot vehicle is always a bad idea. Keep in mind these risks when transporting e-evidence to the lab:

- **Heat:** Never let the evidence sit in a hot car! Severe heat warps disc drives and makes evidence unreadable.

- **Sunlight:** Direct sunlight can damage evidence by raising heat levels quickly.

- **Static electricity:** Vehicle carpets and low humidity generate static electricity that causes massive amounts of electrical mayhem to any evidence. Use rubber mats.

- **Momentum:** A vehicle in motion has brakes. Its contents have momentum. To avoid bashing around the evidence, secure it!

- **Environmental factors:** Be alert to what's in your car and what you put into it. Electromagnets, high-wattage radios, or anything that generates energy either magnetically or by way of radio frequency has the potential to harm computer evidence.

Part II
Preparing to Crack the Case

In this part . . .

Almost every task in an investigation begins with a planning step. Unfortunately, it's human nature to skip the planning and jump right to the task at hand. In Chapter 5, you find out how to avoid the ready-fire-aim approach. Poor planning adds unnecessary risk, delay, and expense to an investigation and can stress you out. Take a tip from construction crews who "measure twice, cut once" — wood can't be uncut. Acquiring e-evidence makes full use of that principle, as you read in Chapter 6. Even when you're improvising, you need to follow a do-no-harm defensive methodology. The safest (least harmful) methodology is one that prepares you for the worst-case scenario. With a lot of unknowns in your case, such as who's involved and the timeframe, you need to know what to consider. If you consider these factors in your planning decisions, you then treat every case like a criminal investigation with the strictest evidence rules.

You prepare to make smart choices that crack the case but not your credibility. You find out how to handle yourself as well as the e-evidence. In Chapter 7, you learn how to examine electronic content to find the evidence relevant to the case. You're the master of this thinking and deductive stage of the investigation process. You perform your work in the style of the famous master of deduction, Sherlock Holmes.

You go head-to-head in Chapter 8 with attempts to stop you from finding e-evidence. You recognize attempts to hide evidence behind passwords, encryptions, and steganography — and how to overcome them.

The most exciting phrase to hear in science, the one that heralds new discoveries, is not "Eureka!" . . . but "That's funny. . . ."

— Isaac Asimov (1920–1992)

Chapter 5

Minding and Finding the Loopholes

*L*egal hardball is expensive, irrational, and rampant. Parties involved in commercial or civil litigation often defy rational behavior. (Commercial litigation covers business and employment disputes.) In contentious divorce actions, the crazy-meter can go off the chart. Litigation cases range from relatively simple matters to complex, money-burning sagas that take years to resolve.

For all types of cases at all times, the devil is in the details. Small items in an investigation, if overlooked, open loopholes that the opposing side can use to undercut your results and make you look incompetent. Loopholes may be either party's best or only chance of winning. Learn how to harness loophole power. The opportunity to harm the case or be humiliated on the witness stand is unlimited, for either not following standard procedure or not being able to defend what you did or did not do. By making informed choices about forensic methods and work habits, you defend your analysis and opinions from fact-spinning by the opposition.

In this chapter, we begin by discussing your entree into civil or criminal cases. The focus is mostly on cases where you aren't working with a prosecutor (see Chapter 3) or securing a crime scene (see Chapter 4). You decide whether to take a case, and if you do, what arrangements are involved. Then you view cases from the perspective of your client, the lawyer who's considering hiring you. After these preliminary tasks are finished and you're on the case, you find out about legal loopholes whose existence and size are determined by your defensible forensic methods. Here's to a favorable outcome to your cases.

Deciding to Take On a Client

You may come up against tricky situations. For example, a lawyer facing an upcoming court date may want a preliminary expert opinion from you about the strength of the prosecutor's e-evidence, which would be delivered on CD to you by the next morning. Don't make hasty commitments. Unless you're experienced enough to know that you can perform the review properly by the deadline, you put yourself and the case at risk if you agree.

You shouldn't accept, without consideration, every case that's offered to you. The field of forensics is labor intensive and deadline driven, which limits the number of cases you can take on at a time. In addition, not all cases are appropriate for every investigator, nor is every investigator appropriate for each type of case. You'll face cases and clients that you're willing and able to take on and also face some that you're not. How do you decide? You start by learning about your prospective client's case, priorities, and resources.

Taking on only one type of case and client, such as only criminal cases involving assault or harassment for the defense, can be risky because you could appear to be an expert for hire or a professional witness.

Learning about the case and the theory

You need to know what type of case you're being asked to take to determine whether it's within your area of expertise. For example, in a contract dispute, the lawyer knows which documents need to be retrieved. But a fraud case requires familiarity with a chart of accounts or ACL (auditing) software, so you should refer the attorney to a forensic accountant or suggest that one also be retained.

If you cannot accept a case, admit it politely and immediately to save everyone's time and to protect confidentiality. Before the call ends, you might identify your areas of expertise for future cases or follow up with a mailing.

Find out which evidence has been confiscated or taken into custody and when. Most likely, the lawyer will explain what happened and who was involved. Ask about any DIY activity.

Take good notes and label them, but do it quickly. Neatness doesn't count here, and you don't need to write out every word. Sketch a timeline or chart relationships among people, if appropriate. For the most part, you're listening and limiting your questions only to clarify points. For example, if computers were confiscated, you might ask whether only the defendant had access to devices that were confiscated or if any others had access too. Considering how long it takes for a case to reach trial, don't be surprised to hear that events happened more than a year earlier.

If the case involves suspected possession of child pornography (CP), law enforcement will already have confiscated all computers and equipment. Ask for, or at least mention, that you would need the name and contact information of the prosecutor's computer forensic investigator.

Each case has a *theory* — a theme that unifies the evidence to tell a believable or compelling story. Ask about the theory and try to identify which, how, and whether e-evidence can support it. A common defense theory used in wrongful termination cases, for example, is that the employee was fired because of poor performance. Ask to review the plaintiff's (former employee's) performance reports and those of comparable employees, the metadata of the files (see Chapter 11), access logs, and hard copies of those digital reports. If performance reports were edited to manufacture e-evidence showing that the firing was for poor performance, the metadata indicates the date of the edit. No matter how hard one tries, mistakes in editing documents get made. You need to find them. By comparing the hard copy to the digital copy, you can detect those human mistakes or oversights that lead to inconsistency between the paper and digital versions. Look for volatile (changing) fields within the document or its headers and footers that are automatically updated, such as the Today field (or =TODAY() function) that inserts the current date. Paper doesn't update itself!

When theories go wrong

Correct theories are critical to a case. But incorrect theories are sometimes formed. The following list summarizes two theories in the 1995 O.J. Simpson case:

- ✔ **The prosecution theory:** Simpson was angry with his ex-wife on the day of the murders. (Defense attorney Johnnie Cochran effectively disproved this theory by showing pictures from that day of Simpson smiling and greeting his former in-laws.)

- ✔ **The defense theory:** Simpson was framed by the former police detective Mark Fuhrman. (The prosecution claimed in closing arguments that Fuhrman wasn't important to the case, which was a weak rebuttal of the defense's theory because the prosecution had used Fuhrman as a star witness during the trial.)

The plaintiff's theory in the infamous McDonald's coffee lawsuit, in which a 79-year-old Albuquerque woman was severely scalded and had to have skin grafts after spilling coffee in her lap, was that McDonald's was negligent and disregarded human safety. Note that this theory wasn't based on sympathy for the elderly woman. Testimony by one of McDonald's quality assurance managers that management was aware of the risk of serving dangerously hot coffee and that they had no plans to turn down the heat or to post burn warnings supported the theory. According to *The Wall Street Journal*, McDonald's callousness was the issue, and even jurors who first thought that the case was just a tempest in a coffeepot were overwhelmed by the evidence of negligence against the corporation.

Avoid cases where the plan is to tamper with the e-evidence to make it fit the theory after the fact. Without fail, mistakes will be made. It's like trying to commit the perfect crime: Something is always overlooked. In a wrongful termination case, a company instructed its human resources (HR) department to change the fired employee's evaluations from Commendable to Poor. Evaluation forms were formatted Excel spreadsheets with Date and Time fields in the headers and footers. When a user works in Excel, the header and footer aren't visible on the screen, so the HR person making the edits overlooked the updated dates that appeared on the pages as they were reprinted. The company submitted the tampered performance reports — showing that they were all printed on the same day just weeks earlier.

Every case brought before a jury should have a memorable (short) theme based on the theory of the case. A theme can be crafted around an answer to a question, such as "If no [pick one: harassment, discrimination, negligence, policy violation] occurred, why are we here?"

Finding out the client's priorities

Investigations run up against the usual limits of available time and money. Many legal deadlines exist for case filings, responses to case filings, and court appearances. Lawyers may not plan for your services far enough in advance of their court-imposed deadlines, such as filing with the court or appearing before a judge. If you can do the work by the deadline, consider accepting the case subject to the issues discussed next. You need time to think through the elements of the case. You also increase the risk of making mistakes or overlooking vital issues if you're in too much of a rush.

You cannot perform investigative miracles, but you might be expected to. Tradeoffs apply to the quality, time, and cost of your work. Here's a simple law of investigative work:

> Quality work takes more time and costs more money.

When presented with a case, find a smooth way to lay out three factors and ask the client to "pick two." The client may want all three, but that's not feasible. Have the client pick the type of work to be done:

✔ Fast (time)

✔ Cheap (total cost)

✔ Right (quality of work)

Be sure to get a response so that you know which factors are important to the people paying for your expertise. Clarifying these issues up front might make getting paid easier, when the client gets your bill (see Chapter 17). The client can't deny being informed that a quality investigation takes more time, as reflected in the final tally. You can't guarantee that the forensic method (see the "Keeping a Tight Forensic Defense" section, at the end of this chapter) of acquisition through reporting of e-evidence can be done right, quickly, *and* cheaply.

Litigants may be driven by strong emotions, possibly called *principles*, that defy rational behavior. Individuals whose emotions are inflamed tend to make bad decisions, even rejecting amazingly generous settlement offers given the strength of the e-evidence. (The party on the receiving end of this emotional battle may want to settle the case as soon as possible and may not care or may not be aware of how much e-evidence has been found.) Plaintiffs may refuse to follow their lawyers' advice and want you to keep digging. You're neither legal counsel nor therapist. Confine yourself to your area of expertise — the e-evidence.

Timing your work

Limits apply to how fast an investigation can be done because of the devices to be forensically examined. Travel time and your availability are obvious to the client. Key factors influencing the elapsed time to forensically investigate a computer that clients may not know about are described in this list:

- ✔ **Speed of the hard drive being imaged:** A major choke point of imaging a computer is the speed of the hard drive being imaged. You can't begin to search until after the hard drive has been forensically imaged.

- ✔ **Clarity of the search and volume:** In some cases, a person knows what they need, and search terms lead to the documents, e-mails, and other evidence. In other cases, a person suspects or wants to find out what's going on — fishing expeditions looking for e-evidence. Consider the difference in these two scenarios:

  - A business owner needs to recover the original copy of a contract that he only recently learned had been altered. He had composed and e-mailed it to a longtime contract worker. The worker altered the terms of the contract and e-mailed it back when the owner was out of town. The owner didn't inspect the document and never saw the changes. Over a year later, the contract is being enforced. The owner wants a computer forensic investigator to recover the original contract from the computer and e-mail.

- An individual in the process of a divorce suspects that his spouse, who uses several computers, is hiding assets or indiscretions. You don't have much material to work with — just the individual's suspicions.

✔ **Contamination by do-it-yourselfers (DIYs):** If a do-it-yourselfer starts to investigate hard drives or e-mail and contaminates the evidence, you might have to figure out some way to work around the contaminated data, such as finding e-evidence on the recipient's computer or backups somewhere off-site.

Defining the scope of work

From watching news of the crimes and misdemeanors of high-profile individuals or companies, you know that new e-evidence oozes out as cases unfold. An event that starts off as a minor violation can erupt into multiple felony charges. By now the entire world should know that text and e-mail messages might, in effect, be carbon-copied (CC'ed) to major news organizations, such as CNN, Fox News, and *The New York Times*.

Before agreeing to a case, define your scope of work. You use two standard documents for this purpose:

✔ **Case intake form:** The case intake form is similar to a questionnaire. You collect information to set up an investigation. Questions differ according to the type of case: civil, criminal, matrimonial, insurance, or private.

✔ **Letter of agreement:** This letter describes your fee, payment details, and perhaps a retainer.

To see an example of an intake form for use by law enforcement, see pages 58–61 of the *Forensic Examination of Digital Evidence: A Guide to Law Enforcement,* by the Department of Justice (DOJ), at `www.ncjrs.gov/pdffiles1/nij/199408.pdf`.

Be alert to changes in scope because a client may not be willing to pay more in legal fees, including your fee, than the amount stipulated on the contract. This advice sounds simple enough, and it is — as long as the scope of the work for the lawsuit doesn't change. If the value of the case spikes, the scope of the case changes, in addition to your fee. Certain types of lawsuits spiral outward, such as negligence cases. If the contract doesn't address what happens when the scope of the cases changes, you may cheat yourself out of a fee.

Determining Whether You Can Help the Case

Lawyers want to know whether you can help prove their case, build a case, or defend their clients. Crimes aren't crimes and rights aren't rights without proof. A careful lawyer always has an eye on which information can be proved and who can prove it.

Typically, before discussing a case with you, a lawyer reviews your résumé to make sure that you have the proper credentials or qualifications. Keep your résumé updated and honest because you may be asked about it under oath in court or in a deposition. Lawyers also need to verify that no conflict of interest exists. You cannot have ties to any party involved in the case. Bias creates a loophole.

Serving as a resource for the lawyer

Sound like a pro. The lawyer is now uncertain about you and the e-evidence. Most likely, if the lawyer is familiar with the concept of forensic software, she has already mentioned it in this call. To be a helpful coach, explain the computer forensic process as you would explain it to a jury — in simple-to-understand language using analogies (see Chapter 17). By doing so, you're also demonstrating your ability to explain technical topics to a jury.

Be sure to explain these basic concepts of how computer forensic cases work:

✔ **Forensic imaging is done by the prosecution, not by the defense in criminal cases.**

The DA's office or law enforcement confiscates computers and devices. Forensic imaging is done by the DA's computer forensic experts or by experts at a regional computer forensic lab (RCFL). The government doesn't give back computers that contain contraband. Explain that only one forensic image is needed. Each side examines the image, if it's allowed by law. A government office or the DA's office provides a copy of the image unless it contains contraband (such as child pornography). In those cases, the defense may receive the report only on a CD or DVD that has been produced by FTK, EnCase, or similar software.

The defense may receive a paper copy of the report with some redacted sections, a digital copy of the report produced in an Excel spreadsheet on CD in hypertext, and a listing of filenames, dates, and locations.

✔ **Make clear that your role in criminal cases focuses on reviewing the reports and materials provided by the DA's computer forensic expert.**

All the lawyer has to do to view the e-evidence is insert the CD or DVD into a computer and click on the reports to open them in a Web browser. Evidentiary documents, photos, e-mail messages, files, and Registry entries, for example, are all available in a readable format with the click of a mouse.

Taking an active role

As an investigator, don't expect to simply be an order-taker. Clients don't say "Check this out and get back to me." They may not realize what they don't know. You're much more valuable when you take both active and educational roles. The types of help you might be asked to provide are described in this list:

✔ **Find e-evidence to prove that something happened.**

You might be looking for e-mail indicating sexual harassment, financial files indicating fraud or IRS violations, or file transfers indicating theft of intellectual property.

✔ **Find e-evidence to prove that someone did not do something.**

You might prove that image files of child exploitation on a person's office computer could have been downloaded by another person because the computer had no password or firewall protection.

✔ **Figure out what the facts prove or demonstrate.**

This advice includes the discovery of harassing jokes that had been routinely circulated or forwarded by way of the company's e-mail system or of files and e-mail indicating patent violations.

✔ **Examine the prosecution's or opposing counsel's e-evidence for alternative interpretations.**

You might prove that an allegation that the defendant manipulated accounting software isn't supportable by the e-evidence that has been provided.

✔ **Assess the strength of the e-evidence against a suspect.**

Sometimes the client and the accused need to know what the prosecution knows in order to decide whether taking the plea deal or probation is the right choice. Pleading guilty carries less jail time than being found guilty.

✔ **Scrutinize experts' report for inconsistencies, omissions, exaggerations, and other loopholes.**

Cases involving e-evidence usually have two computer forensic investigators — one for each side. The prosecution or plaintiff's side has the burden of proof, so their investigator prepares a report. Regardless of which side you're on, you need to evaluate, and possibly rebut, the opposing expert's report. (See Chapter 16.)

Not getting caught in a lie isn't the same as telling the truth. Judges and juries don't like being fooled with. When you take on a case, recognize that you might have to raise your right hand and swear to tell the truth about the investigation and what you did.

Answering big, blunt questions

Depending on whether the lawyer interviewing you represents a plaintiff or a defendant and the type of case, you might hear various versions of the question "Can you help my case?" You might be asked these types of questions:

✔ Is there another explanation for how the files got there?

✔ How can we prove that the e-mail wasn't sent from a computer by way of the company's network?

✔ How do we prove the geographical location of the machine used to send or receive files?

✔ What else could the e-evidence mean?

✔ What other theory can explain why the files were deleted or missing?

✔ Was my client's computer capable of viewing the images or downloading those files?

✔ Which statements or allegations in the affidavits are vague?

✔ How might the opponent's expert mishandle or taint the e-evidence?

If e-discovery and the production of electronic documents are involved, you're asked to provide expertise on those issues too.

We've seen alarming misinterpretations of e-evidence — based on ignorance or false hope or just plain deliberately. Sometimes e-evidence, like physical evidence, by itself or out of context just cannot be interpreted. For example, a manager might accuse an employee of stealing customer files before resigning. Technically, copying a file to external removable media (a CD or flash drive) creates a .lnk (link) file. Suppose that a lot of .lnk files are found on the former employee's laptop using forensic software such as EnCase or FTK. But that analysis was done on the laptop after another employee had been using it for weeks. For the client, that's sufficient proof that the employee stole intellectual property (IP), but it has no evidentiary value. It's possible that a specific employee can be associated with .lnk files and the IP, but only if someone finds the device on which those files were copied. Otherwise, too many degrees of separation — or breaks in the chain of evidence — exist between the former employee and the IP files on the reused laptop. No defensible interpretation about the .lnk files is possible.

Signing on the dotted line

If you believe that you can perform an investigation fairly, impartially, and thoroughly and state your findings in a signed document, do the following:

✔ **Say "I accept."**

A clear reply indicates to that client that you made a decision. Don't assume that you gave enough signals for the client to figure out your intention.

✔ **Sign an agreement or a contract that details, as much as possible, tasks to be done, deadlines, costs, and payment schedules.**

Be sure that it's clear who is responsible for paying your invoices. All parties must read and sign the contract so that if something goes wrong, no one can plead ignorance.

 At some point, you report your findings with an introduction that begins something like this: "Within the bounds of reasonable computer forensic certainty, and subject to change if additional information becomes available, it is my professional opinion that. . . ."

Passing the Court's Standard As a Reliable Witness

Most 21st century litigation relies on the testimony of experts — including computer forensic experts. Expert testimony plays a deciding role in a lot of litigation, so it's not a surprise that the U.S. Supreme Court has ruled several times on who qualifies as an expert and the admissibility of expert scientific testimony in a federal trial. These rulings ensure that your testimony is reliable and can be evaluated by a judge and jury.

Getting your credentials accepted

The reliability standards began in 1923, with the Supreme Court decision in *Frye v. United States,* which began tests of expertise for experts. The Court held that, to be admissible, expert testimony had to

✔ Rely on principles that were "generally accepted" by the scientific community

✔ Be able to meet the standards of peer review

As a result of *Frye,* your reputation and achievements in the forensic field comprise the central question of admissibility of your testimony. It's an objective standard for courts to apply when trying to distinguish your legitimate testimony from fantasies of quack and crank scientists. But *Frye* created a problem when lawyers began gaming the system. *Frye* didn't or couldn't protect against experts-for-hire.

Tougher federal regulations and Supreme Court precedents replaced *Frye* — primarily *Daubert* and Rule 702. In the 1993 *Daubert v. Merrell Dow* opinion, the Supreme Court set stricter criteria for the admissibility of scientific expert testimony. State courts' set their own standards based on Frye, Daubert, or Rule 702.

The *Daubert* test is primarily a question of relevance or fitness of the evidence. For testimony to be used, it must be sufficiently tied to the facts of the case to help understand the disputed issues. (See the blog on *Daubert* issues at http://daubertontheweb.com/blog702.html.) But *Daubert* didn't apply to nonscientific expertise.

To fill that gap, in the 1999 *Kumho Tire v. Carmichael* opinion the Court extended *Daubert* to also include nonscientific expert testimony. For technical or other specialized knowledge, Fed. R. Evid. 702 applies.

Rule 702 broadly governs the admissibility of expert testimony. The rule

✔ States "If scientific, technical, or other specialized knowledge will assist the trier of fact to understand the evidence or to determine a fact in issue, a witness qualified as an expert by knowledge, skill, experience, training, or education, may testify thereto in the form of an opinion or otherwise."

✔ Permits nonscientific expert testimony as long as it helps the trier of fact.

✔ Imposes these requirements on technical or other specialized knowledge witnesses:

> • *The witness must possess such a relevant form of knowledge.*
>
> • *The knowledge must assist the trier of fact.*
>
> • *The witness must be qualified as an expert.*

Expect opposing counsel to question your credentials. See Chapter 18 for ways to add to your qualifications.

Impressing opinions on the jury

When an expert's analysis is based on an objective metric or standard (for example, the standard in Italy that fingerprints are a match to a person if they have 17 points of similarity), jurors decide for themselves whether the expert's conclusions are valid. If the expert can show only a 13-point match, the jury can make a comparison. But as Chief Justice William H. Rehnquist pointed out in the 1997 case *General Electric Co. v. Joiner,* when the standard is subjective, the jury has to accept an expert's conclusion as *ipse dixit* (the only proof of the fact is that this expert said it). The jurors lack a standard against which to assess and decide whether a conclusion was reached correctly.

The court in the *Daubert* case pointed out that the availability of data about a technique's error rate is important to decide if an analytic method is admissible. For example, when juries know that a computer forensic toolkit has a 3 percent error rate, they're better able to intelligently determine the believability of the expert's opinion that is based on that toolkit. But without knowing about the toolkit's reliability, a juror may decide solely on the expert's personality, credentials, or other irrelevant factors.

Going Forward with the Case

After you accept the case and the lawyer is satisfied with your credentials, it's time to get started with the case. In this section, we discuss how to get up to speed with the case, how to organize your files, and how to search for background information on the case.

Digging into the evidence

The first thing you must do is obtain permission from the lawyer to call the district attorney's (DA's) forensic expert to discuss the case.

To conform to the Adam Walsh Child Protection and Safety Act of 2006 (often abbreviated as AWA), you may need to make arrangements to view the e-evidence. Section 504 of the AWA states that

> *(1) In any criminal proceeding, any property or material that constitutes child pornography . . . shall remain in the care, custody, and control of either the Government or the court.*
>
> *(2)(A) Notwithstanding Rule 16 of the Federal Rules of Criminal Procedure, a court shall deny . . . any request by the defendant to copy, photograph, duplicate, or otherwise reproduce any property or material that constitutes child pornography . . . so long as the Government makes the property or material reasonably available to the defendant.*

Reasonably available to the defendant means that the government provides ample opportunity for inspection and examination at a government facility by the defendant, his attorney, and anyone who will provide expert testimony at trial.

Defense lawyers have criticized the AWA for limiting their two most frequent defenses:

- ✔ Whether a digital image depicts an actual child and isn't a virtual image or a digitally altered adult

- ✔ Whether the defendant knowingly possessed or received the image. That is, that the contraband images had not been transferred or downloaded to the hard drive by malware or some other source unbeknown to the defendant.

You're not a digital imaging expert, nor do you want to possess contraband. Inspect the log files detailing dates and times of file uploads or downloads, file sizes and access dates, locations of files and how they were stored, and password protections to form an opinion regarding whether someone or something other than the defendant could have led to the images being stored on the hard drive.

You should also suggest a conference call with the lawyer and client. You have to ask questions about computer use (for example, times of day and Internet habits), user access, password sharing, and issues related to the circumstances. If that's not an option, discuss the possibility of e-mailing questions for the client to answer.

Organizing and documenting your work

Being a computer forensic investigator means never saying "I can't find the computer file." Follow these steps to get organized:

✔ **Create a cases folder.**

Give it a memorable name, such as `All CF Cases`.

✔ **Create a case folder for each case inquiry, which becomes your case folder if you get the case.**

All case folders are nested within the `All CF Cases` folder. Folder names should include the case name (`Plaintiff v Defendant`), the lawyer's name, the month and year, and a descriptive identifier — for example, `Acme v Zena Robson July 20## NY fraud case`.

✔ **Save a copy of every e-mail sent and received about the case.**

Use descriptive filenames. Cases tend to span long periods, and people forget what was decided or communicated. When a call comes in from a lawyer who needs to discuss a case, you can easily find it later.

✔ **Scan paper documents and hard copies into the appropriate folder.**

You may receive hundreds of pages of texting, e-mail, depositions, affidavits, and reports. An *affidavit* is sworn testimony. Keep these documents organized and protected in a filing cabinet so that they stay "clean." You may need to use them in your deposition or in court. Coffee or spaghetti stains send an unfavorable message about you.

✔ **Create a spreadsheet template for tracking timeframes and descriptions of your work.**

Starting with the first call, use the template to start a tracking file. Track the start and end times and dates of everything. Include everything even if no charge is associated with the activity. For example, list the first call for consultation and mark it No Charge. Figure 5-1 shows a spreadsheet you can design to track your activities. Include all details, which you can edit before submitting it as your invoice for professional services. After using your tracking spreadsheet as your invoice, start another tracking sheet in the same workbook so that you don't accidentally double-charge.

	A	B	C	D	E
3	Date of first inquiry	October 31, 2008			
4	Invoice #:	1234			
6	Case #:	103108			
7	Case name:	Plaintiff vs. Defendant			
8	Attorney:	Will Wynn			
9	Firm name:	Law Office of Wynn			
10	Firm Phone & Fax:	Phone: (800) 555-6789 | Fax: (800) 555-5678			
11	Client:	Name of Client(s)			
12	Expert/Consultant:	Your Name			
13		Your Address			
14		Your City, State, Zip			
15		Your Tel #, Fax #, e-mail address			
17	**Dates**	**Description of Services Performed**	**Hours**	**Rate per hour**	**Net**
18	Oct 31, 2008	Discussed issues of the case.	0.0	$ 200	$ -
19	Nov 24, 2008	Reviewed materials sent by Wynn on Nov 15, 2008 and received on Nov. 17, 2008. Materials: depositions; Forensics Analysis Case Summary; police reports; and transcripts of messages. Read: REPORTER'S TRANSCRIPT OF PRELIMINARY HEARING, date/time: July 20, 2007, 1:15pm. Prepared report of material issues and statements.	5.5	$ 200	$ 1,100
20	Nov 27, 2008	Reviewed Encase, FTK, and MySpace evidence files received from the prosecutor's office; prepared notes for use in final report.	2.5	$ 200	$ 500
21				$ 200	
22				$ 200	
23		**Total Services**	8.0		$ 1,600
24	Nov 27, 2008	Expenses: Expedited Shipping of documents			$ 35
25		**Total**			$ 1,635
26					

Figure 5-1: Spreadsheet for tracking work and time.

Researching and digging for intelligence

You want basic knowledge about the parties involved in a case, similar cases, or characteristics of the crime or lawsuit. The military calls this process *intelligence*. Doing research is necessary, is a slow process, and may be frustrating. With practice, you get good at it, so do research for every case to keep sharp.

Don't bill for research you do to get up-to-speed on general issues.

Your search strategy includes several tools:

- ✔ **Search engines:** For specific topics or companies that are new to you, start with a search engine, such as Google (www.google.com) or Yahoo! (www.yahoo.com) to pick up background information and ideas for more precise searches. Your results will form the equivalent of a data dump.

Try a search on exactly the phrase you're thinking about. For example, a search on **how to defend against charges of fraud** or **electronic evidence in divorce cases** may result in some useful information or threads. If you need to search for information about child pornography, do it *very* carefully, by using related terms, such as **prosecuting child exploitation crimes**. Search engines don't know your intent. Engines cannot distinguish between someone trying to research the crime and characteristics and someone looking to find and download contraband images.

These two examples show what you can learn from research into the use, or attempted use, of e-evidence in divorce proceedings:

- *In Florida:* A wife installed spyware on her husband's computer and later tried to use the information she collected in their divorce case. The e-evidence was inadmissible because Florida bans the interception of communications.

- *In New Jersey:* A wife was granted $7,500 during divorce proceedings after her husband wiretapped her computer to keep track of her transactions and e-mails.

Set your Internet security to a higher setting before such a search to avoid accidentally accessing contraband images. If you stumble across images, expect to receive cookies on your computer from those sites followed by annoying spam or pop-up windows.

✔ **Government agencies:** Use the search engine to find .gov Web sites. The U.S. Department of Justice (www.usdoj.gov) and the National RCFL program's Web page (http://rcfl.gov) offer up-to-date cases and Webcasts.

✔ **LexisNexis or Westlaw online database (for-fee services):** If information exists, it's probably accessible from these online services. Current news, business information, company directories, trade journals, federal and state laws and regulations, legal cases, and medical references are available at an incredible level of precision. Training is required, or else you waste time and frustrate yourself. For intense research, these databases are indispensable.

✔ **Legal encyclopedias and dictionaries:** Find good, practical information that you can use to quickly look up a term or verify that you're using or spelling a term correctly.

✔ **Law school libraries:** An amazing amount of law school content can be understood by nonlegal minds. And, the sites have search engines so that you can get in and out quickly.

Digging is the process of searching for information about a party involved in a case. The following list describes not only places to dig for information but also how a person leaves digital traces. Because the mantra for many of these social networking sites is "Find and get found," the search engines provided at each of these sites make searching for what you need quite easy.

- **Social networks, such as MySpace (www.myspace.com) and Facebook (www.facebook.com):** Typically, a MySpace user's Web page can be viewed by any other MySpace user. Further, any MySpace user can contact any other MySpace user by using internal e-mail or instant messaging on MySpace. Access to private text messages among members is available to law enforcement officers who have subpoenas. Confessions and admissions made while texting have been hard to refute and have even destroyed alibis.

- **Video-sharing sites, such as YouTube (www.youtube.com) and VideoEgg (www.videoegg.com):** People post evidence of their crimes in public. In fact, UK police officials monitor YouTube for evidence of crimes. Several incidents of videos posted to the site have led to arrests. In many cases, perpetrators of illegal acts filmed themselves and then posted material to the Internet. Showoff videos aren't sufficient on their own, but they provide a good start or boost to the case.

Keeping a Tight Forensic Defense

No matter which side you're on (prosecutor/defense or plaintiff/defendant), you have to defend your methods, interpretations, and conclusions.

Maintaining the integrity of e-evidence requires a standardized defensible approach to data handling and preservation. Figure 5-2 shows your target — admissible evidence that isn't excluded because of a rule or loophole.

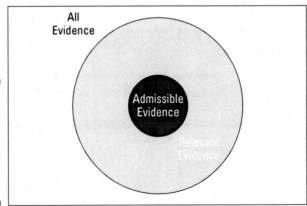

Figure 5-2: Visualization of an investigator's target — admissible evidence.

The opposition tries to find mistakes in your approach. Your defense, discussed in detail in Chapter 7, is that you

✔ Acquire the e-evidence without altering or damaging the source.

✔ Authenticate the acquired e-evidence by verifying that it was the same as the original.

✔ Analyze the data and files without altering them.

Also, as part of your defensive strategy, your work is

✔ Performed in accordance with forensic science principles

✔ Based on current standard best practices

✔ Conducted with verified tools to identify, collect, filter, "tag and bag," store, and preserve e-evidence

✔ Documented thoroughly and in detail

Plugging loopholes

Any wrong action you take can possibly blow out a case. Figure 5-3 shows the standard processes you should perform during your forensic examination. You see these forensic processes in action throughout Part III.

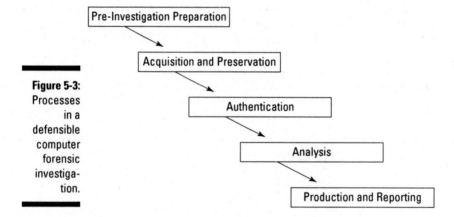

Figure 5-3: Processes in a defensible computer forensic investigation.

Pre-Investigation Preparation

Acquisition and Preservation

Authentication

Analysis

Production and Reporting

Preinvestigation preparation

The key to effective data searches is to prepare and plan carefully. Quite simply, poor preparation can lead to mistakes or compromises or other compensations. Take time to understand and carefully plan which information is critical to an investigation or case.

Before acquiring potential e-evidence, you should do some fact-finding:

✔ **Interview members of the IT staff.**

You need to find out how and where data has been stored. Though helpful, many times such a conversation with these people may be inappropriate. Have this conversation with caution. You don't want to tip off unauthorized people about the investigation, especially in a corporate environment.

✔ **Identify relevant time periods and the scope of the data to be searched.**

You use this information to define and limit the scope of your investigation of the e-evidence. You want to be sure to cover the entire period and not waste time reviewing irrelevant materials.

✔ **Identify relevant types of files.**

The case may not involve every type of file. Some investigations pertain only to documents, images, music files, or e-mail. Obtaining this information saves time.

✔ **Identify search terms for data filtering, particularly words, names, or unique phrases to help locate relevant data.**

Filter out irrelevant information. Metadata can help in the filtering process.

✔ **Find out usernames and passwords for network and e-mail accounts.**

To get past password-protected files and accounts, you may need this information. Password-cracking software is part of most computer forensic software packages, but cracking can take a lot of time and isn't always successful.

✔ **Check for other computers, devices, or Internet usage that might contain relevant evidence.**

Ask questions about each of the other potential sources of useful evidence. People involved may not know that handheld devices, flash drives, or social networks are sources of e-evidence.

Document only the facts. Don't treat documentation like a diary of your thoughts or gut feelings.

Acquisition and preservation

You cannot work with the original material, so you must create an exact physical duplicate of it. The creation of a forensic copy is the *acquisition*. A *forensic copy* is the end-product of a forensic acquisition of a computer's hard drive or other storage device. A forensic copy is also called a *bitstream copy* or *image* because it's an exact bit-for-bit copy of the original document, file, partition, graphical image, or disk, for example. All metadata, file dates, slack areas, bad sectors — everything — are the same in the image as in their original forms.

Acquisition isn't the same as copying files from one medium to another. You cannot use a Copy command because dates aren't preserved. Make a copy of a .doc file on your computer; and compare the time stamps for the files. Notice the differences. Using normal operating system utilities to make a copy is a mistake.

Make several forensic copies in case something happens to the image.

A drive can be imaged without anyone viewing its contents. You can make a forensic copy in several ways, all requiring specialized software. This list describes two imaging methods:

- ✔ **Drive:** This means of evidence preservation captures everything on a drive. One method of capturing or copying all data on a drive is to make a non-invasive *mirror image* of the drive. Slight variations in definitions of a mirror image exist. A mirror image might be an exact copy of a hard drive, but not necessarily. Mirror images are meant for backup purposes. To be safe, assume that a mirror image isn't a forensic image.

- ✔ **Sector-by-sector or bitstream:** This more advanced method starts at the beginning of a drive and makes a copy of every bit — zeros and ones — to the end of the drive without in any way deleting or modifying the contents of the evidence. The file slack and unallocated file space that often contain deleted files and e-mail messages are acquired too. This method creates a forensic image of the e-evidence.

Authentication

Failure to authenticate a forensic image may invalidate any results that are produced. Creating a forensic copy with the FTK Imager or EnCase tools authenticates the image. These programs store a report that includes two digital fingerprints, called MD5 and SHA1 hash values, that uniquely identify and authenticate the acquired data. Hash values enable you to prove that the evidence and duplicate data are identical. If data was altered, the hash values would also change.

Authenticating e-evidence also requires you to demonstrate that a computer system or process that generated e-evidence was working properly during the relevant period.

Analysis

Your methods of analysis depend on which type of forensic you're performing — computer, e-mail, network, PDA, or cellphone, for example. A forensic image is, in effect, a single file. This handy format lets you perform keyword searches to find information or review thumbnail-size pictures that had been on the original hard drive. To survive an opponent's challenges:

✔ Use analysis tools according to the manufacturer's directions or recommendations.

✔ Test or verify that the results of the forensic tool are consistent before using.

If you use a generally accepted forensic toolset, these verifications are carried out for you, but you need to know what the software is doing.

Production and reporting

You need to produce your results or findings to your client or the court. Working with your client to determine the design and content of a report is smart and helpful.

Your reports aren't intended for all to see. Work on a need-to-know basis, and don't give or show the report to anyone without approval.

You can submit reports on a CD or DVD with hyperlinks to supporting information that's contained on the CD/DVD. This effective, self-contained method lets you concisely deliver the report and supporting information.

Writing that is logical and organized and that uses proper grammar, capitalization, sentence structure, and punctuation has become an ancient or arcane art. But try to recall a time when sentences were used. Resist the urge to use slang. Your results can be improved if you

✔ **Write the 1-minute sound bite story.**

No matter how complex the issue, the news media delivers it as sound bites. You have to do the same. Think of your summary as a story. If your story doesn't persuasively explain why your opinion is reasonable, keep working at it.

✔ **Test your explanations and summary.**

Be sure to test your story on people who are unfamiliar with the case and are technology-illiterate. If they think that your analysis is reasonable, you're headed in the right direction to persuade a judge and jury.

Writing a report takes time, concentration, and lots of editing. Leave enough time to write your report. Keep in mind that you use your own report to refresh your memory about what you did. Be good to yourself by minding the details.

Chapter 6

Acquiring and Authenticating E-Evidence

The foundation of a computer forensic investigation isn't the damaging e-mail you find that implicates a company CEO of embezzlement. Your investigation depends on how you forensically transfer the evidence from one location to another without contaminating it and then prove that you found the evidence the way you present it to the judge and jury. Without this foundation to work from, all subsequent work on a case can be called into question and potentially thrown out of court as possibly being tainted. This chapter explains how to prevent this situation. Although the concepts we describe are fairly simple, applying them often stymies even the best investigators.

The bottom line is that you're extracting and fingerprinting potential evidence in a way that is incontestable and easy for the average person to understand.

Acquiring E-Evidence Properly

Because the acquisition of data in a forensically sound manner is the cornerstone of a good computer forensic investigation, you should acquire evidence in the most professional manner possible. The primary obstacle to creating a sound forensic copy of potential evidence is the possibility of changing the data while you're attempting to duplicate it. Due to the large number of devices in circulation that hold data, the equipment you use to duplicate data varies by device type. We can't stress enough that, as a computer forensic professional, you need the proper equipment and training (which you can find out about in Chapters 18 and 20) in order to effectively duplicate data in a manner that leaves no possibility of it's being changed and to prove it in a court of law. The tricky part is doing it with all the various media out there and not messing up!

The first rule to follow when working a computer forensic acquisition is to document *everything* you can. In Chapter 4, the documentation process is covered in detail, so read that chapter if you need more information.

After reviewing the first rule of computer forensics and committing it to memory, your next step is to begin the process of acquiring a forensic copy of the evidence. The process in a generalized format is:

1. **Determine which type of media you're working with.**

   You might be working on a magnetic storage device such as a hard drive, on an optical device such as a DVD, or with volatile memory such as a mobile phone.

2. **Find the right tool for the job.**

   After you know the type of media you have, you have to ensure that you have the correct tools to retrieve the data from the media in a forensically sound manner.

3. **Transfer the data.**

   You're using the appropriate equipment to transfer the data from the original device to sterile media (if necessary) and ensuring that the process to check the integrity of the transfer is in place.

4. **Authenticate the preserved data.**

   Digital data is easy to change, and court systems like to ensure that the data doesn't change after it's acquired. You do that by *authenticating* — running a checksum — after the data is in your possession.

5. **Make a duplicate of the duplicate.**

   After the data is safely off the original device, you can make a *duplicate* copy of the evidence from the copy so that you have a working copy of the evidence. This step is critically important, no matter which type of media you're working with, because you need the working copy.

Always follow this standard rule: Touch the original once, the forensic copy twice, and your working copy as many times as needed.

We discuss each of the preceding steps in more detail in the following sections.

Step 1: Determine the Type of Media You're Working With

The first step in any computer forensic investigation is to identify the type of media you're working with. The various types of media you might encounter are described in this list:

✔ **Fixed storage device:** Any device that you use to store data and that's permanently attached to a computer is a *fixed storage device*. The type of storage device you're probably most familiar with is the classic magnetic-media hard drive, which is inside almost every personal computer (see Figure 6-1). Traditional hard drives are mechanisms that rotate disks coated with a magnetic material; however, new technology uses chip-based storage media known as the solid-state drive (SSD), shown in Figure 6-2. It's as though your thumb flash drive is 1,000 times larger than its current size!

Figure 6-1: The classic magnetic-media hard drive.

✔ **Portable storage device:** Most people consider floppy disks (remember those?) or flash memory drives, shown in Figure 6-3, to be the only true portable storage devices, but *any* device that you can carry with you qualifies. iPods (shown in Figure 6-4), MP3 players, mobile phones, and even some wristwatches are also portable storage devices.

Unlike fixed storage, where most interfaces are standardized, mobile devices have different interfaces, which adds to the complexity of your case. We discuss the complexity of mobile devices in Chapter 12.

Figure 6-2:
A solid-state
drive.

Figure 6-3:
A typical
Flash drive.

Figure 6-4:
The Apple
iPod.

✔ **Memory storage area:** With the move from desktop computers to mobile
devices, investigators are seeing increasingly more evidence that's
found *only* in memory. The obvious type of device is a mobile phone
(such as the Apple iPhone, shown in Figure 6-5) or personal digital assistant that often saves data only in volatile memory. After the battery dies,
your data evidence also dies. Not-so-obvious places to find evidence in
volatile memory are the RAM areas of regular computers and servers as
well as some network devices.

✔ **Network storage device:** With the growth of the Internet and the expo-
nential increase in the power of network devices, data can be found on
devices that until now haven't held forensic data of any value. Devices
such as routers (see the Cisco routers shown in Figure 6-6), switches,
and even wireless access points can now save possible forensic information and even archive it for future access.

Figure 6-5:
The Apple
iPhone.

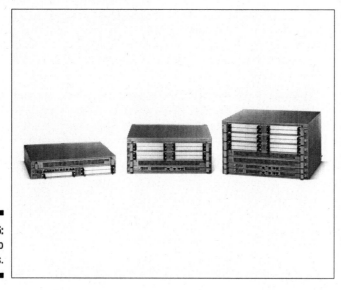

Figure 6-6:
Cisco
routers.

✔ **Memory card:** In addition to using built-in RAM memory, many devices
now use digital memory cards to add storage. Common types are SD
(shown in Figure 6-7) and MMC flash cards. To read this type of memory
device, you often have to use a multimedia card reader.

Figure 6-7:
An SD card.

Step 2: Find the Right Tool

When you acquire a forensic image, you're making a *bitstream copy*. In this rather simple process, you copy every bit of the original media, from the physical start of the media to the physical end of the media. The concept is simple, but the execution in practice can be difficult unless you have the proper equipment that's designed for the purpose.

Acquiring a bitstream image is difficult for two reasons: An operating system doesn't recognize the entire hard drive where data may be lurking, and the integrity of the system might be compromised. We discuss both problems in the following sections. Then, we go into the tools we find indispensable when acquiring images.

Finding all the space

Operating systems allocate space on their storage media, but a little part of the hard drive is always left over and not accessible by the operating system. For example, a Microsoft Windows operating system might recognize 55.8 gigabytes (GB) of hard drive space, when in fact the hard drive measures 60GB of physical space, as shown in Figure 6-8.

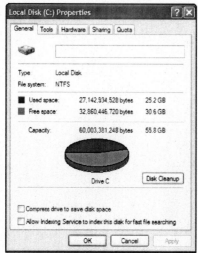

Figure 6-8:
Hard drive
usage
statistics.

This statement doesn't mean that you can't access the "extra" space by using the right software tools; it just means that the operating system cannot.

Because most operating systems work this way, you must rely on a tool that doesn't use the operating system to retrieve the bits from the storage media. A tool made specifically for computer forensics, such as FTK or EnCase, is a good candidate for the job.

If you're a power user and know how to use tools such as Linux dd, you're in good shape, but you should always use the right tool for the right job such as:

- ✔ **FTK/EnCase/Paraben:** Tools for working with most operating systems such as Windows, Linux, and Apple. Also extremely easy to use for relatively newer users.

- ✔ **Hex editors/system level utilities:** Software tools for digging deeper into the structure of file systems and their files. Power users use these tools for deeper analysis, but require a fair amount of knowledge of file structures.

- ✔ **Disk duplicators:** Hardware devices such as Logicube's Forensic Talon duplicate storage media quickly and forensically to the tune of 4 gigabytes per minute.

- ✔ **Write protectors:** Devices such as Weibetech's Forensic Ultradock keep you from accidentally writing to storage devices during a preview or acquisition from a suspect's media device.

This loss of storage space doesn't occur only in storage media such as hard drives — it also occurs in storage media such as flash drives, cameras, and even mobile phones. Rarely does an operating system use every last bit at its physical disposal.

A write-protect device

If writing to the original media where the potential evidence is stored is disastrous, what can you do? The answer to this technological dilemma is the use of a *write blocker* that (obviously) blocks any attempts to write to the original media. The process sounds simple, but what happens in the background is complex.

To put this concept in practical terms, the write blocker responds to the write requests of the operating system with the responses that the operating system is expecting as though the write operation had really taken place on the storage device. The write blocker is telling the operating system what it wants to hear. To see an eye-opening example of this process, you can format a hard drive (pick one you don't need) with a write blocker attached. Notice that the operating system formats the hard drive, just like in a regular format operation, but if you reboot the computer system and plug the hard drive back in, the hard drive looks like it was never formatted! Of course, if it did format, your write blocker isn't working, and you have a big problem, forensically speaking.

Two forms of write blockers exist, and both work in the same conceptual fashion but use different mechanisms:

✔ **Physical:** Physically intercepts the data signals that leave the data bus on the computer and responds with the appropriate data signals by way of the data bus to the operating system. Write blockers of this type are operating system independent and can be classified even further as either native or tailgate:

  • *Native:* Has the same media interface on both the target and acquisition sides.

  • *Tailgate:* Can be a combination of IDE, SATA, USB, FireWire, and even wireless.

  Figure 6-9 shows a typical write block device that you install in the drive bay of a desktop forensic workstation.

✔ **Logical:** Usually bundled with computer forensic software as part of its feature set; works by intercepting write calls at the software level and responding to operating system calls. This type of write blocker is operating system specific — a Linux software write blocker doesn't work on a Windows computer, for example, and vice versa.

Figure 6-9:
Desktop
write block
device.

Sterile media

It's always embarrassing when you find smoking gun evidence of a crime only to find out that the evidence you found was left over from a previous case on media that you didn't properly erase or wipe.

Imagine that you have on videocassette tape a movie that you don't want to view any more and you decide to record your child's birthday party over the movie. Unless you erase the cassette, whichever part of the movie the birthday party doesn't record over is still on the tape. So, immediately after the birthday party footage ends, the movie pops up on the screen and rolls the credits for you. The same concept is obvious in storage media on a computer in that you mix two different cases on one examination media.

The use of wiping software on storage media is necessary to make sure that no cross contamination of cases or evidence occurs because not to do so dooms the investigation and your credibility in one fell swoop. The basic process to wipe a drive is to write a sequence of binary digits over the media in its entirety to make sure that no pre-wipe data is on the storage media.

Wiping software is usually included with any professional computer forensic tool, but you can find third-party wiping software quite easily. Here are two:

- ✔ **LSoft Technologies Hard Drive Eraser** (`www.lsoft.net`): Conforming to the Department of Defense (DOD) standards for data destruction, this free tool works fairly well.
- ✔ **White Canyon's Wipe Drive 5** (`www.whitecanyon.com`): This wiping software is not free, but it is so inexpensive for the features it includes it might as well be free.

Most wiping software do the job of cleaning up a storage device fairly well because all they really have to do is write over the storage device. The only problem you encounter with every software wiper that actually works is that they take a *long* time to complete their job. On large devices, it may take days to wipe a storage device!

An excellent source of information for computer forensic investigators and others who need to wipe storage media is the National Institute of Standards and Technology (NIST) at `http://csrc.nist.gov/publications/nistpubs/800-88/NISTSP800-88_rev1.pdf`.

Step 3: Transfer Data

You can take data off a computer in many ways, but only a few are forensically sound. The use of any one of these forensic techniques is dictated in large part by the circumstances around your computer forensic investigation. The biggest decision you have to make is whether to do the work in the field or in your lab. Those two differing environments dictate to a large degree what your toolkit looks like — a simple toolkit or full-blown field kit that requires a small RV for transportation. (It's the geek version of a SWAT team.) The methods described in the following sections are commonly used by computer forensic examiners.

Transferring data in the field

The following steps illustrate how the process of making a bitstream copy works. By using a field kit and professional forensic software, these steps illustrate a forensic situation in the field:

1. **Determine the media you're working with.**

   In this case, the media is an EIDE hard drive.

2. **Position the write blocking hardware and hard drive.**

   In Figure 6-10, an EIDE write block device is positioned to connect to the target media. The power is turned off. Notice that the hard drive and write block device are placed on an antistatic mat.

Figure 6-10:
Positioning
an EIDE
write block
device and
an EIDE
hard drive.

3. **Connect the data and power cables to the acquisition hard drive.**

   Connect the data cable to the hard drive, and connect the power cable as shown in Figure 6-11. Make sure that no power is applied to the write block device yet.

Figure 6-11:
Data cable
and power
cable
connected
to the
acquisition
hard drive.

4. **Connect the data cable to the write-protect device.**

   In Figure 6-12, the adaptor to connect the EIDE interface by using the EIDE data cable is being connected.

Do not bend the pins or stretch the cable!

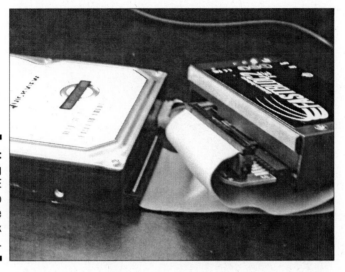

Figure 6-12:
Connecting
the EIDE
adaptor to
the write
block
device.

5. **Make sure that all cables are connected correctly.**

   Double-check to ensure that all cables are securely connected, as shown
   in Figure 6-13. Note the red line on the data cable. If you don't see the
   red stripe on Pin 1, the connection doesn't work. If you did it backward,
   take off the connector and reverse it.

Figure 6-13:
The properly
connected
setup.

6. **Power on the write blocker.**

After all the cables are connected, you can power on the write block device (see Figure 6-14). Within a couple of seconds, the computer forensic workstation detects the presence of a new drive and lists it as an available drive if it can read it. Don't worry if your operating system doesn't see the hard drive — the computer forensic software detects it.

Figure 6-14:
The write block device is powered up!

7. **Acquire the bitstream image with your computer forensic software.**

Depending on which computer forensic software package you're using, the details of how each software tool acquires a bit stream image will vary, but the general principles still apply. In Figure 6-15, the computer forensic software is being set up to acquire the bitstream image and to make a hash (which is explained in greater detail later in this chapter) of the data being transferred.

8. **Acquiring the bitstream copy.**

Most computer forensic software keeps you up-to-date on the progress of the transfer — notice the status indicator in the lower-right corner of the window shown in Figure 6-16. As a secondary way to double-check whether your software is accessing the hard drive, check the write-protect device for any telltale LED lights.

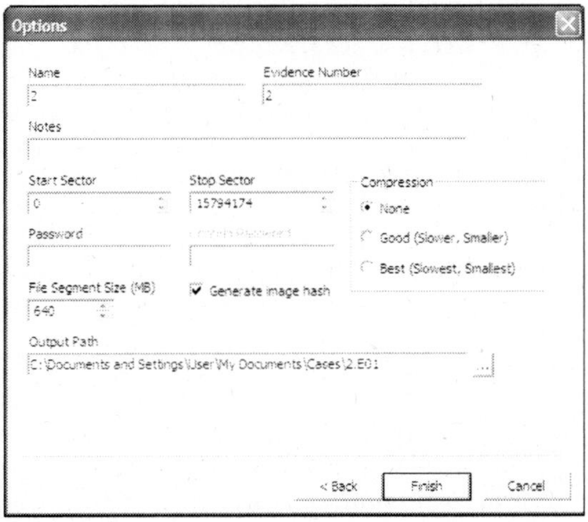

Figure 6-15:
Transfer settings to ensure that a hash value is computed.

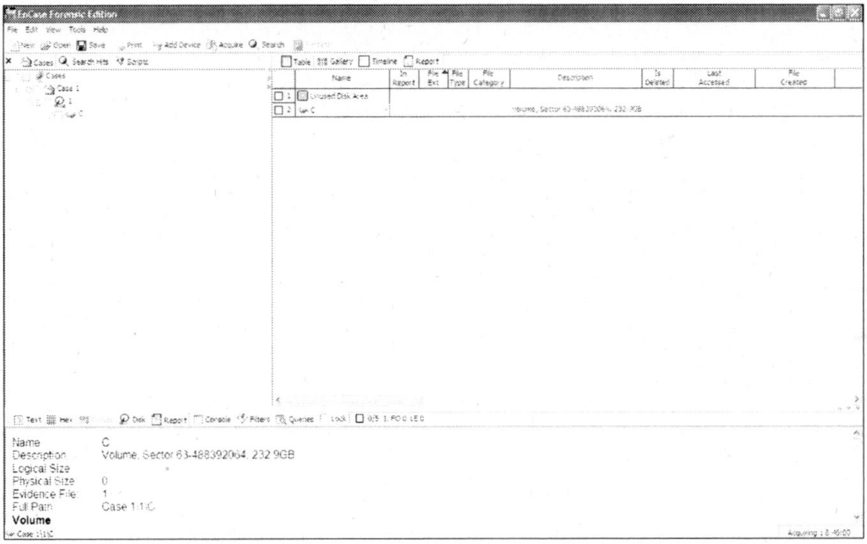

Figure 6-16:
An acquisition in progress.

9. **Wrap things up.**

   After the forensic software has finished the acquisition and the software reports the hash values match, save the new image file. After making sure that the image file is saved, turn off the power to the write block device and reverse the process to disconnect all cables. Put the hard drive in a secure storage area.

From computer to computer

In a computer-to-computer acquisition, you use the suspect computer as the platform to extract the data to your forensic examination computer. Of all the data-transfer methods, this one is most likely to cause accidental data corruption, because of the manner in which data must be retrieved.

Unless you have experience in performing this procedure or have practiced it until you can do it in your sleep, we recommend using a different method.

You use one of these two cable options to link the two computers:

- ✔ **Parallel:** The slowest method, but the best one to use if you have the time. Most computer geeks recognize the parallel cable as the one you normally use to connect your computer to a printer. The only difference here is that both ends have the connection designed to be connected to the back of the computer and not to the printer.

- ✔ **Network:** Slightly faster than using a parallel cable and typically used to connect computers to a network. If you look behind your computer and see an oversized phone jack with a couple of blinking lights next to it and a skinny-looking cable attached, that's your network cable.

A limiting factor in both these methods is the restricted amount of data you can transfer at a time. Both methods are useful, however, for previewing a data drive forensically to see whether it has obvious evidence, although they're extremely slow to forensically copy entire drives that are larger than 50GB.

Another problem is the potential for a catastrophic data-corruption event — or *tainting* the evidence. Using this method, you boot (load) the operating system on the suspect computer with forensic boot media. It acts as the software write blocker that links to your forensic computer to enable the data transfer. The boot media can be a floppy disk, compact disc (CD), digital video disc (DVD), or even USB device.

Unless you follow the extraction procedure exactly, chances are good that the computer will boot up using the suspect's hard drive and potentially erase data that might be useful in your investigation — and possibly affect the credibility of your case.

To copy data between two computers using the parallel or network cable method, follow these general steps:

1. **Unplug the power source to the computer.**

2. **Open the computer case and disconnect the storage device power supply from the computer.**

   You have to ensure that there's no physical way for the storage device to boot up during the computer power-up.

3. **Reconnect the power supply on the computer, boot the computer, and enter the BIOS setup area.**

   How you enter the BIOS setup area is determined by the computer manufacturer. Some computers require you to press F1, and others want you to press F2. Still others use combinations of keyboard keys. Check with the manufacturer to make sure that you know which keyboard sequence works.

4. **Look for the Boot Sequence tab or page.**

5. **Change the order in which the computer boots to the boot media you're using so that your boot media is number one on the list.**

   You can choose a floppy disk, CD, DVD, or USB boot media depending on which one you use to boot your computer.

6. **Save the changes you made to the boot sequence.**

   Don't connect the suspect storage device yet.

7. **Insert the bootable media you're using and then restart the computer. Make sure that your bootable media boots correctly and that the software runs properly.**

8. **After everything is working correctly, turn off the computer and reconnect the suspect storage device to the computer.**

9. **Turn on the power and carefully watch the computer to make sure that it boots from your forensic media.**

   If at any time you think the computer is booting from the suspect storage device, pull the power plug from the back of the computer and troubleshoot why your forensic media didn't boot first. Then begin from Step 1.

10. **If all devices boot correctly, use your forensic software to connect, and then begin to either preview or acquire.**

From storage device to computer

Acquiring data by copying it from a storage device to a computer is faster than using the computer-to-computer method, because better safeguards are in place to prevent the writing of data to the original storage device. Also, the circuitry is much faster at this level of technology.

Always check with the manufacturer of the forensic equipment — and your own policies and procedures — for any detailed steps you need to complete in your unique circumstances.

The following step list shows how to extract data while you transfer it from a storage device to a computer:

1. **Figure out the type of media you're working with.**

   The type of media dictates which equipment you use, from EIDE, SATA, or SCSI connections for hard drives to the type of interface you need for devices such as mobile phones, cameras, or even MP3 players. (Playing *MacGyver* or flying by the seat of your pants isn't an option!)

2. **Use the proper write blocker.**

   Having the proper write blocker while you're working in the field can be a challenge simply because some forensic field kits limit their selection of interfaces. On the other hand, if you have a forensic workstation in your lab, chances are good that you have just about every interface type attached to it.

   If you're using equipment that connects to the forensic workstation by using the USB port, see the Technical Stuff paragraph at the end of this step list.

   Check your write block equipment monthly to ensure that it's still working correctly. Document your maintenance checks in a log, if possible.

3. **Use your forensic software.**

   After all your connections are secure and the media is connected correctly, open your forensic software and follow its instructions to acquire an image or make a transfer.

4. **Disconnect the media.**

   The image is transferred, and all the integrity checks indicate perfection, so now you have to disconnect the media and put it in a secure storage facility. Be sure to save the image file or data transfer *before* you disconnect.

   Always turn off the suspect media device power source before you begin to disconnect data cables. Unless you have a hot swappable device, pulling cables while electricity is still running can damage either the media or your equipment.

5. **Make a working copy.**

   If you have made an image file, all you have to do is copy the file and run the integrity checks to ensure that no changes have been made. If you created a duplicate disc, the process is the same as before except that the copy is now in the place of the original.

In some instances, you use equipment that connects to the forensic workstation by using the USB port. When you use it, you must write-block it. You can use Windows XP with Service Pack 2 or Vista for this task by changing these Registry settings:

1. **Back up your Registry by using a restore point or the Export function within the Registry Editor (RegEdit).**

   To open RegEdit:

   a. Choose Start ⇨Run.

   b. In the dialog box that appears, type regedit *and press Enter.*

   c. To save your Registry settings, choose File⇨Export.

2. **Navigate to My Computer/HKEY_LOCAL_MACHINE\SYSTEM\ CurrentControlSet\Control.**

3. **Right-click Control, and then choose New⇨Key. Name the key** StorageDevicePolicies.

4. **Right-click StorageDevicePolicies and select DWORD. Name the value** WriteProtect **and press Enter.**

5. **Right-click WriteProtect and set the value to 1 to enable the write-protect feature.**

To reverse this process, just put the value 0 in the WriteProtect value instead of 1. To automate this process, choose File⇨Export and save the Registry file in USB Write Protect On format. Go back and change the WriteProtect value to 0, and when you export the Registry file, save it in USB Write Protect Off format.

Step 4: Authenticate the Preserved Data

Because digital data is extremely easy to change, court systems have demanded a way to ensure that the data doesn't change after it's acquired and analyzed. For this purpose, several methods are used to prove conclusively the integrity of the potential evidence after it's in the hands of investigators.

The primary method used by all major forensic software packages to accomplish this integrity check is the use of a *checksum*, which is simply a method of performing a calculation on the entire original suspect data to generate a sum. When the data is transferred to the forensic computer, the same operation is performed on the data in its new home, and if the calculated sum is the same, the assumption is that the data hasn't changed. Not just any algorithm can be used for this type of operation because some checksum algorithms are easy to "fake out" or bypass.

The key to a good hash value is to use cryptographic *hashing* — an algorithm that can be used in only one direction. In other words, there's no way to reverse-engineer the original data stream based on the computed value. Cryptographic hash algorithms are designed to run an algorithm on an input block of data and then produce a fixed-length sequence of characters. Theoretically, the chances of two different input values having the same output value are in the range of 2^{65} (which equates to a number with lots of zeros behind it).

As of this writing, the two most popular cryptographic hash algorithms have some security issues that can be exploited, but the statistical probabilities of this happening are so small that the insecurities are considered an acceptable risk. As computing power increases, the probability that these insecurities will be exploited increases.

Cryptographic algorithms you commonly use for now (new algorithms are always in development) are described in this list:

- **Message-Digest algorithm 5 (MD5):** The most commonly used cryptographic hashing since approximately 1991. It has been shown to have a flaw in its design, but because no other hash has been shown to be flawless, MD5 is still actively used.

- **Secure Hash Algorithm (SHA):** Developed by the National Security Agency (NSA) as a family of cryptographic hash algorithms to replace the MD5 hash. SHA is in fact slightly more secure than the MD5, although a flaw has been discovered in the SHA-1 algorithm family. Increasingly more forensic investigators are migrating to this standard because of its increased security over MD5.

To see how this process works, a hash value is generated from the input of a block of data, and a sequence of characters is generated that's unique to that input string. Suppose that you make a slight change in the letter case of the first letter of each word in the phrase *computer forensics*:

```
MD5 Hash: ("Computer Forensics") = 7e48ea010d29aa81311d0fa10afa9ea4
MD5 Hash: ("computer forensics") = 982952ca09c9f9a6e11f0db4ed4c1b39
```

The hash values are dramatically different after a change only in the upper- to lowercase values of the input string! Even though only two bytes (not a bit) have changed, the hash value output is obviously different.

From a purely practical point of view, if your hash values match, there's no way that the data could have been modified in the normal course of your investigation.

Sometimes the hash values don't match, for technical reasons that you must articulate to a judge. The two most common reasons are described in this list:

- ✔ **The acquisition media you're extracting data from begins to fail.** Usually, the problem is that your software has taken a hash value from the original media and because the software cannot copy the data correctly because of physical errors on the media, the software generates a different hash value. In this scenario, you have to prove that the original media is failing to prove the discrepancy.

- ✔ **You're using faulty transfer equipment.** The original media may be stable, and the target media may be stable, but the transfer media, such as write protect devices or wiring, may be failing. (This reason is much less common than the one described in the first bullet.) The equipment may introduce errors in the transfer and change your hash value by default.

These causes of mismatched hash values aren't common, but you need to be aware of them in case you encounter these situations. The basic idea used in making most bitstream copies is to generate a *checksum* report on the source media that is then used as a comparison against the data after it is copied to the destination. Here's how a checksum works in practice:

1. The software applies an algorithm to the original media and generates a sum.

2. You transfer the data, and the software generates a sum for the transferred data.

3. The software program compares the original sum with the calculated sum to ensure that they match.

   If the two sums match, the assumption is that the data wasn't altered in any way. If the sums don't match, you know with mathematical certainty that the data changed during the transfer and that the potential evidence therefore was also damaged or changed during transfer.

As with other operations in the computer forensic world, this one appears to be simple, but the exception to matching checksums will always occur when you're working with live operating systems, such as those found in mobile phones, or with mobile computing devices, such as PDAs. The original data can change by the second because the time function creates a new checksum literally every second. In most of these special cases, courts have allowed some leeway, but be aware that a smart attorney can always argue that the checksums are different and convince the judge and jury the evidence is tainted unless you can explain the reasons why the checksums are different. If you have no plausible argument to counter that argument, your case may just sink.

Step 5: Make a Duplicate of the Duplicate

In an earlier section, you read that making a copy of your forensic copy is a deal breaker in computer forensics if not done. The reason for this is quite simply that you want a working forensic copy of the evidence in case there catastrophe occurs. If you accidentally destroy your first copy without having a working copy, you would have to access the original media and then run the risk of contaminating original evidence.

To make this duplicate, use the forensic software to duplicate your first forensic copy as though the first copy were the original evidence. This strategy serves two purposes:

✔ A hash value is computed for comparison.

✔ The computer forensic software probably saved the first copy in a proprietary format, and the computer forensic software can read its own proprietary file to make the copy correctly.

From this point forward, all you do is use the working copy to do your analysis.

Chapter 7

Examining E-Evidence

Digging through a suspect's data, documents, memos, e-mail, instant messages (IMs), Internet histories, financial files, photos, and other information is what most people think of when they hear the term *computer forensics* — and for good reason. What you've done up to now, (getting subpoenas, lugging computers back to the lab, preserving evidence) has been in preparation for this big event — examining the e-evidence and figuring out what it says.

The stage is set. You made forensically sound images (see Chapter 6). What you have now is a forensic image *(forensic copy)* of each device to review and analyze. For evidentiary purposes, the images are on recordable-only CDs or other read-only media to retain the exact information that's copied and nothing more.

Examining e-evidence marks a shift from the *science* of forensics to the *art* of investigation. It's a demanding art. No technology or artificial intelligence exists that can pick up the scent and assemble clues, test theories, follow hunches, and interpret e-evidence. Human intelligence and determination are needed to find e-mails or files that are smoking guns of guilt or white knights that exonerate.

In this chapter, we explain the e-evidence examination process. Your objective is to search for and analyze the facts in full, interpret what they do (or maybe do not) mean, and present your findings without judging what you found. Expect to defend the actions you did and did not take, the inferences you drew, and any limitations of your search tools or methods under unfriendly crossfire in court possibly years later. Obsessively document everything as though the case depends on it.

The Art of Scientific Inquiry

Scientific inquiry is a process that's more art than science. It calls for rational and creative thinking, for which (most) humans still retain the exclusive. Computers can't think, fortunately. Imagine squaring off against HAL from *2001: A Space Odyssey* or Gort from *The Day the Earth Stood Still.*

Acquisition and preservation make up the technical side of forensics. After the forensic images are properly made, you have a big pile of evidence, an unknown portion of which is relevant to the case. When you have a lot of e-evidence (for example, five 120GB images), a thorough file-by-file search of each image can't be done: Your available time and sanity won't allow it. It would be similar to making a door-to-door search of an entire city to find suspects — it's not possible, or at least not practical.

Although you develop your own strategies to deal with cases, the way you navigate the examination typically goes like this:

1. **Ask questions and observe as much as possible.**

   Examinations shouldn't be scavenger hunts, but they can be if you can't get answers to your questions. If you don't already know (if you haven't been involved from the outset), ask questions to gain a fundamental understanding of the elements of the case, e-evidence, chain of custody, and actions that are expected of you. Whenever possible, try to interview the person you're accountable to and the person whose data and files you're about to review. An *interview* is a conversation with a purpose. Your purpose is to get information.

2. **Design your review strategy of the e-evidence, including lists of keywords and search terms.**

   When you learn about the case, decide how to allocate your time and effort. You may need to become familiar with or focus on images, and then e-mails, and then Internet viewing history. Search terms are discussed in detail in the "Getting a Handle on Search Terms" section, later in this chapter.

3. **Review (examine) the e-evidence according to the strategy you designed in Step 2.**

   This is the main event. Execute your strategy, making adjustments as you discover clues to follow. Clues are like threads: You find a thread and then follow it to see where it leads. Clues may lead to locations or evidence not captured in the image under review. Follow up. (For more information, see the section "Looking beyond the file.")

4. Formulate explanations, interpret them, and draw inferences.

People are relying on you to explain what happened and how it could have or could not have happened, and to do so in a way that they and juries can understand.

Be alert to the distinction between what you observe during your review and what inferences you make. In general, *observed* evidence can be viewed and verified by others, such as a specific e-mail found on the hard drive. But *inferences* are drawn based on how you interpret what you observe. Inferences can vary greatly from one person to another (such as when an e-mail shows abuse). The middle process, *interpretation*, makes your inferences more difficult to verify.

5. Reflect on your findings and your methods.

Does this step surprise you? We're basically telling you to sleep on it. Consider this period your timeout to review and consider the evidence you discovered. You're checking your work. Ask yourself questions about your methods, strategy, results, interpretations, and missed opportunities, for example.

6. Report on your findings.

Yes, we're talking about the dreaded topic of report writing. We recommend that you read about the specifics of clear legal writing in *Paralegal Career For Dummies* (Wiley Publishing).

These steps aren't completed in sequence. You may have to go back to an earlier step as you learn from the evidence. You might, while reflecting on your findings (Step 5) have an "Aha" epiphany moment and want to review the evidence again (Step 3).

You don't have an unlimited length of time to complete the analysis, either. Resource constraints will (and, typically, should) influence how much time you spend doing your work. You need to make inferences (Step 4) and base them on what you reviewed and analyzed (Step 3). You might not notice a gap until you're writing the report (Step 6). Go back because that gap is also a loophole — and no one — except for the opposing side — wants to hear that particular *L* word.

Gearing Up for Challenges

No analysis tool can interpret the e-evidence or provide the clues that link the e-evidence and elements of a case. *You* provide that expertise. In this section, we discuss the challenges that can add nonstop excitement to this stage of the investigation.

Google M for murder

A March 2007 article at Slashdot.org warned in its title, "Don't Google 'How to Commit Murder' Before Killing." The article referred to a 2007 murder trial in New Jersey in which Google and MSN searches were used against a woman accused of killing her husband in 2004. Prosecutors claimed that the defendant, days before her husband's murder, searched for the phrases "how to commit murder," "instant poisons," "undetectable poisons," "fatal digoxin doses," and gun laws in New Jersey and Pennsylvania." The husband was killed with a gun bought in Pennsylvania. His body had been sliced into four pieces with a power saw, packed into trash bags, stuffed into the couple's luggage set, and tossed into the Chesapeake Bay.

How did the prosecution show that the defendant did the searches? By using police techniques and the information on her computer as a starting point. The defendant's Google and MSN search histories were obtained from her computer and used as strong forensic evidence. By looking at her Internet history (which you find out about in Chapter 9), investigators found her poison-related searches and her visit to www. walgreens.com/storelocator. With this clue to follow, they found the pharmacist who filled the prescription for chloral hydrate. Allegedly, the prescription was written by the defendant's boyfriend, a doctor.

Because investigators couldn't link the chloral hydrate she bought as that which was used on the husband, it became a smoking gun, but no finger pulling the trigger! The gun was never recovered. Other evidence included conflicting alibi statements, tollbooth records, forensic analysis of hairs and garbage bags, surveillance tapes, and phone taps.

The woman was convicted.

How well prepared you are to start looking for relevant evidence depends on multiple factors, some beyond your control. As in any other profession, you follow standard methods, keep up with your learning, and get better as you gain experience.

If you're a TV detective show fan, you see investigators facing a uniquely perplexing situation during each episode. But the investigators follow the same methods to solve each of their cases. Factors influencing the challenges you face are listed in Table 7-1. This list isn't exhaustive. You run into these factors in various combinations. Consider each combination a learning experience. To ease your pain, always view painful experiences as learning ones.

Table 7-1   Factors Influencing the Challenge of the Investigation

Your Role	Type of Case	Working Conditions	When You Got Involved
To support plaintiff	Civil	Friendly	Before any legal action
To support defendant	Criminal	Neutral	During e-discovery
To serve as neutral party	Employment	Nonsupportive	During capture and imaging
To investigate for a private party	Divorce	Hostile	During image review and analysis
To investigate for a private party	Fraud	Stealth mode	Just before the trial began

Here are four examples of situations you might face. (We already faced them, so we disguised them here.) In the last two examples, we also describe the analyses:

- ✔ **A hostile environment:** You're hired by the plaintiff's attorney in a case involving the theft of engineering drawings by a former employee of a manufacturer. Management suspects that the employee gave copies of the drawings to his new employer, but no other information is given to you. You arrive on-site to capture files and e-mail from the suspect's office PC and network logs and to review them.

  Immediately, the IT staff resents you for being there, because they were responsible for controlling access to confidential files and filtering e-mail — and they hadn't done so. Adding stress, the lawyer doesn't show up, so you're there alone; and the network had crashed that morning, so no one has time to talk to you. In this example, you're reviewing for the plaintiff in an employment case under hostile conditions after having captured the evidence yourself.

- ✔ **Stealth mode:** The director of human relations (HR) hires you to inspect an employee's computer to find out whether the employee is violating company policy by viewing pornography. HR needs the investigation done without alerting the employee or anyone else. In this case, you work for a private party in stealth mode after 10 p.m., when the office is empty, to acquire the image, and then review it later, off-site.

✔ **Neutral environment:** A defendant's attorney sends you a CD containing the image of his client's computer that had been made by law enforcement. You also receive `.xls` files listing details about cookies and recently used files. The defendant is alleged to have bought or purposefully downloaded child pornographic (CP) images — a criminal case.

Review and analysis show the presence of a small number of possible CP images, all with file sizes smaller than 10 kilobytes (K), and most smaller than 5K. The file sizes indicate thumbnail-size images. What's also important is what there's *no* evidence of. (See the "Finding No Evidence" section, later in this chapter.) There's no evidence of typical indicators of CP behavior (for example, image files weren't organized; no bookmarks, usernames, or e-mail names indicating interest in CP; and no file sharing). The review shows many visits to adult pornographic sites (which is an objective observation that can be seen by others), at which time the CP thumbnails could have been downloaded unknowingly (which is an inference that is subjective and that another person may not agree with).

✔ **Friendly or nonsupportive environment:** Just one week before the jury trial begins, a prosecuting attorney asks you to confirm that the suspect in custody had in fact sent e-mail threatening federal agents, which is a criminal offense. The threatening e-mails would corroborate other types of evidence (letters, faxes, and in-person threats). You ask the prosecutor these two questions, "How did you tie the e-mails to your suspect? How do you know it was him and not someone else who sent the e-mail messages?" But no one on the prosecution team can come up with an answer that would stand up in court. You proceed to do the analysis. E-evidence shows the e-mail had been sent from an account that the suspect used, but you cannot link the suspect to the messages. Prosecutors are spared making a mistake in front of the jury. The suspect was still found guilty because the e-evidence was correctly used to corroborate the physical evidence rather than to stand on it own. On its own, that e-evidence was insufficient.

In any type of case, the defendant may frankly admit that he's guilty. His lawyer may want you to analyze the data and determine how bad the evidence is against the client. You may be asked to make a judgment call on whether the client should take the plea deal. You're not a lawyer nor a judge or jury.

Getting a Handle on Search Terms

Because you can't read the image file by simply clicking it, you have to use forensic software to open the file. You can use forensic software to structure a query and catalog your results, but the final results depend on you. You need to know exactly how to do what you want to do.

Overall, you're _querying_ the forensic image to discover what has happened and how it happened or could have happened. Querying is a structured search approach. Unless you have very few files or an infinite amount of time, your examination depends on your querying ability.

The effectiveness and efficiency of your searches improve the more you observe and understand the elements of the case, the characteristics of the crime, and the people involved. That's why you start the examination by asking questions. Use your knowledge to build the list of keywords or search terms to find respondent files.

It's not unusual that only a few responsive e-mails exist in a pool of many thousands. Even if you find every single one of those e-mails, you still can't be sure that you got them all. Unless you have the time and the attention span to read each e-mail, you use your judgment to determine that you've done a reasonably thorough search.

Be prepared to defend your search strategy by keeping a detailed explanation of your search protocols, procedures, search list, and tested hypotheses.

Keyword searching is a tricky process. You have to zero in on precise terms but not exclude necessary terms. And that doesn't account for human error in developing a keyword list.

In the following section, we discuss putting together search lists and then explain how forensic software can overcome some search-related limitations.

Expect to make several passes through the image using various search filters. It's not likely that you can do a single search and retrieve all relevant files. You might find out something new from each pass.

Defining your search list

Your search results depend on your list of search terms. You can reduce uncertainty by attempting to know as much as possible about these three Cs:

- ✔ **Characters:** Understanding the people involved — the accuser and the accused — and their possible motives gives you context for the search. The cast of characters may be unique, but motives and tactics are not. Law enforcement is experienced and skilled in figuring out motives. It's not uncommon for a person to unfairly accuse another of harassment or fraud. It's too easy to frame others or attempt a cover-up using e-mail or forged documents.

✔ **Circumstances:** A timeline of activities or surrounding circumstances can help identify the puzzle pieces and how they fit together. Ask for dates to narrow your search to events that fell within that range. Determine whether one party had physical or remote access to the other party's computer or e-mail accounts.

✔ **Characteristics of the crime or legal action:** You need to know the possible interpretations of what you find. You may need to research the crime to understand its characteristics to draw inferences. Some crimes may be beyond your expertise or tolerance. For example, if you don't understand how accounting systems work and how fraud schemes are carried out, don't investigate fraud unless you're working with someone who does know.

You can also add search terms to your list during pretrial conferences and depositions:

✔ **Using Rule 16 results:** Detailed information about characters, circumstances, and characteristics may also be available for you. Litigants hold a pretrial meeting to address e-evidence to better understand the opposing party's electronic data. From that meeting, you may get details such as the location, format, and status (active, archived, or deleted) of an opponent's data. (See Chapter 2 for more information about Rule 16 and pretrial conferences.)

The parties may have agreed to file extensions, keywords, metadata, or dates. For example, the parties may agree to a search for all e-mail containing specified search terms, keywords, or other selection criteria needed to narrow huge data sets to a manageable size. You can then limit the search-and-review process based on those agreements.

✔ **Using depositions:** A *deposition* (or *depo*) is testimony under oath in the presence of a court reporter before the case gets to court, but not in court. Depositions are part of discovery. Attorneys may set up depositions to get sworn testimony from someone who knows something relevant to the case. Transcripts of depos are an excellent source of search terms, names, dates, and other information. You may get deposed as an expert, which you can read about in Chapter 15.

Using forensic software to search

One of the computer forensic software kits, which may or may not have been used to acquire the image, is commonly used to search and identify files that you need to review. Search capabilities continue to improve, but tools themselves can't perform the review.

During the acquisition process, the software may have created an index of *terms,* which are basic units of a search. A term can be a single character or a group of characters, alphabetic or numeric, and have a space on either side. Indexing increases the time it takes to acquire the image, but it expedites the search.

Get trained in using the software before you use it. Keep a copy of the manual and refer to it as needed. Software versions change, so you should keep the manual for each version you use.

Searching by Keyword

Two types of *search options* to use with your keywords or search terms are described in this list:

✔ **Broadening options** apply to words:

- *Stemming:* Searches for variations of the root of the search word; for example, a search for *poison* also finds *poisonous.*

- *Synonyms:* Searches for synonyms of the search term; for example, a search for *money* also finds *cash* and *funds.*

- *Homonyms:* Searches for words that sound the same; for example, *manner* also finds *manor;* and *serial* also finds *cereal.*

- *Fuzziness:* Searches for different spellings of a word or misspellings; for example, *lethal* also finds *lethel* and *leethal.* Searching for *flavor* also finds *flavour* and *flaver.*

  Fuzziness is useful for finding misspelled words or mistakes in numbers. For example, if you're searching for numeric references, such as *product X7447,* a fuzzy search would catch *X7747* if that mistake had been made. You can specify the degree of fuzziness; 1 is the least fuzzy. If you're searching for the word *subpoena,* for example, use a high degree of fuzziness because that word is commonly misspelled. Fuzzy searching makes sense for first and last names, city names, company names, and other proper nouns.

✔ **Limiting options** apply to dates and file sizes. You can specify

- Data ranges for either the range of dates when the files had been *created* or when they were *last saved* (or both)

- File sizes or a range of file sizes

Other keyword searching options may be available depending on your software. You can use various options in combination to extend the word search *and* limit the number of files. The broader your search filter, the greater the expected number of results. And, eventually, you need to read through your resulting list of files.

Expressing a search with Boolean

You can link search terms using connectors. You can use Boolean searching, as it's called, to develop a search expression to filter your results. If you understand how Boolean connectors work, you can improve or expedite your search by using these standard connectors between your search terms:

- ✔ **AND:** Narrows your search by requiring that the file contains both search words. For example, the search for *X7447 AND carbon* produces only those files that contain both *X7447* and *carbon* anywhere in the file. As a general rule, use AND when it doesn't matter where the search words appear in a file. If the search terms are fairly unique, the AND connector can find files related to your case.

- ✔ **OR:** Expands your search by broadening the resulting set of files. Files that contain either search word or both words will be found. In effect, using the OR connector in a single search (for example, *hydrogen or nitrogen*) is similar to making two separate searches (one search for *hydrogen* and another search for *nitrogen*) at one time. You can broaden the search by increasing the number of times you use the OR connector; for example, *hydrogen OR nitrogen OR carbon.*

- ✔ **AND NOT:** Subtracts files that have the specified word in them. For the phrase *and not hydrogen,* files containing *hydrogen* are excluded from the search results.

  When you use AND NOT, be sure that it's the last connector you use in the search expression. Everything after this operator is excluded from the search results.

You can combine these operators, but do so carefully because these tiny words are powerful. You might exclude files unexpectedly or create unintended results. If you use two or more of the same connector, they operate from left to right. An order of priority may exist: For example, if OR has the highest priority, the OR connectors are processed first and then the AND connectors.

After you put on a filtering operator, it might stay on even after you've started a whole new search. Check the directions in your forensic software for removing any filter you applied.

Each computer forensics software toolkit has its unique search methods that are based on the Boolean search. Check the software manual for its search features and tools.

Assuming risks

Search engines and their options are based on assumptions. You make many assumptions in your career, or else you can't proceed. If those assumptions are wrong, the results are too, unless you're darned lucky. You make four main assumptions while searching:

- ✔ The person writing the messages or documents didn't use slang or code words, possibly to avoid detection.
- ✔ The evidence wasn't planted by someone else who managed to get access to the drive.
- ✔ Any user of the computer hadn't visited a site that dropped or downloaded content onto it without the user knowing about it.
- ✔ The computer hadn't been compromised by malware that left it vulnerable to use by others.

For these reasons, you need to do a direct visual inspection of the contents of the files on the image.

You can pick up clues by looking at thumbnail images or reading e-mails to use in keyword searches. It's an iterative process. What you discover by directly reviewing files can help focus your keyword search, and keyword searches can find files for you to review.

Forensic software enables you to view the contents of files even if they were deleted (unless the files were overwritten; see Chapter 1). The software also organizes the files according to categories or status, letting you choose to examine only these elements:

E-mail messages	Folders
Documents	Slack space
Spreadsheets	Encrypted files
Databases	Deleted files
Graphics	Files from the Recycle Bin
Executables	Data-carved files

Data-carved files are files carved out from unallocated file space. Data-carving tools search unallocated space for header information, and possibly footer information, of known file types and then recovers that block of data. The files themselves don't exist, even as deleted files, so they must be carved out of that space. If you're interested in finding out more about data carving, visit the site of the Digital Forensics Research Workshop (DFRW), which sponsors forensic challenges as part of its annual conferences. The DFRWS 2006 and 2007 Forensics Challenges focused on data carvings, the results of which you can review at www.dfrws.org/archives.shtml.

A basic data-carving test created by Nick Mikus is available at http://dftt.sourceforge.net/test12/index.html.

Sneaking a peek: Data sampling

When numerous volumes of data exist, a party might want to do a preliminary check by sampling the data. By *data sampling*, you can check for responsive material without "breaking the bank" by doing a full review. If a data sample doesn't bring expected results, the retaining lawyer can decide whether to expand the search or call it off.

If evidence can't be found, legal counsel may settle for a dismissal. For example, a sample of the data might show that relevant documents don't exist for a particular period, making it unnecessary to continue the case or the search.

Challenging Your Results: Plants and Frames and Being in the Wrong Place

You found the incriminating files. Hurray for you. Now move on to the report. Not so fast. Great detectives, like yourself, look for planted evidence and attempts to frame a client.

Knowing what can go wrong

What would the investigators on the TV show *CSI* do when examining evidence and trying to interpret it? They would consider the following risks, and more, as they became apparent:

- ✔ If your computer were forensically investigated, consider whether you would be willing to bet the farm that there's absolutely no evidence of wrongdoing on it. Unless your computer is brand-new, has never been used, or was never exposed to the Internet (all improbable situations), don't take the bet. You would be playing Russian roulette with no missing bullets.

- ✔ Planting evidence to frame others can be done with e-evidence as easily as with physical evidence.

- ✔ No malicious or deliberate attempts were made to personally implicate your client, but the client got caught up in the e-evidence. Here are some situations that can get out of control:

    - An employee quits and her computer is given to your client without being forensically wiped clean.

- Your client buys a used laptop from eBay. All kinds of creepy crawlies could reside on that hard drive.

- Your client has sloppy computer and Internet hygiene habits — or shoddy click-impulse control. Although it wouldn't always happen, the defense strategy "The malware did it" can be the truth.

Looking beyond the file

Figuring out what happened is tough, but it's still easier than showing how it happened or who did it.

Finding planted evidence or attempts to frame others is tough. An important aspect is keeping an open mind. It's easy to make a mistake and stop the investigation after the evidence is found on the initial suspect's computer, but it may implicate the wrong person. You need to verify your results by trying to disprove them yourself.

Here are some verification tests to perform or questions to be answered depending on the elements of the case:

- ✔ Follow the vendor's or manufacturer's directions regarding the use of the product. Chapter 20 lists the types of products used by computer forensic investigators.

- ✔ Test the product or the results of using it before you use it on the evidence.

- ✔ Check the target computer for the necessary operating capabilities or software to open or create the files. Finding Microsoft Word or Excel 2007 files, for instance, on a computer that cannot open those files raises a red flag.

- ✔ Verify that the target computer is capable of viewing the pictures, editing the document, or printing it.

- ✔ Make sure that the suspect's computer works and that all the drives work.

- ✔ Verify which types and versions of e-mail and accounting programs, for example, were in use at the time.

- ✔ Determine whether the suspect had access to the computer at the time that illegal files were downloaded. Verify that the computer's clock is set correctly and for the proper time zone.

- ✔ Make sure that the programs or devices needed for exporting the suspect files are on the computer.

You find out how to search for and verify e-evidence in the riveting specialty forensic chapters in Part III.

Finding No Evidence

It's tempting to do, but you cannot draw conclusions or make judgments outside your area of expertise. For example, you cannot judge whether a photo is child pornography or a spreadsheet shows hidden assets, because you're not an expert in that type of identification.

No matter how obvious something is to you, stop and reflect on what you've analyzed.

You may find no evidence that something happened. Or, you may find no evidence that something did not happen. The case may depend on what you found *no* evidence of.

You need to report what you did not find. Someone will ask you about what you did not find. The following two sections show you two examples of what you need to report not finding.

No evidence of who logged in

Passwords do not authenticate who's logging in. After a username is entered, the system authenticates that the correct password for that username is entered. What do a username and password prove? Not much. They're supposed to authenticate who's logging in, but they don't. Unfortunately, password guessing, sharing, and findings take the air out of that evidence.

Who was logged on a computer at a particular date and time? Unless the computer is biometric-capable or clear camera images were captured, you cannot "connect the dots." If the computer is biometric-capable and the user made use of biometrics when logging on, you have traction. Biometrics can point the finger at the user logged in at a particular time, like the secret handshake to get let into a clubhouse. Biometrics uses an individual's physical characteristic, often a fingerprint, to authenticate that person for access to the computer. Typical biometrics, in secure facilities, include fingerprints or handprints.

No evidence of how it got there

You can report on which images you found in a file, but you might not be able to report on how the images got there. Likewise, finding supporting evidence in a user's browser history doesn't make the user guilty, although it can close the window of reasonable doubt a little.

E-evidence may not prove that a crime was committed, but it can support motivation or intention to commit that crime. You know the drill. Be careful, exact, and don't jump to conclusions.

Reporting Your Analysis

Reporting your findings is a critical element to your success as a forensic examiner. You cannot avoid reporting. No matter how whiz-bang brilliant you are as an investigator, if you can't write out your findings in an organized report that's easy to navigate, read, and understand, your forensic talents may get wasted. You may need to submit one of these items:

- ✓ **Working papers:** Prepare your working papers in such a way that they're understandable to independent reviewers — juries, for example. From an efficiency perspective, consider that the purpose of a working paper is to document the procedures you performed and the conclusions you reached. Be neat. If the document you create is clear, accurate, and readable, it qualifies as a working paper.

- ✓ **Preliminary report:** If your work involved data sampling or the attorney asked for a preliminary report, label your report as such. If your analysis isn't complete, do not label the report as final.

- ✓ **Final report:** Consider submitting this report the same as testifying under oath, because that's where you may have to explain and defend it.

Figure 7-1 shows an example of the types of information in a report and the structure of the report.

Be sure to spell check and proofread before you submit the report. Also, be sure to check and correctly fill in the properties of the document.

> **Description of Case or Investigation**
>
> **EXAMINER'S REPORT** _____ **Month ##, 20##**
>
> **A. INTRODUCTION**
>
> Describe the issues in broad and general terms. Sometimes say right up front what is alleged to have happened.
>
> <u>Describe your scope of work:</u> This investigation was performed to determine if...
>
> *Example: The purpose of my investigation was to determine if there was evidence to indicate intellectual property theft on the part of <Name>.*
>
> **B. MATERIALS or EQUIPMENT AVAILABLE FOR REVIEW**
>
> List all information, equipment, or other materials you were given that related to this case. List materials that are case specific. Do not list reference standards or other content that you researched.
>
> *Doing this will be very convenient for you at later stages of the case.*
>
> 1. Should you want to list multiple items in outline form, this would be the appropriate format.
>
> 2. Materials or Equipment
>   a. item 1
>   b. item 2
>   c. item 3
>
> **C. BACKGROUND**
>
> If you have background information on the case, computers, people, etc, include it here. Write the background as a complete series of facts, and just the facts with no emotion or judgment.
>
> If you want to include a quotation that is greater than 3 lines, it should be inserted as an excerpt:
>
> The excerpt would set apart and indented as follows, without quotations, and should be no more than a paragraph.
>
> Try to limit this to relevant facts. Everything you say should have some meaning to you in your analysis and findings, or at least be there to set the scene for the reader. Use references to photographs and diagrams sparingly to help your description, and include them at the end of the report.
>
> If you have different items you would like to list out separately, create a sub-heading using an underline. This would be appropriate when listing related, but separate, items.
>
> **D. ANALYSIS**
>
> Your fully described analysis goes here. Use your notes or working papers so you don't forget anything. Expect to re-write and edit this section several times.

E. FINDINGS

Within the bounds of reasonable computer forensics certainty and subject to change if additional information becomes available, it is my professional opinion that: (list)

1.   Statement 1.

2.   Statement 2.

3.   Statement 3.

Go back to your description of scope of work and make the scope match with the findings.

REFERENCES

Include via footnotes or table after findings.

FIGURES, PHOTOS, APPENDICES or ATTACHMENTS

Include things that you would want to show to our client or to the jury to show the basis for your opinion. Include sketches or photos if relevant; e.g., not just to fill up a report.

Include extracts from documents to show the standard of care that you think should have applied.

Label and order these as Figures, Photos or Attachments. Do not use other terms, including Exhibits.

_____

Name, Title

Figure 7-1:
A sample report of your examination and findings.

Chapter 8

Extracting Hidden Data

*A*s a computer forensic investigator, you eventually run into evidence whose very existence is hidden (unseen) or that has been hidden in plain sight (disguised). That is, you're confronted with *invisible electronic evidence.* Criminals may hide their files so that you don't even know that the files exist — at least not without effort. When insidious camouflage tactics are in play, you're not only involved in detective work — you're also engaged in combat plus detective work.

Your challenge is to discover covert attempts and break through them to extract hidden information. This area of computer forensics is arguably the most intriguing. You're matching wits with a criminal mind and playing mental chess games using digital pieces. Outsmarting someone who has gone to great lengths to hide data feels good, but you have to pay a price for this excitement. You also face the dull wait for software to come back with a clue to help you break the code — a password or hidden piece of data. You may experience the agony of defeat if cracking the password or defeating the encryption is beyond the technical means at your disposal. Then you might need to use alternative means of extracting the evidence. In this chapter, you find out how data can become hidden or disguised and how to extract it.

Recognizing Attempts to Blind the Investigator

Cyberspace is also, in part, criminal space. It's a medium where criminals apply ancient methods in digital disguise to remain undetectable.

Hiding data has been done by criminals and governments for thousands of years using techniques such as a *wrap-around cipher* (shifting the base alphabet over such as A=B, B=C, and so forth) used by Julius Caesar to today's *stego* (covered writing) data hiding techniques. The Greeks used to tattoo a message on a person's shaved head and a decoy message in his hand. When the inked person's hair grew back, he was sent out and had his head shaved again by the recipient to reveal the message.

The goal of data disguise is to hide the message. Hiding is done using one or more of the following three tactics. For simplicity, the term *hiding* refers to all of them. You can hide a message by making it

- ✔ **Invisible:** Make the message unseen to hide its very existence.

- ✔ **Disguised:** Hide the message in an object or item that looks innocuous so that the message isn't detected, such as in the image of a book cover.

- ✔ **Unreadable:** Use techniques to make the information undecipherable to anyone except the intended recipient without attempting to hide its existence or disguise what it is. An example is the use of encryption.

The recipient would know of the scheme, be able to locate the message, and have the code key or ability to convert the message into readable form. In drastic cases, the message or messenger could get destroyed if the data was tampered with.

If the data is hidden, how do you know it's there? You don't know unless you try. (Now intrigue comes into play!) No magic formula or marker exists to guide you in the detection of hidden data. Fortunately, detection and cracking tools can analyze images for signs, such as overly large files and uneven bit mapping. You need to know when and where to use these tools. There are so many ways to hide data that you need to use various tools and techniques to ferret out hidden data.

As the computer forensic investigator, you have to look for signs that data hiding techniques are being used. For example, an engineering firm suspected that an employee was stealing valuable intellectual property (IP) by transmitting it from the firm's network. Investigators began looking for e-evidence on the local hard drives, but didn't find any. The next logical item to check were the company's e-mail logs. Investigators found two e-mails with harmless-looking image attachments sent by the employee of interest — the suspect. (When steganography is used to hide content in image files, the size of the files can become huge.) Sending huge file attachments creates suspicion. Using stego detection software, the investigators revealed that the images were hiding two of the company's high-value IP engineering specifications. The suspect had used stego to hide the IP within image files.

Encryption and compression

Cryptography is the science of writing in secret codes. The formal definition for cryptography is the practice and study of hiding information with the purpose to protect information from being read or understood by anyone except the intended recipient. In computer forensics, you deal with two types: encryption and compression.

Both encryption and compression make use of an algorithm to rewrite the initial data. They differ in the uses they're designed for and how they're analyzed:

- ✔ **Encryption:** Readable plain text (data, a message, or any type of file) is scrambled by applying an algorithm (the cipher) to it to convert it into unreadable ciphertext. The ciphertext, plus its key, converts the text back to its original, readable form. Encryption has one and only one purpose: to make information unreadable to anyone other than the intended recipient. Encrypted files are fairly easy to spot because they usually have common file structures or extensions.

- ✔ **Compression** is related to encryption in that a content-altering algorithm is applied to the data or message. But compression has a different purpose: to shrink the size of the file. The result is a file that's unrecognizable from its original form, although the reason is compression itself and not any form of data hiding. Compression adds a layer of complexity to forensics, but compressed files aren't themselves suspicious.

Don't confuse compression with encryption. The nontechnical difference is the intent of the user. Other differences are described in this list:

- ✔ **Compression saves space by reducing file size.**

  Encryption increases file size.

- ✔ **Compression software packages may put a password on a compressed file, but it's in no way an encrypted file.**

  In fact, encrypting a compressed file increases file size, which makes the compression moot! Most password-protected compressed files are so weak that shareware password crackers are usually sufficient to crack them.

- ✔ **Compressed files can be uncompressed without any keys.**

  All you need is the software and — voilà — it's uncompressed.

Two encryption methods affect computer forensic investigators:

✔ **Asymmetric:** This two-key system uses a public key and a private key. As shown in Figure 8-1, the public key is used to encrypt the data. The recipient's private key is the only key that can decrypt the data. During encryption, the private key is produced by creating a key-pair. The genius of this system is that the user gives half of the key to the world by way of the public key but keeps the private key *private*. No one else can decrypt the data easily, or at all, without the private key.

This method is a bit more complicated to implement, but after the asymmetric system is in place, it is — unfortunately for forensics — one of the more secure methods of encrypting data.

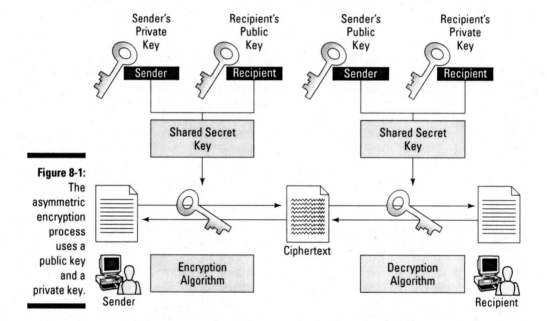

Figure 8-1: The asymmetric encryption process uses a public key and a private key.

✔ **Symmetric:** In this one-key system, the single key is shared by the sender and receiver, as shown in Figure 8-2. The same key is used to encrypt and decrypt the data, which makes the security of the key harder to protect.

In addition to making it harder to protect the keys from falling into the wrong hands because of a one key design, symmetric keys tend to be shorter and easier to crack with the right equipment.

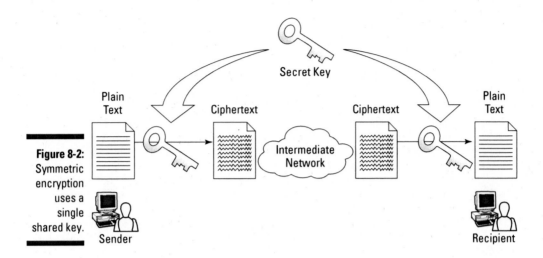

Figure 8-2:
Symmetric
encryption
uses a
single
shared key.

Data hiding techniques

So many methods of hiding data exist that even an entire book on the subject would be incomplete because a new technique would come to light before the print was dry — or the last word typed. In this section, we show you the basic techniques used by most people who try to hide data. This list isn't complete by any means, but it gives you a fighting chance by giving you an idea where to start looking.

Each of these tactics (with the exception of steganography) is fairly simple to spot, and can be defeated with specialized tools when used individually. Real problems occur when savvy criminals use a combination of data hiding techniques to obliterate their tracks. For example, someone could encrypt a file using asymmetric encryption such as PGP, and then embed the file in an audio file with the stego program S-Tools.

File extensions

A widely used and popular method of hiding a file type is to simply change the extension at the end of a filename. Try it:

1. **Change the `.doc` extension on an unimportant Word document to `.xls`. Click Yes when the warning message appears.**

   The icon changes from a Word icon to an Excel icon.

2. **Double-click the file to try to open it.**

   Because the extension indicates that the file is an Excel file, Excel opens. But the file fails to open because Excel can't open Word files.

3. **Launch Word and then open the file with the `.xls` extension.**

The file opens.

4. **Change the `.xls` extension back to `.doc` and notice that the icon changes too.**

5. **Double-click the file to open it.**

It opens!

To find out whether an extension has been changed, you need to compare the file header to the file extension to make sure that they match. The *file header* is a sequence of bits at the beginning of a file and is used by programs to determine whether they can open the file. Chapter 11 covers file headers in greater detail.

Even when the file extension is changed (as you just did), the appropriate program still opens the file. On the other hand, when the file header is changed, the program no longer recognizes the file.

Advanced users can change the file header easily by using a hex editor to make the file readable or unreadable. A hex editor is a program that can access data directly where it is stored without the need to know what type of format it is. Hex editors literally read data byte by byte and have the ability to change files at the byte level.

Hidden files

All operating systems assign attributes to files. One particular type of attribute is the ability to hide files, or more precisely, to mark files as hidden, which is comparable to files being marked for deletion. Hidden files are no more hidden than deleted files are deleted.

If you use Microsoft XP or Vista, you can show any hidden files by selecting the Show Hidden Files and Folders option in the Folder Options dialog box (see Figure 8-3). If you have an older file system, such as Microsoft Disk Operating System (DOS), use the `Attrib` command to either hide the file or make the file viewable.

Hidden shares

Hidden shares are shared areas on a network where files are stored but the shares are hidden. Hidden shares can be found on a local computer, but with networks everywhere, savvy criminals can use hidden shares on remote computers rather than risk using their own machines. Finding hidden shares is a bit more difficult than finding hidden files, but if you have the proper software, such as Legion V2.1 (www.packetstormsecurity.org), the process is straightforward. In addition to hiding shares, users sometimes also put passwords on hidden shares to protect them in depth.

You can add a dollar sign symbol ($) to the end of the share so that it appears hidden and not visible from a network browser.

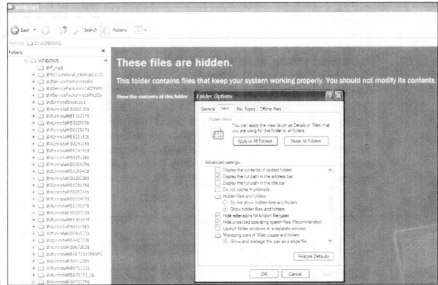

Alternate data streams

The uncommon data storage concept of *alternate data streams (ADS)* started with Windows NT version 3.51 and was introduced as a compatibility fix for the Macintosh HFS system. The implication of this fix is that you can piggyback data onto an existing file without changing the attributes of the first file — with the exception of the time stamp.

These data streams allow multiple forms of data to be associated with a file. A clever user can hide nefarious files in this manner because the files don't show up using a DIR (directory) command, nor do they appear in Windows Explorer. A few antivirus programs can pick up ADS information, but for the most part the majority of the computer world is oblivious to the existence of ADS. One ADS scanner you can try — it's free — is from Pointstone (www.pointstone.com).

Layers

The simplest example to demonstrate the use of a layer is to overlay a picture on text in a desktop publishing program. At first glance, you can see only the picture. After you move the picture, however, the text underneath is revealed. Another simple example is to change the font color of a document to the same color as its background. Open the file and all you see is what appears to be a blank page.

If you come across a blank file (a file which appears empty when you open it such as a blank Microsoft Word page), print it. Hidden text may appear on the hard copy.

Steganography

Steganography (or *stego*), a complex version of layering and data hiding, is a modern-day version of an ancient communication method. Stego refers to covered writing, such as invisible ink. In the digital world, this technique involves hiding a message inside an innocuous image, music file, or video that is posted on a Web site, e-mailed, or stored on a hard drive.

Imagine downloading an image of the Brooklyn Bridge from the Internet. As a suspicious investigator, you use your stego-detecting software to extract the message it's hiding. The problem is that, because many algorithms are used in stego, and without knowing which one was used, extracting the hidden information — or even knowing that it's there — is quite difficult.

Encryption blurs admissible evidence in child porn case

One case, believed to be the first of its kind to reach a U.S. District Court, raises an unresolved question about how to balance privacy and civil liberties against the government's responsibility to protect the public. Sebastien Boucher, a 30-year-old drywall installer who lives in Vermont, was stopped at the U.S.–Canadian border in 2006. Border officials searched his laptop and found evidence of child pornography. In the initial search, Boucher had helped the agents log in to his computer, but a subsequent search after Mr. Boucher was arrested was stopped cold: Investigators couldn't gain access to the Z drive content because it was PGP protected.

PGP encryption software is used by government agencies in the U.S. and around the world and is widely available online for use by your average person to help protect their privacy. PGP, like all encryption algorithms, requires a password of some type for decryption. In the case of PGP, a passphrase is used to add complexity. For more than a year, the government has been unable to view Boucher's Z drive. A grand jury subpoena was issued to force Boucher to surrender the password to federal agents. It put him in the forbidden trilemma: Incriminate himself, lie under oath, or find himself in contempt of court. The subpoena was eventually struck down by a federal magistrate on the grounds that it violated Mr. Boucher's Fifth Amendment rights.

During testimony before the federal magistrate, agents testified that they needed the password because using brute force (see the later section "Defeating Algorithms, Hashes, and Keys") to crack the encrypted data would take years and be impractical. As of this writing, the controversy continues and the case remains pending. It may set a precedent regarding the authority to compel individuals to surrender passwords in criminal investigations.

Defeating Algorithms, Hashes, and Keys

When you encounter evidence that has been hidden in some way, your first decision is to decide *how* it was hidden. Was steganography used, or was the suspect using Windows Encrypting File System (EFS)? Much depends on what you find because if you use the wrong tools to attempt an extraction, you waste a lot of time and might even accidentally destroy your evidence.

Always work with copies of the evidence and not the originals. If you destroy a copy, you can always make another one from your backup copy.

You can use several methods to defeat data hiding, and each one has its pros and cons. Often, the only way to find the key is to get it from the suspect! When you can't do that, you have to circumvent the crucial password by using one of these methods:

- **Brute force:** Be brutal. In this procedure, you try every possible combination until you find the right one and crack the password. It involves trial and error. For simple hashes or algorithms, brute force works fairly well. As the key length increases, so do the number of possibilities. As you can tell from the following table, a 512-bit key has more than 154 zeros behind it!

Key Length in Bits	Number of Possible Combinations
8	256
40	1,099,511,627,776
128	18,446,744,073,709,600,000
256	$1.15792 * 10^{77}$
512	$1.3408 * 10^{154}$

With the advances in cryptography algorithms and long key lengths, finding a key by brute force is often impractical. It's your last resort to password cracking.

- **Dictionary attack:** Throw the book at them. This word-based trial-and-error method uses a dictionary of passwords or hashes that are compared to the hash value stored on the suspect's password file. Dictionaries contain not only standard words but also the names of celebrities, sports teams, TV shows, and Klingons (for *Star Trek* fans). Despite how often people are told to use good passwords, they don't. The most common passwords found in the field are *password, letmein, 123456,* and *qwerty.* Other popular passwords are the user's first name, the names of children or pets, addresses, phone numbers, and even Social Security numbers.

Using a dictionary doesn't mean that you're limited to words or even letters. Most password cracking software uses letters, numbers, and even special characters as part of their dictionary attacks. In a good password-cracking software program using a decent dictionary, the word *hello* and the character substitution *h3110* are cracked in less than a second.

✔ **Rainbow tables:** These extensions of dictionaries are much larger hash databases that reside either on the Internet or with a private party. Rainbow tables let you use a larger database of possibilities than could be stored on a forensic computer.

✔ **Keystroke logger:** Sometimes the best solution isn't to try to crack the encryption but, rather, to resort to sleuthing — when it's legal to do so, of course. Use a keylogger to capture the encryption keystrokes when the suspect types them. This method works well when you know that the person you're watching in a case is using some form of encryption. Keylogger features vary, but they all record the keystrokes typed on a computer keyboard. You can install keyloggers manually or use Trojan software (software that looks like it's for one purpose, such as playing a game, but in reality inserts another program on the computer).

In addition to software keyloggers, physical keyloggers are installed between the keyboard and the back of a computer. This type of device is more difficult to install but cannot be detected by antivirus, anti-spyware, or anti-malware software.

✔ **Snooper software:** This type of software is used in the same fashion as software keyloggers except that snooper software logs not only keystrokes but also almost any activity that occurs on the computer. Everything from screen shots to printouts, to chat sessions to e-mails, and even how many times you turned on the computer is archived. As you might imagine, this type of software takes up quite a bit of room on the storage device, but can be extremely useful when re-creating passwords or passwords on a suspect's computer. This method works well in a situation where you know ahead of time that the suspect is using a computer for illegal activities.

✔ **Suspect questioning:** The suspect may be your only option to gain access to a password or passphrase. Although most people don't initially supply their passwords, after some legal arm-twisting, it sometimes does occur. In serious crime cases, though, don't count on a suspect helping you out!

✔ **Application specific integrated circuit (ASIC):** This type of computer chip is specifically programmed to perform a task. The sole purpose of programming an ASIC decrypting system is to crack a specific type of encryption. Most computer forensic investigators don't have access to computers of this type, but government agencies do, and they can chew through a 40-bit encryption key in only seconds!

✔ **Cache checking:** Certain applications and operating systems may put passwords in a *cache* temporarily — it's a smart place to search. Users who allow their systems to save their passwords so that they don't have to type them repeatedly are often saving their passwords in plain text mode in a cache area.

Finding Out-of-Sight Bytes

To hide information, criminals use special software programs to identify the least significant bits (LSBs) in a file and change them to contain hidden content without altering the file in a detectable way — in the background color of an image, for example. The best candidates for steganography (described at the beginning of this chapter) are byte-intensive digital pictures and audio files because they have a good supply of insignificant bits. Even a plain text document can hide content within the structure of the file. Certain areas in files (depending on whether they're video or audio or some other type) can be modified without compromising the quality of the file to the human eye or ear. The major forensic issue is exposing the presence of hidden data.

You have several methods to find clues to whether a file *might* have a hidden message in it:

✔ **Look for steganography software on the suspect's computer.**

A blatant clue is finding stego-creating software on the suspect's computer. The trick is to recognize the different types (experience is needed here) or known hash values of stego software using hash analysis. Many investigators have no clue how many steganographic software packages exist and may overlook the software as being "just part of the system." Figure 8-4 shows the steganography software JPHS for Windows. Notice that the software gives you details about the original file, the hidden file, and, toward the bottom, the new file with the stego.

✔ **Look for duplicate files.**

When you're making a forensic analysis and find a huge number of duplicate files, it's a glaring red flag. Stego often produces duplicate files because the original file is often left behind by sloppy criminals. When you find two files that look the same or are named the same, you have some major clues to work with. The types of files you find indicate the type of steganographic software that's used. Certain types of steganographic software work with only specific file types, such as video or audio files. Using forensics software, compare the files on a bit-for-bit scale with a hexadecimal editor to find the differences and further narrow the possibilities of which steganographic software was used.

Because you now have two files to work with, you can also run a statistical analysis to see which file falls outside the expected digital signatures of a typical file of its type.

✔ **Use stego detection software.**

Software such as Gargoyle (www.tucofs.com) can be used to detect files that have steganographic signatures. They may not always detect it, though, if a new algorithm was used or the algorithm is so good that it escapes detection.

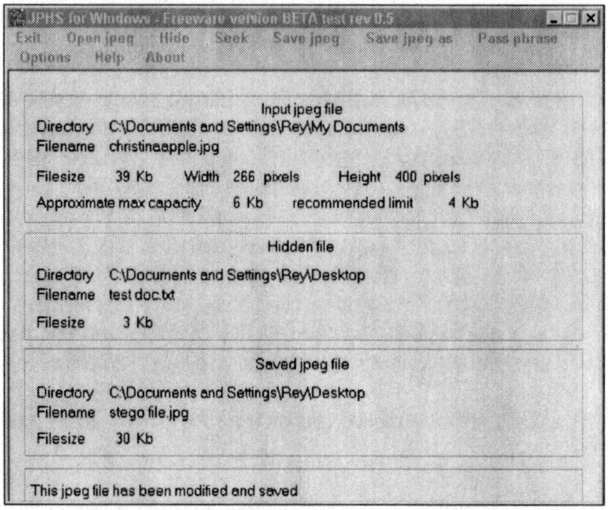

Figure 8-4:
Stego
software
found on a
computer.

You use these basic tools to find files that have been used to hide data — and to discover the stego software that was used. Unless you use the same software, the chances of extracting the hidden data are zero.

Cracking Passwords

Passwords aren't of equal strength and may be only part of an attempt to authenticate a person's attempt to gain access to a computer or file they are protecting. From a user's perspective, a password is easy to remember but hard to guess. It can be a word, phrase, hash, or even biometric (something unique about someone biologically, such as a fingerprint or voice print). From a computer forensic investigator's perspective, a password is a barrier to get past to complete the investigation.

In most password applications, the password isn't even used to authenticate; rather, a hash value is used. A *hash value* (or simply *hash*) is the result of applying a one-way algorithm to a password. The reason for the one-way algorithm is to keep would-be intruders from reverse-engineering the hash back into the password. In other words, when you type a password, the computer is hashing the data you typed and comparing the result to the hashed password that's already saved. If both hashes match, the password is the same one that was entered originally.

Why use a hash in the first place? The most obvious reason is that storing plain text passwords isn't secure. Replace plain text passwords with a one-way hash value, and you exponentially increase the security of your passwords. To put this concept into perspective, suppose that an MD5 hash is used to hide a password. Roughly 8.5 billion combinations for an 8-character password exist, give or take a billion. Years would pass before you could hit all those combinations!

An even more secure version of a password is a *passphrase,* a phrase or short sentence that increases the number of possible combinations to strengthen the cryptographic hash. PGP (Pretty Good Privacy), a type of encryption software, is famous for the use of a passphrase and the difficulty of cracking the PGP hash. The MD5 has only a 128- bit key size, but PGP with passphrases can use, for example, a 2048-bit key size. Simply put, cracking the encrypted data or even the pass-phrase by using a brute force method is almost impossible.

Knowing when to crack and when not to crack

As in other areas of life, time and money determine the choices that are available to you. Whether you decide to crack a password or try other means to obtain data depends on how much time remains on the meter and how much money is on the table. The biggest obstacle to cracking encrypted passwords is the time it takes to crack a well-defended password. Money plays a role because it determines how many toys you have in your arsenal — and how big they are! For example, using a standard home computer, cracking a 40-bit key cipher takes from a day to several weeks. The deep-pocketed and well-equipped NSA spends less than one second cracking a simple 40-bit key cipher to several seconds for a well-defended 40-bit key cipher. If you have neither time nor money to waste and need to crack a password, be sure to read the rest of this chapter.

Disarming passwords to get in

You might have tried to no avail to obtain a password from a suspect and the e-evidence of the crime is sitting in the file you need to access. Because time and money are always an issue, start with simple solutions first and save the most time and money consuming solution for last. Use these guidelines not only as directions but also to inspire ways to work "outside the box:"

✔ **Crack the easy passwords first.**

Human nature dictates that few people use different passwords for all the files or accounts they are trying to protect. Most people simply reuse their passwords repeatedly and change them slightly every time. This situation can work to your advantage because some applications are much easier to crack than others. Cracking a password in a word processing or spreadsheet program is so easy that certain shareware programs can accomplish this task quite easily. After you have one of these passwords, try the password you cracked on the more difficult algorithms to see whether you have a winner. You might be surprised at how often this technique works. If it doesn't work, try substituting characters or variations of the password.

✔ **Grab clues.**

When a user asks the browser to remember a site password to avoid having to type it repeatedly, you catch a break. Look in the cache for the passwords. Usually they're not the ones you want, but they can give you a clue to the target password or hints to how the user thinks. In Figure 8-5, the Cain & Abel software shows a typical password cache dump. Pay attention to the line that reads Default Password: It shows you the password to access the Windows operating system.

✔ **Bring on the brute force crackers.**

If all else fails, you have to use password cracking software, such as Cain & Abel (www.oxid.it) or John the Ripper (www.openwall.com/john). They can crack a password by brute force or use a dictionary, depending on which clues you picked up during your search. Any hints you find to reduce the number of possibilities save you processing time in spades! If necessary, create a custom dictionary just for this case with all possible passwords that this particular user may have used. Be sure to check pet names and favorite teams.

Figure 8-5:
Cain's
Secrets
Dumper
reveals
passwords.

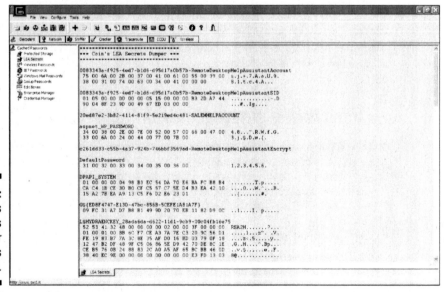

Circumventing passwords to sneak in

Getting around passwords can either be a preventive measure or a night-mare. Usually, nothing exists between those two extremes.

If you can, install a keylogger or snooper software *before* a computer is seized and while the suspect is still using the computer.

If you have a bunch of evidence sitting on your desk with passwords pro-tecting them, you might be able to peek into them depending on the type of application. Applications such as word processors, databases, and spread-sheets often save their data in formats that can be read with a hex editor. For example, you can view the file contents in raw form using a hex editor such as WinHex and not even have to break the password. Keep in mind that the formatting disappears and you see strange characters, but some of the data is in human-readable format.

Other extremely technical methods exist for attacking a file and working around a password. The cost in time and money, however, often isn't worth the effort unless your organization's initials are in the three-letter formats FBI, DHS, CIA, or NSA.

Decrypting the Encrypted

In many ways, trying to decrypt a file involves Hollywood hype more than it involves reality. Most cryptographers agree that a better solution is to break the key and use the "cracked" key rather than try to decrypt an entire file.

A good way to look at this quandary is to take a look at this chapter. This chapter alone has more than 34,000 characters in it, and trying to decrypt every single one with a strong key cipher would take literally thousands of years! Suppose that you create a key that's strong enough to withstand only a couple of months of analysis or that you're careless in storing the key. The bottom-line question is whether to crack a single key or an entire document? No clear-cut answer exists. Answers are based on a diagnosis of the situation and an educated guess at probability. Or, you might find a careless criminal.

Sloppiness cracks PGP

Another factor to consider in cracking encryption is that even heavily armored encryption algorithms, such as PGP, have been cracked at the key level. In the case of PGP, it wasn't the PGP system that was faulty — the users' careless use of the keys was their undoing. A chain is only as strong as its weakest link, which in this case happened to be the human link.

You can crack the key by using a keylogger. The user may actually leave a key stored on the computer allowing you easy access to cracking it, or (as is often the case) a user may not understand how the key really works and creates a weak or faulty key. You could even try tricking the user into revealing the key!

Desperate measures

One issue that most computer forensic analysts have no experience in handling is the *self-destruct mechanism*. Software self-destruct mechanisms are harder to detect than physical threats and are even harder to prevent. (After you pull the trigger, you can't call back the bullet.) A *self-destruct system* is usually a software program that destroys all evidence if a set of parameters are met such as wrong passwords or incorrect usernames.

If the sophistication of a suspect indicates that they *may* have installed a piece of code or a password fail-safe, make a backup copy of the backup copy and call in a professional who deals with software coding or security issues of this type. The last thing you need to happen to your evidence is to watch it disappear because the password fail-safe was set to wipe any data if you missed the password three times!

Just as in steganography, this type of defense mechanism is hard to spot if you aren't looking for it. You might receive a warning, and you might not, but much depends on how your procedures are set up to handle this contingency. If you follow the proper protocol of using a copy of the copy of the e-evidence, the payload can self-destruct and you can just reload and try again. If and when this happens to you, have a professional handle the "defusing" of the logic bomb.

Part III
Doing Computer Forensics Investigations

The 5th Wave   By Rich Tennant

"Good news! I found a place where the router works with the PC upstairs and the one in the basement."

In this part . . .

You forensically find the tracks that even the most digitally devious desperadoes leave behind that connect them to the case or crime. Whether it's e-mail messages exposing illegal or illicit behavior, chat conversations meant to be forever confidential, data hidden in the caverns of unallocated space, documents and drafts in electronic landfills, or e-evidence on the run, you find and use these bytes as clues to figure out what happened, whodunit, and how, where, when, and maybe even why.

The six chapters in this part explain computer forensic investigations and subspecialties. You find out how to investigate the most incriminating of all evidence — e-mail and instant messages (see Chapter 9). The urge to e-mail is an investigator's best friend. Chapter 10 describes how to use data forensics to find hidden evidence. Chapter 11 covers document forensics, which team with e-mail forensics to keep litigators in high demand. The fastest-growing branch of forensics mirrors the indispensable, got-to-have-one-of-those personal devices. Power users of these devices surrendered their privacy when they plugged in (see Chapter 12). Network and exotic forensics expose evidence hoarded by devices we don't give thought to (see Chapter 13), but printers, SUVs, and home entertainment centers all have digital memories. Read on.

There is no branch of detective science which is so important and so much neglected as the art of tracing footsteps.

— Sherlock Holmes, *A Study in Scarlet* (1888)

Chapter 9

E-Mail and Web Forensics

E-mail plays the lead or support role in most civil and criminal investigations. Federal and most state law allows for a review of e-mail in every case. These laws, mixed with people sending badly-thought-out e-mail, have made e-mail forensics the leading type of forensics. Don't expect your investigation to be a slam-dunk because verifying the sender's identity isn't always easy to do.

E-mail and Web-based e-mail (*Web mail,* for short) can spread far and wide. E-mail-evidence has helped put people in jail or on the losing side of a lawsuit because of head-in-the-sand attitudes about the risk of unintended destinations and readers of their messages.

In this chapter, you find out how e-mail and Web mail sent to or from someone who accesses e-mail over a public ISP can be recovered. ISPs such as Google and AOL are served thousands of subpoenas and search warrants each month from investigators as they try to identify subscribers or review their e-mail — and the companies must comply. Even companies that have zero-tolerance e-mail policies, when faced with legal action, face high odds that their e-mail will be searched and incriminating evidence found.

Opening Pandora's Box of E-Mail

Ray Tomlinson sent the first network e-mail message in 1971. When his invention was teamed with the newly invented PC ten years later, they unleashed widespread e-mailing. The areas of business, law, entertainment, relationships, and personal and criminal behavior were transformed. For organizations and people in general, e-mail became a Pandora's box that, when opened, created an uncontrollable source of grief and valuable e-evidence.

In this chapter, we cover how e-mail gets sent, its volume, and its starring role in divorce cases. Then we describe the technological side of e-mail and Web mail forensics.

Read the Google Gmail privacy statement at `http://gmail.google.com/mail/help/privacy.html`. Google's privacy policy specifies that deleted e-mail messages "may remain in our offline backup systems" in perpetuity. It doesn't guarantee that backups are ever deleted.

Following the route of e-mail packets

Every e-mail message is sent as a series of byte-size packets, as described in Chapter 1. In the networks transporting these packets (*packet-switched* networks), each packet carries these elements:

- **Source address:** The IP address of the originating or sender's computer, unless that IP address has been disguised
- **Destination address:** The IP address of the destination or recipient's computer
- **Payload:** The data or message

Routers are positioned at nodes where one segment of the network connects with another segment. As their name suggests, routers forward packets along the network toward their destination. Figure 9-1 shows the simple path of a packet through a series of routers. Of course, routers need to look into the packet to see its destination IP address to know where to send the packet next.

Becoming Exhibit A

E-mail messages routed over the Internet make up the majority of Internet traffic, and more than 1 billion of the world's 6.6 billion inhabitants are Internet users, according to Internet World Stats (`www.internetworldstats.com`). To estimate the average number of e-mails sent per day, consider how many you send — and then multiply that number by 1 billion.

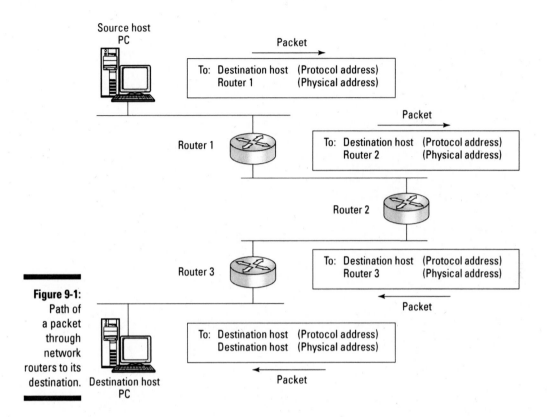

Figure 9-1:
Path of a packet through network routers to its destination.

But volume alone doesn't explain why e-mail is often Exhibit A in a courtroom. People are candid, careless, and delusional in believing that nothing they send by e-mail will ever be looked at by unfriendly eyes. The courts recognize what users write about themselves as truthful. It's up to the jury to

consider and weigh the relevance of all evidence.

Review ten e-mail messages that you had expected to stay strictly confidential. Would you find it difficult to explain away your comments? Would it be easy for a stranger to misinterpret or misunderstood them? If your messages became an exhibit in legal action, you probably would want to provide some context or explanation. Remember this feeling when you're reading other people's e-mail.

Other advice to keep in mind so that you don't compromise the strength of your case or get blasted on cross-examination are described in this list:

✔ **Keep an open mind.**

Your job is to find the truth about what did or did not happen.

The unique nature of e-mail communication

In 2007, Nevada District Judge Herndon suppressed telephone conversations between District Attorney (DA) Gammick and the accused killer Darren Mack because they were obtained unethically. The judge also ruled that e-mail sent by Mack to the DA could be introduced as evidence because it was unsolicited. On June 17, 2006, Mack had sent the DA e-mail from Mexico with the subject `Darren Mack's surrendering himself`. The DA's testimony that Mack set conditions for his surrender in the e-mail was allowed in court. Why different rulings?

✔ The e-mail arrived without any action from the DA.

✔ The judge ruled that it was part of the DA's duty to read the e-mail message.

✔ For telephone conversations, the DA could have either immediately warned Mack that he was represented by counsel or stopped the conversation.

✔ **Don't jump to a conclusion based on a few messages.**

Your conclusion taints the way you read and interpret other e-mail.

✔ **Don't assume that the registered user sent all the messages.**

In many work environments, for example, co-workers share computers or post their passwords so that others can access their accounts when they're away from work.

✔ **Pay attention to whether the writing style is casual (candid) or formal (official).**

Those messages may contradict each other.

Because e-mail is used extensively, e-mail forensics often provides the "smoking gun" that attorneys look for to win their cases.

Tracking the biggest trend in civil litigation

E-trails are the biggest trend in civil litigation in decades. Not surprisingly, e-mail is a leading source of evidence in divorce cases. Soon-to-be-ex-spouses collect e-mails, instant messages, and transcripts of online chats. When marriages go from bliss to bust, e-mail messages on laptops, cell phones, and BlackBerrys are used to build cases.

In divorce cases (high emotion + desire for revenge + financial stakes), one party can way too easily frame or spy on the other party's e-mail. Employment cases are similar because a manager can find out other employees' passwords without consequence. E-mail forgeries and frames are the key reason to keep an open mind. Fortunately, the person trying to impersonate another almost always makes a mistake. If something seems strange, dig deeper and wider.

The Electronic Communications Privacy Act (ECPA), a federal law, bans anyone from disclosing "to any other person the contents of any wire, oral, or electronic communication" that was obtained illegally. This law is tricky. Attempts to suppress e-evidence acquired using a keystroke logger may fail, in part because keystrokes, when recorded, haven't yet traveled in interstate commerce. In 2007, U.S. District Judge Thomas Rose said that ECPA doesn't permit courts to disallow such evidence.

Scoping Out E-Mail Architecture

E-mail messages are composed of several identifying components. You need to be able to interpret what these components reveal and what they don't.

E-mail structures

E-mail works much the same way as U.S. Postal Service mail. The central post office corresponds to the e-mail server, and the computers connected to it are the clients. Two types of e-mail systems are client/server and Web-based. E-mail systems can also be differentiated according to use: business and personal. ISP systems such as Gmail, AOL, Yahoo!, and Hotmail are used for personal e-mail, and most businesses have their own, internal e-mail system using a client/server setup (although you do find small businesses using Web-based e-mail because the cost is so low). Here's how a client/server setup works:

- ✔ **Client:** The computer that's receiving or sending the e-mail. Think of the client as your home mail box.

- ✔ **Server:** The computer that's storing e-mail it receives until the destination client retrieves them. Think of the server as your local post office where mail is sent and received.

E-mail addressing

The structure of the e-mail address, as originally designed by Ray Tomlinson, consists of these two parts, separated by the familiar @ symbol:

- ✔ **Mailbox:** The part on the left, often referred to as the *username*
- ✔ **Domain (or *host*):** The part on the right; the name of the domain server

For example, `Computer-forensics@ForDummies.com` has the mailbox `Computer-forensics` and the domain `ForDummies.com`.

Under this two-part structure, e-mail servers can find an e-mail's destination quickly by looking up the IP address of the domain in a domain name server (DNS). A DNS translates domain names into IP addresses. Internet traffic depends on the functioning of the hidden DNSs.

E-mail lingo

Each and every e-mail message travels from source to destination in the same way. E-mail systems have a unique language when they communicate, consisting of these protocols:

- ✔ **Simple Mail Transfer Protocol (SMTP):** The language e-mail uses to send messages to an e-mail server. SMTP *pushes,* or delivers, the messages to their intended e-mail servers.

- ✔ **Post Office Protocol (POP):** The language an e-mail system uses to retrieve messages from an e-mail server. This protocol is referred to as *POP3,* but you also see it listed simply as POP. When POP *pulls* (retrieves) messages from the e-mail server, it deletes the original message from the server and downloads a copy to the destination computer. POP has these two important features:

  - • You have the option to delete e-mail messages or store them indefinitely on the server, but the user has to make the selection when setting up the POP account.

  - • POP is designed to work with only one user at a time. Multiple access to a user's mailbox isn't possible with POP.

- ✔ **Internet Message Access Protocol (IMAP):** The newest kid on the block with regard to e-mail retrieval. IMAP differs from POP in the way it handles e-mail. Here are a few Important IMAP features:

  - • IMAP is designed to handle multiple users on the same mail account.

  - • IMAP downloads all e-mail messages to the local destination without deleting the e-mail from the e-mail server until the user deletes them purposely.

- IMAP is newer than POP, but not as widespread or popular.

✔ **Messaging Application Programming Interface (MAPI):** A proprietary protocol used by Microsoft to power the de facto workhorse of the e-mail world: Microsoft Outlook. MAPI sends and receives e-mails as a single protocol instead of using two separate protocols such as SMTP and POP. In addition to handling e-mail communication, MAPI also manages the organizational structure of the client system such as inboxes and storage folders.

E-mail in motion

After you know the e-mail vocabulary, you can take a look at the physical process of sending and receiving e-mail. Suppose that you're at your laptop, composing an e-mail to your best friend, and have just pressed the Send button. Here's what happens:

✔ Your laptop looks for and finds the e-mail server assigned to it.

✔ Your laptop uses SMTP to upload the e-mail message to the server for storage.

✔ The receiving e-mail server stores your message until either the e-mail account gets full or your best friend accesses the account to retrieve the e-mail.

✔ When your friend checks e-mail, her computer connects to the e-mail server and downloads your message to the local computer using either POP or IMAP. She can then read your message.

Figure 9-2 illustrates how the process works.

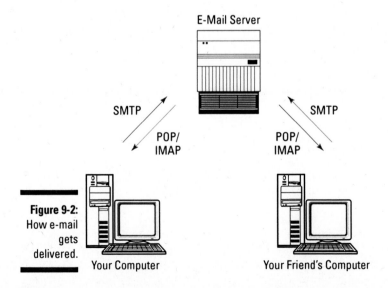

Figure 9-2: How e-mail gets delivered.

Seeing the E-Mail Forensics Perspective

From a forensic point of view, client/server e-mail systems are best for finding information because messages are downloaded to the user's or local computer's hard drive. Because you have ready access to this computer, your investigation is easier. You usually have access to the server too, from which you can access e-mail messages and logs of e-mail activity.

Production e-mail servers are hard to shut down to investigate because companies can't afford to be cut off from their e-mail systems; e-mail has become such an integral part of business today. For example, if Dell's e-mail system crashed, chances are the business would grind to a halt until the system was back up. Your first step should be to look at backups of the e-mail system and if all else fails then take down the live (production) e-mail server.

Dissecting the message

This list describes the two parts of an e-mail message, as shown in Figure 9-3:

- ✔ **Header:** Like the outside of an envelope, contains the source and destination addresses. You use header information to track an e-mail back to its source or sender.

- ✔ **Body:** Contains the actual message and often has the "smoking gun" information that attorneys love to see.

When you're looking at an e-mail message, you see only these two parts and not the packets that were used to deliver the message because you're looking at it after delivery. Anyone who wants to capture packets of e-mail en route from source to destination can do so by using packet sniffer software. Unless it has been encrypted, e-mail is sent in plain text and is readable like a post card.

Do not have anyone forward the e-mail to you; doing so alters the header information!

Expanding headers

Most e-mail clients display by default only regular header information. Here are the basic four fields of information in the header:

- ✔ **From:** The sender's address. Be careful about relying on this information. This field can be *spoofed* (disguised) to make it look as though another person sent the e-mail while hiding the IP address of the real sender.

✔ **To:** The recipient's address, which can also be faked or spoofed.

✔ **Subject:** Sometimes left blank or contains misleading information.

✔ **Date:** Recorded from the sending computer, but may not be accurate if the sender's computer clock was set incorrectly.

Obviously, you cannot trust header information. You may not be able to verify the real information. To confirm the information, you need to expand the header.

Header

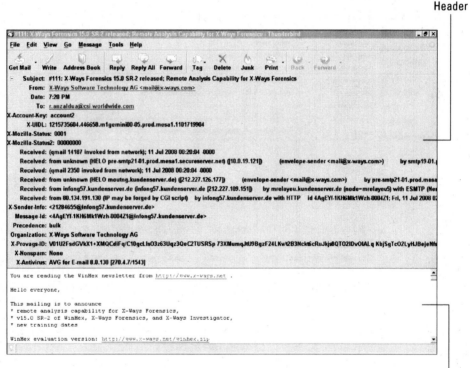

Figure 9-3:
E-mail
message
with head
and body.

Body

The expanded mail header has quite a bit more information that's needed by routers to deliver the e-mail to its destination. For the most part, e-mail client software doesn't show you full headers unless you specifically ask, and even then you may have to look at the raw e-mail to find all the headers you're after. Figure 9-4 shows the type of information you can glean from a full e-mail header.

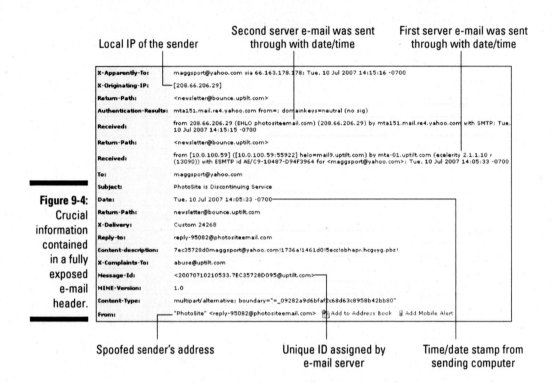

Local IP of the sender

Second server e-mail was sent through with date/time

First server e-mail was sent through with date/time

X-Apparently-To:	maggsport@yahoo.com via 66.163.178.178; Tue, 10 Jul 2007 14:15:16 -0700
X-Originating-IP:	[208.66.206.29]
Return-Path:	<newsletter@bounce.uptilt.com>
Authentication-Results:	mta151.mail.re4.yahoo.com from=; domainkeys=neutral (no sig)
Received:	from 208.66.206.29 (EHLO photositeemail.com) (208.66.206.29) by mta151.mail.re4.yahoo.com with SMTP; Tue, 10 Jul 2007 14:15:15 -0700
Return-Path:	<newsletter@bounce.uptilt.com>
Received:	from [10.0.100.59] ([10.0.100.59:55922] helo=mail9.uptilt.com) by mta-01.uptilt.com (ecelerity 2.1.1.10 r (13090)) with ESMTP id AE/C9-10487-D94F3964 for <maggsport@yahoo.com>; Tue, 10 Jul 2007 14:05:33 -0700
To:	maggsport@yahoo.com
Subject:	PhotoSite is Discontinuing Service
Date:	Tue, 10 Jul 2007 14:05:33 -0700
Return-Path:	newsletter@bounce.uptilt.com
X-Delivery:	Custom 24268
Reply-to:	reply-95082@photositeemail.com
Content-description:	7ec35728d0maggsport@yahoo.com!1736a!1461d0!5ecc!obhapr.hcgvyg.pbz!
X-Complaints-To:	abuse@uptilt.com
Message-Id:	<20070710210533.7EC35728D095@uptilt.com>
MIME-Version:	1.0
Content-Type:	multipart/alternative; boundary="=_09282a9d6bfaf2c68d63c8958b42bb80"
From:	"PhotoSite" <reply-95082@photositeemail.com> 🖼 Add to Address Book 🖼 Add Mobile Alert

Figure 9-4:
Crucial information contained in a fully exposed e-mail header.

Spoofed sender's address

Unique ID assigned by e-mail server

Time/date stamp from sending computer

The piece of information most useful to you is the originating IP address (source IP address) or domain. You can use this address to try to track down the person who sent the e-mail — unless it has been spoofed or faked.

A *unique ID* is assigned to the message by the first e-mail server that the e-mail passes through. You can find the e-mail's footprints on the servers it had passed through using this ID. If you can catch the e-mail server logs before they're overwritten, you can literally track the true date/time of the e-mail as it passes through the network.

In most full headers, the path of the e-mail starts at the bottom and works its way up. For example, in Figure 9-4, by following the date-and-time stamps, you see that the e-mail traveled through two e-mail servers to arrive at its destination. If the full e-mail header isn't clear or the header is written upside down, following the e-mail by using its listed date-and-time stamps often clears up in which direction the e-mail has traveled.

E-mail has a truth serum effect or a delusion-of-privacy effect that seems to apply to anyone regardless of age, occupation, or gender. See the nearby sidebar, "Judge allowed use of e-mail as evidence."

Judge allowed use of e-mail as evidence

In the *SEC v J.P. Morgan Chase & Co.* case, Chase was charged with knowingly helping Enron Corporation manipulate its reported financial results through *prepays*. These false transactions were used to disguise loans to inflate its financial results. Specifically, prepays were transactions used by Enron to report loans from Chase as cash from operating activities. The SEC needed to prove that Chase knowingly helped Enron falsify financial reports, which would show that Chase had not been duped by Enron. The SEC recovered and produced as evidence many incriminating internal Chase e-mail messages, including one from vice chairman Donald Layton, who wrote in an e-mail: "We are making disguised loans, usually buried in commodities or equities derivatives (and I'm sure in other areas). . . .With a few exceptions, they are understood to be disguised loans and approved as such. But I am queasy about the process." Chase tried to have the e-mail messages excluded, essentially contending that the colloquial meaning of the words didn't convey what the writers' intended. The judge allowed the e-mails. The outcome from the frank messages: J.P. Morgan Chase agreed to pay $135 million to settle the SEC allegations that it helped Enron commit fraud.

Checking for e-mail extras

In addition to checking the header and body of an e-mail message, check it for these other potential sources of information:

- ✔ Attachments, such as .doc or .xls files or images
- ✔ People who have been carbon copied (cc) or blind carbon copied (bcc)
- ✔ People to whom the message was forwarded
- ✔ Original messages or series of messages that the e-mail is in response to

Examining Client-Based E-Mail

The process of forensically extracting e-mails in a client/server environment follows general steps. Human-friendly graphical user interfaces (GUI) used in e-mail client software makes the process much easier than it was even five years ago. Press a button or two in the computer forensic software and out come the e-mail messages.

Extracting e-mail from clients

Most e-mail systems use SMTP, POP, or IMAP. The use of these protocols makes e-mail transport fairly standard. Your challenge is to extract e-mail from different e-mail client software. Here's a description of the two most common e-mail client systems:

- ✔ **Outlook:** The big brother to Outlook Express and bundled with the Microsoft Office Suite. Outlook is much more than a simple e-mail program. It can act as a data assistant with features such as a calendar, a task list, and contact management. When you investigate cases where Outlook has been used to manage the day-to-day affairs of a suspect, you find enormous detailed information! Unlike Outlook Express, Outlook saves all its data into a single identity using a `.pst` file extension. You need a viewer or forensic software to view the contents of this file. FTK and EnCase offer the most complete method for extracting Outlook files.

- ✔ **Outlook Express:** From Microsoft, stores data in files with a `.dbx` file extension and requires you to have a viewer to read them. Additionally, each account created in Outlook Express is assigned a hexadecimal sequence of numbers, which Microsoft uses to identify the account. Depending on the version of Windows, these account identities are located in subfolders of the `\Documents and Settings` folder if the user hasn't customized or changed the folder location.

In Outlook Express, Outlook, AOL, Eudora, and Thunderbird, e-mail is stored on the local client computer, which helps your investigation tremendously. But you also have a server somewhere to look at. Although the client may have the e-mail downloaded to a local computer, the server has the logs that tie that e-mail to this server using the unique message ID. Using this ID, you can find the tracks of the e-mail through the server and literally begin building a chain that shows how the e-mail traveled through a network. Having the smoking gun e-mail is useful, but you can build a more solid case by showing how the e-mail arrived at the suspect's doorstep.

Getting to know e-mail file extensions

In some instances, you need to be able to extract just the file required to view the e-mail, or you might need to copy a file and transfer data to another computer. Table 9-1 lists the file extensions used by the most common e-mail clients. Forensic software often opens these files for you and extracts the e-mails. You always have the option to use the suspect's e-mail system to extract files, but the use of forensic software makes it much easier to automate the process for easier analysis and report generation.

Table 9-1	File Extensions for Common E-Mail Clients	
E-Mail Client	*Extensions*	*File Type*
AOL	.abi or .arl	Organizer file
	.aim or .bag	Instant messenger
Eudora	.mbx	Message base
Outlook	.pab	Personal address book
	.pst	Compressed personal folder
	.wab	Address book
Outlook Express	.dbx	Compressed database
	.dgr	Fax page
	.e-mail	Mail message
	.eml	E-mail
Thunderbird	.msf	Mail summary file

You have several options for reading these various file types and extracting e-mail from them:

✔ **E-mail client:** You can use an e-mail client such as Microsoft Outlook or Eudora to view files that are native to the computer you're investigating.

✔ **Third-party viewer:** Software such as Outlook Extract Pro or Outlook Export is available to view different mailbox formats.

✔ **Forensic software:** Forensic software such as FTK and EnCase has built-in viewers that extract the contents of e-mail client databases and allow you to export the information to other media for analysis.

Of these three options, the last one is the easiest to use and the best one from a forensic point of view. Forensic software can open almost all e-mail formats and offers you the convenience of being able to

✔ Perform powerful and precise searches

✔ Extract header information

✔ Print e-mail messages in their entirety, including headers

✔ Group messages by data or other data classification

When you use any of these options, you aren't extracting from the original e-mail — you're using either an image or a restored copy of the potential e-evidence.

Copying the e-mail

The first step after you obtain a forensic image is to copy the e-mail messages you want from the e-mail client. Figure 9-5 shows how Outlook lists e-mails.

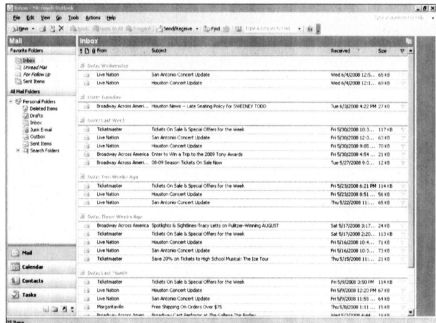

Figure 9-5:
Copying
e-mail from
Outlook.

Follow these steps to copy the e-mail:

1. **Open the e-mail client and select the folder of interest to you, such as Inbox or Sent Items.**

2. **Open Windows Explorer and make sure that the drive or folder where you're saving the e-mails is displayed on your screen.**

3. **Arrange the e-mail client and Microsoft Explorer windows on your desktop in either a horizontal or vertical manner.**

   Right-click the taskbar on your desktop and choose Tile Windows Horizontally or Tile Windows Vertically.

4. **Click and drag an e-mail message over to the area where you want to save it.**

   Now you have an e-mail file with an .eml extension ready for analysis. What you are going to do with this copy of the e-mail is open it up and search the headers for evidence and, if the body of the text is your evidence, make that part of your report.

Another way to extract e-mail from a suspect's computer is to use forensic software, such as FTK or EnCase, to extract the e-mail for you in an automated script or a program feature. Depending on the program you use, the software gives you the option to extract e-mail messages and save them as bookmarks or extract them to external media for further analysis. The power of using this type of forensic software makes the extraction of e-mail from e-mail client software extremely easy and forensically sound and in reality is the preferred method over the manual method.

Printing the e-mail

After you save or copy e-mail messages, print hard copies of them for reference. This step is usually done after making the forensic copy, but sometimes you want to print an e-mail message before you make a forensic image of it, such as when an employee receives an e-mail message that violates policy. You should take this precaution because a person who doesn't understand how e-mail headers work can accidentally alter important header evidence by forwarding the e-mail message. In cases when a nontechnical person has concern about an e-mail message, by all means have him print it!

To print e-mail from a GUI file system, follow these steps:

1. **Open Windows Explorer.**
2. **Navigate to the folder or drive where the e-mail message is located.**
3. **Double-click the e-mail to open it.**

   The e-mail client software opens the e-mail for you. If the client software doesn't start, a dialog box might open and ask which program to use. Select the e-mail client that's listed.

4. **Choose File⇨Print.**
5. **Make sure that the selected printer in the dialog box is the correct one and click the Print button to finish printing the e-mail.**

If you're using forensics software, simply click the Print icon.

Investigating Web-Based Mail

Users often rely on Web-based e-mail for personal communication. The major providers of Web mail are Yahoo!, Hotmail, and Google, which provide their basic services for free. Web mail can be used without e-mail client software. The only software that's needed is the free Web browser already installed on most computers. In reality, Web mail is a client/server system. Figure 9-6 summarizes the basic e-mail interactions on a Web mail server.

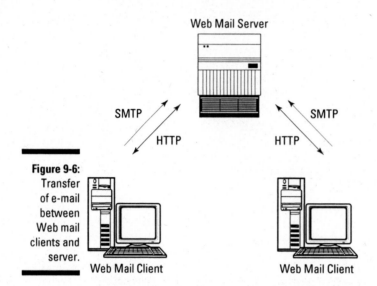

Figure 9-6:
Transfer
of e-mail
between
Web mail
clients and
server.

Behind the scenes, the Web mail system uploads e-mail using SMTP and downloads it using POP or IMAP. The biggest technical difference is that Web mail isn't normally stored on the local computer unless the user requests that it be stored that way. As a computer forensic investigator, you have to work harder to find any local files.

If you have access to the e-mail account at the server or can get the e-mail provider to release the account details, you reduce your workload. But don't count on a company the size of Yahoo! or Google to retrieve from their servers for you any e-mail messages that were deleted six months ago. The amount of data written to their servers precludes the ability to find any meaningful data.

The caching of data stored in RAM has been the saving grace for many forensic investigators, and its use in e-mail forensics isn't an exception. When a user checks her e-mail or composes a message, the operating system caches the data that's on the screen to the hard drive, especially if the e-mailer is taking a while to write. Therefore, the best places to find Web mail are

✔ In the temporary file area such as the system swap file or file cache.

✔ In the unallocated space after the temporary files have been erased

Forensic extractions into the temporary file area and unallocated space take more time and expertise because you're digging deep and reconstructing Web pages from raw digital space! You must have patience and skill in equal measures to sift through HTML formatting unless you have FTK or EnCase to carve out the relevant data. Even using one of those toolkits, you might need to fine-tune the data that the forensics software finds.

The easiest way to view the contents of a person's Web mail account is to get permission from that person. But the odds of that happening are unlikely. Instead, you can find data by using forensic methods on the local machine.

When you're looking for Web e-mail, you're looking at a Web page that just happens to have e-mail functionality. You're looking not for files with e-mail extensions, but, rather, for files with `.html` extensions.

Extracting every Web page that a suspect has ever visited would be foolish. The results could run into hundreds of thousands of pages, pushing the time it would take to view all those pages into the next decade. Here are two ways to structure an efficient Web mail search:

✔ **Use key words or phrases in conjunction with Web page tags.**

Suppose that you're looking for e-mail messages for `joe@123.com` pertaining to a bank fraud investigation. Using forensic software, you set up a search of `joe@123.com` and limit the search to only Web pages with key words or phrases related to the specifics of the fraud investigation. In this way, you eliminate extraneous Web pages and focus on those with Joe's e-mail address. You may still get hundreds or thousands of e-mail hits in this way, but your results are narrowed.

✔ **Focus on the type of service the suspect used, such as Yahoo! or Hotmail.**

Yahoo! and Hotmail Web mail uses words or phrases unique to their service. You can search for those unique identifiers to open only Web pages from those services. The fortunate or unfortunate key to this process (depending on how you look at it) is that these key words or phrases change after updates or urgent technical changes are made. Be aware of changes! Yahoo!, for instance, uses the wording *Yahoo Mail* in its Web mail. You may be able to search for this phrase and focus just on Yahoo! e-mail pages.

The steps involved in using this method to search for Web mail varies depending on the forensic software you use. FTK and EnCase automate the retrieval of Web mail by using dialog boxes that ask which keywords you're looking for within Web pages. Figure 9-7 shows a dialog box which is used by EnCase to search for Web pages.

There's no such thing as subpoena-proof e-mail. A version of Google Toolbar uploaded users' documents to Google servers "to enable searching from any of the user's computers." When data is held by ISPs, it's subject to different laws than data on personal computers. A search warrant is needed to view the contents of a computer. In contrast, data on an ISP's servers require only a subpoena, which is easier to get.

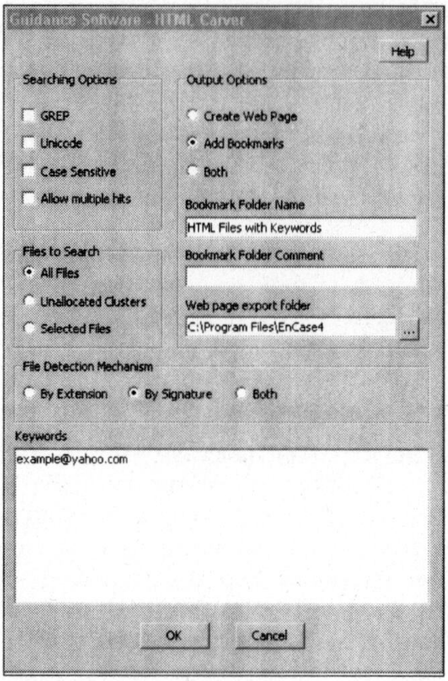

Figure 9-7:
Retrieving
e-mail with
EnCase.

Searching Browser Files

Besides e-mail, Internet browsers, such as Internet Explorer, also keep a temporary copy of data that has come from the Internet. Most users never see this side of Internet Explorer because the files downloaded in the background. The part most users can see is the browsing history showing the Web sites the browser has visited.

Temporary files

The temporary files created by applications sending and receiving data over a network are temporarily stored by the operating system. The files are first stored in RAM. When RAM becomes full or the operating system pushes that data down the priority list of data to be retrieved by applications, the files are written to the storage device.

There is no single area for temporary files on modern day computers because some applications also create temporary files in addition to the operating system. For example, Internet Explorer handles temporary files downloaded from the Internet through settings in the software as shown in Figure 9-8. Not only do you find the location of the temporary files, but you also find the number of days Internet Explorer keeps the history of the Web sites you visited.

If you look at the temporary files stored directly on the storage device, the file types run the spectrum from Web pages to individual pictures (see Figure 9-9).

If the application doesn't have the ability to temporarily store files for use later, it often lets the operating system handle this function via the swap file or virtual memory. The *swap file* is an operating system function that acts like RAM, but uses the hard drive or storage device instead of memory microchips. If the application needs the information in the swap file, the operating system retrieves the information and deletes the information off the storage device.

Because the swap file is written and then deleted, the information is still physically on the storage device and retrievable by you. Figure 9-10 shows the control dialog box for the virtual memory settings in Microsoft Windows. Virtual memory is just a big file that is size adjustable and can be written and deleted similarly to any other file on an operating system.

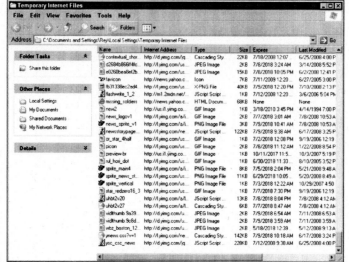

Figure 9-9:
Temporary
storage
space used
by Internet
Explorer.

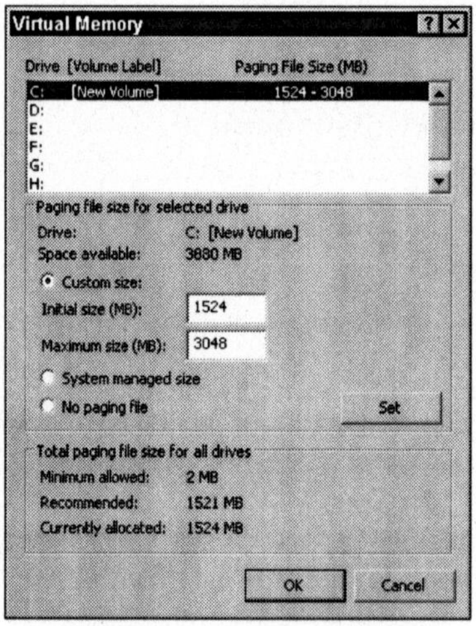

Figure 9-10:
Virtual
memory
control
settings in
Microsoft
Windows.

Internet history

Internet Explorer has the ability to keep track of where the Web browser
has visited. The user has quite a bit of control and can adjust the number
of days the browser hangs onto the list of Web sites (the Internet history).
Most users think that deleting the history deletes the files forever! The part
most users cannot control is the index.dat file. Internet Explorer uses
the index.dat file to create a database of Web sites visited, cookies, and
assorted other details pertaining to the use of the Web browser.

You can extract data from the index.dat file and re-create the tracks of where you have been, often going back to the first day you ever surfed the Internet on that particular computer. Other Web browsers, such as Mozilla and Opera, also have the ability to keep these types of files.

Because most Web browsers keep histories, computer forensic software is designed to open these types of files to extract the data quite easily. In the case of EnCase and FTK, the process is automated to the point where the software not only looks for active database files, but also deleted files in unallocated space that contain web surfing histories. Figure 9-11 shows multiple `index.dat` files on one computer detailing the history of Internet Web browser use.

	Name	File Ext	Is Deleted	File Type	Description	Last Accessed	File Created	Last Written	Entry Modified
☐ 6223	index.dat	dat		Data ASCII / Binary	File, Archive	07/10/08 12:31:26AM	05/07/08 01:58:43PM	07/11/08 01:37:39PM	07/11/08 01:37:
☐ 6224	index.dat	dat		Data ASCII / Binary	File, Archive	07/10/08 12:31:26AM	05/07/08 01:58:43PM	07/11/08 01:37:39PM	07/11/08 01:37:
☐ 6225	index.dat	dat		Data ASCII / Binary	File, Archive	07/10/08 09:54:42AM	05/07/08 01:57:21PM	05/07/08 01:57:21PM	07/02/08 12:24:
☐ 6226	index.dat	dat		Data ASCII / Binary	File, Archive	07/10/08 09:54:42AM	05/07/08 01:57:21PM	05/07/08 08:44:13AM	07/02/08 12:24:
☐ 6227	index.dat	dat		Data ASCII / Binary	File, Archive	07/10/08 10:58:41AM	05/07/08 01:58:39PM	05/08/08 03:06:41AM	07/02/08 02:07:
☐ 6228	index.dat	dat		Data ASCII / Binary	File, Archive	07/10/08 12:41:57AM	05/07/08 01:59:49PM	07/11/08 02:10:49PM	07/11/08 02:10:
☐ 6229	index.dat	dat		Data ASCII / Binary	File, Archive	07/10/08 12:35:32AM	05/07/08 01:59:49PM	07/11/08 02:10:49PM	07/11/08 02:10:
☐ 6230	index.dat	dat		Data ASCII / Binary	File, Archive	07/10/08 09:54:42AM	05/07/08 01:57:21PM	05/07/08 08:44:13AM	07/02/08 12:24:
☐ 6231	index.dat	dat		Data ASCII / Binary	File, Hidden, System, Archi	07/11/08 12:04:55AM	07/11/08 12:04:55AM	07/11/08 12:11:00PM	07/11/08 02:13:
☐ 6232	index.dat	dat		Data ASCII / Binary	File, Hidden, System, Archi	07/10/08 10:16:51AM	07/10/08 01:14:51AM	07/10/08 09:56:59PM	07/10/08 11:27:
☐ 6233	index.dat	dat		Data ASCII / Binary	File, Archive	07/10/08 09:55:57AM	05/28/08 06:11:02PM	06/12/08 10:55:24AM	07/02/08 12:24:
☐ 6234	index.dat	dat		Data ASCII / Binary	File, Archive	07/10/08 10:58:41AM	05/07/08 01:58:41PM	05/07/08 01:58:41PM	07/02/08 02:07:
☐ 6235	index.dat	dat		Data ASCII / Binary	File, Hidden, System, Archi	07/10/08 09:55:57AM	05/28/08 06:11:23PM	05/28/08 06:11:23PM	07/02/08 12:24:
☐ 6236	index.dat	dat		Data ASCII / Binary	File, Archive	07/10/08 10:16:51AM	07/08/08 02:34:13PM	07/08/08 07:54:55AM	07/09/08 11:39:
☐ 6237	index.dat	dat		Data ASCII / Binary	File, Hidden, System, Archi	07/10/08 10:58:41AM	05/08/08 03:06:41AM	05/08/08 03:06:29AM	07/02/08 02:07:
☐ 6238	index.dat	dat		Data ASCII / Binary	File, Archive	07/10/08 10:58:41AM	05/28/08 06:11:02PM	06/12/08 10:55:24AM	07/02/08 12:24:
☐ 6239	index.dat	dat		Data ASCII / Binary	File, Archive	07/10/08 10:58:41AM	05/07/08 01:58:39PM	05/08/08 03:06:41AM	07/02/08 02:07:
☐ 6240	index.dat	dat		Data ASCII / Binary	File, Archive	07/10/08 09:55:58AM	05/28/08 06:11:02PM	06/12/08 10:55:24AM	07/02/08 12:24:
☐ 6241	index.dat	dat		Data ASCII / Binary	File, Hidden, System, Archi	07/10/08 10:16:51AM	07/08/08 08:47:56AM	07/08/08 07:54:56AM	07/08/08 10:20:
☐ 6242	index.dat	dat		Data ASCII / Binary	File, Hidden, System, Archi	07/10/08 10:16:51AM	07/07/08 02:37:25PM	07/07/08 02:29:52PM	07/08/08 04:29:
☐ 6243	index.dat	dat		Data ASCII / Binary	File, Hidden, System, Archi	07/10/08 10:16:51AM	07/07/08 02:37:25PM	07/07/08 02:29:52PM	07/07/08 02:37:

Figure 9-11: List of index. dat files found on a single computer.

Looking through Instant Messages

Instant messaging (IM) has exploded in the dynamic communication arena. Whereas e-mail acts like an inbox, IM acts like a text-based cell call. Texting on mobile devices is the preferred mode of communication for some people.

IM is important to forensic examiners because companies use this form of communication for real-time customer service and internal business communication. On the personal side, people use IM to chat about everything from which recipe is best for roast beef to which hotel is best for a secret rendezvous.

Someone using chat software isn't chatting from his device to another person's device directly. The chat is relayed by way of a server. The same concept is used for IM. IM software works basically the same way as software used by e-mail systems — it's just done in real time.

In any real-time environment, your best chance of finding any data is to log the data as it is being typed. Recovering chat sessions is a hit-and-miss type of recovery because the caching function of the computer is the element that allows you to re-create the chat sessions. Some IM software logs conversations for you, but most people don't activate the logs. If you rely on the caching system to save IM chats, you may get pieces of the conversation or nothing, depending on how the cache archived the data on the hard drive.

IM is migrating to mobile devices, where the technology is somewhat different from desktop computers. The main problem that mobile devices have now is that they don't have the resources or power of conventional desktop computers and they therefore use memory differently. Because mobile devices tend to not cache or archive data in the same way that desktop devices do, retrieving chats is that much more difficult, unless you're recording them as they occur. You may be able to catch some logging information from the mobile clients or even the IM server. But finding a complete conversation in memory is almost impossible unless logging has been turned on.

A relatively new area of computer forensics is the area of Web-based forensics. This area of forensics deals with the use of software to log and track suspects such as child predators in chat rooms while the investigator is using the Internet to pretend they are a 14 year old child. Until recently, real time forensic tracking of live data was problematic because the Internet was a real time environment. Computer forensic software such as WebCase by VereSoft (www.veresoftware.com) is solving this problem by allowing investigators to forensically record IP addresses, chat sessions, and other communication across an Internet connection.

Barrister jailed for fake e-mail

A UK barrister was jailed for trying to frame a man with fake e-mail. Bruce Hyman fabricated evidence that could have sent an innocent man to prison. Hyman represented a divorced woman fighting for custody of her four-year-old daughter. He sent the daughter's father an e-mail that appeared to be from a charity campaigning for father's rights. It appeared to support the father's claim that he should be granted more time with his daughter. The father used the document, which he believed to be real, as evidence in court. At that time, Hyman suggested that the e-mail was a forgery, and it was.

The father, Wall Street banker Simon Eades, was warned by the court that he faced jail time and the loss of his child if the precedent quoted in the e-mail turned out to be fabricated.

An investigation followed. Eades found the location from which the fathers' rights e-mail had been sent to him — an Internet shop in Tottenham Court Road. The shop's owner e-mailed Eades images from the shop's security camera, which identified Hyman as the sender. Hyman was caught by his own e-mail.

Chapter 10

Data Forensics

*T*he recovery of data has taken place since computer users first uttered those immortal words: "Uh-oh." You use the same concepts and techniques that everyone uses to recover deleted files and reconstruct damaged files. The same basic functions are used by forensic investigators — except that you benefit from hashing and write blockers.

To extract data from computers, you must thoroughly understand the basic principles of how and where data can be stored in a computer. The forensic science of using the proper procedure to extract data applies after you know where the data may reside. To put it simply, you may have a hard time forensically extracting data if you don't know where it is!

This process may sound like plain common sense and seem easy to do, but remember that quite a number of operating systems now exist, as well as specialized hardware, with their own way of handling data. The mobile computing industry is on the extreme end, and the regular computer world is somewhere in the middle with only a dozen or so different operating systems. The good news for you is that if you understand the basic concepts of the most popular operating systems, most variants don't stray far from their original design. As a bonus, the majority of operating systems now in use are based on three popular products that cover more than 90 percent of the work in the computer forensic world: Microsoft, Apple, and Linux.

Delving into Data Storage

For the most part, the evidence you're looking for is located somewhere in the storage area of a computer. The areas of mobile forensics and network forensics tend to find the tracks of data or its metadata as it passes through their systems, but computer system storage areas tend to have the relevant data you want to find, such as e-mails and documents. Chapter 13 looks at how networks can capture relevant data, but keep in mind that the bulk of relevant data still resides in computer storage mediums, such as hard drives or RAM space.

To understand the basics of how file systems work, you first have to know the basic concepts of how the computer hardware functions in relation to operating and file systems. Think of it this way: You can have a map of how to get from Los Angles to New York, but if you don't understand the underlying rules of the road, such as traffic signs or the reason the road has a yellow stripe rather than a white stripe, your trip may end up in disaster.

The anatomy of a disk drive

The basic storage medium for most computers is the magnetic disk drive. Its basic design hasn't changed in decades, so the technology is well understood and reliable. Magnetic disk drives use a magnetic material that's polarized into a positive or negative charge that literally spins around like an old-time vinyl record. The two distinct polarities of magnets allow the computer to store binary data (0s and 1s) as magnetic charges and thus are an easy way for a computer to store vast amounts of data on a relatively stable physical platform.

Hard drives of this type have the same basic elements or structure, as shown in Figure 10-1 and described in this list:

- **Head:** A physical element in the hard drive that reads and writes the magnetic material located on the platters. Most, if not all, modern-day hard drives use two heads per platter to read the upper and lower surfaces.

- **Track:** The circular areas on the platter that hold information, just like old-fashioned vinyl records. Unlike vinyl records, though, which literally have a groove, hard drive tracks are magnetic and completely concentric. In the old days, hard drive tracks were a bit wide, and special equipment could read the sides of the track to find any previously written data that was, for all intents and purposes, overwritten. Now the tracks are so close that little remains of previously overwritten data.

- **Cylinder:** The tracks of multiple platters stacked on top of each other. If you think in three, rather than two, dimensions, you can see that the cylinder concept is similar to a stack of pancakes cut down the middle that grow progressively larger toward their outer edge. Each of those new, circular stacks of pancakes is essentially a cylinder.

✔ **Sector:** The smallest unit of storage on a storage medium, in which tracks are broken down into smaller, more manageable pieces. For the most part, sectors contain 512 bytes and usually have a wedge or pie shape when viewed physically on the hard drive.

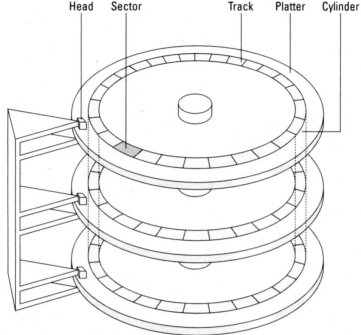

Head   Sector   Track   Platter   Cylinder

Figure 10-1:
The basic geometry of a typical magnetic hard drive.

Hard drive sizes vary depending on their combination of cylinders, heads, and sectors (CHS). Here's the formula for calculating hard drive size:

Hard drive size = number of platters × number of heads × number of sectors × 512.

The modern Basic Input Output System (BIOS) of a computer automatically detects hard drive default manufacturer settings, so you don't have to worry about manually setting the BIOS settings for a hard drive. Most BIOS manufacturers display the cylinders, heads, and sectors if the hard drive has been manually set up versus automatically configured.

A hard drive can be set manually for nonstandard settings if a user has the expertise and knowledge to do so. That person usually keeps the modified settings handy in case the computer loses its settings internally. If you're looking at a computer that has been modified, look around for a record of its storage device settings.

In the following sections, we take a look at how the operating systems for Microsoft, Apple, and Linux work.

Microsoft operating systems

By far the most popular and widespread operating systems are now from Microsoft. Because the company has released several different operating systems over the past 25 years, in some cases the operating systems have backward compatibility. Windows is the dominant operating system, and you need to understand the terms and methods that Windows uses to organize data on a hard drive.

Windows organizes data by using the following physical elements:

- ✔ **Cluster:** A grouping of sectors that reduces the number of entries required to keep track of files on a storage device. The larger the hard drive, the more sectors per cluster to keep the allocation tables at a reasonable size. In modern computers, the size of a cluster is usually 32 kilobytes (K).

  Because sectors are at the hardware level and clusters are at the operating system level, you often hear techie types refer to sectors as "physical address space" and clusters as "logical address space."

- ✔ **Partition or logical volume:** A logical division of the physical storage device. Depending on the operating system, a physical storage medium is partitioned into smaller logical units so that the operating system can function correctly. The use of partitions in computers is now more of a file- or user-organization method than a limitation on the part of the operating system.

  Warning bells should go off when you notice that a large amount of space on a hard drive isn't partitioned. Users with technical expertise often attempt to hide data by temporarily deleting the partition. Another tipoff: finding a partition at the beginning of the hard drive and another one at the end, but a large space in the middle that has no partition defined.

- ✔ **Master boot record (MBR):** The MBR is the area on a storage device that the operating system uses to find a bootable media in order to start a computer. Although the MBR serves a couple of purposes, its main purpose is to hold information about the partitions defined on the physical hard drive. Keep in mind that the MBR is located not in a partition but, rather, in front of the first partition in the main boot record area (MBRA). The MBR can also contain bootstrap information and unique storage device identifiers that you can use to track USB drives that have been attached to the computer system.

Windows has two file systems: FAT and NTFS, which we discuss in the next two sections.

FAT

The original file system developed by Microsoft to organize data on a storage medium is the File Allocation Table (FAT). Because no hard drives were available for personal computers in the early days of personal computers (late 1970s and early 1980s), the FAT system was developed for use with floppy disks. The operating system uses the FAT system to locate files within the computer by pointing to the starting cluster of the file. In addition to providing a way for the operating system to locate files, the FAT contains information such as filenames, time and date stamps, directory names, and file attributes.

The FAT system has several versions with each succeeding version improving on the capabilities of the previous one. For all intents and purposes, the FAT system is no longer used on new computer installations, but is still recognized by operating systems. The distinct versions of FAT are described in this list:

- ✔ **FAT 12:** Used only on floppy disks and released by Microsoft on its first operating system, Microsoft Disk Operating System (MS-DOS) Version 1.0, the FAT 12 system is designed to handle a whopping 16 megabytes (MB) of storage space. (Remember that floppy disks of the time had a 360K storage capacity and measured 5¼ inches in diameter and were truly floppy in that they had no hard plastic sleeves.)

- ✔ **FAT 16:** When personal computers began the transition from floppy disk storage to fixed hard drive storage, the need for a file system that could handle media larger than 16M became critical. The FAT 16 file system could handle, in theory, as much as 2 gigabytes (G) of storage space. The thought at the time was that users didn't need hard drives bigger than 500MB and that a FAT 16 file system should work for a long time. In fact, FAT 16 was the standard Microsoft file system from DOS version 3.0 until Microsoft released Windows 95 version 2. When you run across an older computer, this file system is the one it's most likely to use.

- ✔ **FAT 32:** After the dramatic increases in hard drive size during the 1990s, the need arose for a file system that could handle storage devices larger than 2G. FAT 32 addressed this need: It could handle as much as 2 terabytes (TB) under normal circumstances. Since the release of Windows 95 version 2, the FAT 32 file system was released as an option for all subsequent Microsoft operating systems as a way to provide backward compatibility with previous versions.

- ✔ **VFAT:** Beginning with Windows 95 (and to a lesser degree in Windows for Workgroups), the VxD driver created a method for Microsoft to allow users to work with filenames longer than 8 characters. The interesting part is that while the FAT system doesn't change, the VxD driver acts as an interface to translate the FAT entries to the applications requesting the long filenames.

Even though FAT systems are somewhat ancient by computer standards, you need to understand the basic mechanics of how they work so that you understand how files are stored in older systems. Many older operating systems are still in use now simply because they're stable and can work with simple computer systems, such as ROM-based computers or handheld devices.

Try to keep copies of older operating systems available so that, for example, in case you run across DOS 1.0, 6.22, or OS/2, you can install the operating system to run applications that may work on only that type of system.

FAT systems include a lot of wasted space where data can hide. For example, a 20K file is smaller than a cluster, so it completely fits inside the cluster with room to spare. The extra room in the cluster is *file slack*. The amount of space not used is 12K. But what if the file were really a 33K file? The FAT system would use the first cluster completely and only 1 kilobyte of the second cluster, thus wasting almost an entire cluster, or 31 kilobytes.

Because most files are larger than one cluster, the FAT system has a mechanism to link the clusters: *cluster chaining*. The end of one cluster points to the next link in the chain and so forth until the end of the file is reached. The cluster chaining works well in the direction from first cluster to last, but doesn't work in reverse to show you the previous cluster. Digging deep and trying to reconstruct files from back to front is often time consuming and frustrating if it's done manually on FAT systems. Computer forensic tools can often reconstruct files using scripts or program algorithms designed specifically for this task.

When files are written to a FAT file system, the cluster location is used to identify where the file is located logically on the storage device. When a file is deleted, the FAT file system puts the hexadecimal character sequence E5 in the table to denote that the cluster is now available for use by a new file. Computer forensic tools scan for this hexadecimal character sequence to locate files that have been deleted from the FAT directory but are still physically located on the storage device. The area is *unallocated space* because no files are allocated to its use and are often filled with deleted files or fragments of files that contain useful information. Computer forensic software is the best tool to automatically discover and recover files from this area because modern storage devices often have gigabytes of unallocated space and manually carving out data can take days, if not weeks.

NTFS

Microsoft had a good lock on the residential computer market, but needed an operating system with more stability and security than Windows for Workgroups or DOS could offer for the commercial and business markets. The design goals for the Windows NT operating system were to be as secure as Unix, support long filenames, have network capability natively, and not waste storage space the way FAT systems did. In 1993 Microsoft released

Windows NT 3.1 with NTFS version 1.0, and it has been upgrading the NTFS capabilities with each new release, including Windows Vista.

NTFS is a sophisticated file system in comparison to FAT in a number of respects. The NTFS system has these features:

✔ **Enhanced file attributes:** In addition to the read-only, archive, system, and hidden file attributes, NTFS includes file attributes such as indexed, compressed, and encrypted. In addition to those general attributes, NTFS has increased its control over the permissions of files and folders to provide much more control over how users access files.

✔ **Alternate data streams:** These data structures are attached to existing files. ADS-type data structures can be viewed as metadata, but they can also be independent data sources. In computer geek terminology, the ADS is considered a data fork in that the additional data is connected to the main data, but is logically separate from the main data. In fact, some ADS data can be larger than the original file! ADS technology is completely invisible to the file system and to users unless a user knows to look for ADS information.

Even though the file system doesn't know that ADSs exist per se, quite a bit of data storage can be used by the ADS. In other words, a 2K file may have a 20MB data stream, and you would never know it by looking at the little 2K file. Chapter 8 covers ADS in much greater detail.

✔ **File compression:** NTFS allows for transparent file compression of files using the LZ77 file compression algorithm. Because compression tends to slow things down on a computer system and no real security advantage results from compressing files, most users don't compress files or storage devices unless they're running out of room.

✔ **Encryption:** Unlike the LZ77 file compression, the Encrypting File System (EFS) provides a relatively good level of security for protecting files or folders. The encryption system works transparently to the user who initially encrypted the file or folder by associating the encryption keys with the user account information and encrypting or decrypting at the system level. The Windows system uses a two-key system consisting of a public key and a private key. The user holds the private key, and the operating system holds the public key. Accessing EFS-encrypted files can be difficult but not impossible unless a data recovery agent has been installed, which allows users to reset or bypass their passwords.

✔ **Journaling:** With the release of NTFS, Microsoft introduced change logs to its operating system. The journaling system on NTFS logs any changes made to the metadata associated with files on the system. *Note:* This statement applies only to metadata and not to the actual data in the file! NTFS can therefore redo or roll back changes if a problem occurs and can provide a log of changes for review, if necessary.

✔ **Shadow copy:** This NTFS feature takes snapshots of files or folders at a specified point and saves them for use by either the user or specific applications. Depending on the version of Windows, the shadow copy feature has more or less capability between Windows versions.

✔ **Mount points:** One way to add logical volumes to NTFS without adding another drive letter is to use mount points. For example, you can add an entire new hard drive volume to the existing logical volume C:, thus increasing the logical size of drive C without incurring the hassle and labor involved in adding a new drive letter with all its associated path issues.

The first major difference between FAT and NTFS is that NTFS considers anything on the file system as a file, including the Master File Table (MFT), which is roughly the equivalent of a FAT database table. The MFT handles the addressing issue of files for the NTFS file system, but has quite a bit more information stored as metadata than does the FAT system. The MFT contains information on a file, such as time stamps, cluster addresses, names, security identifiers (SID), file attributes, and even data stream names associated with the file. One thing that truly sets the MFT apart from the FAT is that if the file is smaller than 800 bytes, the file itself can reside in the MFT and not take up any clusters on the storage device. In other words, you can have more files on the hard drive than there are clusters available for files!

You need to recognize attributes that are considered resident and another set of attributes that are considered nonresident. Generally speaking, information located in the MFT is resident, and anything outside the MFT is nonresident.

Files deleted on an NTFS file system are handled in one of two ways:

✔ **The Recycle Bin deletes files by using the Windows GUI interface.**

The file is renamed and moved into the Recycle Bin folder as the first step in the process, and then an entry is made in the Info2 record file, which is the control file that contains metadata about the file, such as path and date-and-time information.

The Info2 file is often a helpful resource for finding deleted files and their links to external media. Most forensic software has the capability to extract and view Info2 files.

✔ **The file system marks the clusters as available.**

NTFS also handles deleted files the same way that older FAT systems do. The clusters are marked as being available for new files, and changes are made in the MFT to signify that the clusters are available too. This also happens when a user empties the Recycle Bin. At this point, the file system marks the clusters as available and considers the files permanently deleted, and the deleted files become part of unallocated space.

HFS+

Developed by Apple in the late 1990s to replace the aging Hierarchical File System (HFS) in use since the 1980s, HFS+ was released with the Mac OS X operating system. One of the more notable features of HFS+ is its use of data and resource forks to separate the data and metadata of a file. The applications write to the data fork where data is saved (such as word processing documents or spreadsheets); the resource fork stores information such as icons and menus. The equivalent in the Microsoft operating system would be the use of Alternate Data Streams, as discussed earlier in the chapter.

The Apple HFS+ system improves upon the original HFS file system by increasing the size of the files that the file system can handle (8 Exabytes) — and uses Unicode for the naming conventions, much the same as Microsoft Windows.

The Apple HFS+ system uses its Catalog File to keep track of all files and folders in a volume. The Catalog File stores data of several types; computer forensic investigators are primarily interested in these five types of data in stored in its File Record area:

- ✔ **CNID (catalog node identification):** A unique number assigned by the HFS+ file system to each file and directory in a volume.
- ✔ **Size:** The size of the file located in the volume.
- ✔ **Time stamps:** The time and date when the file or directory was created, modified, and backed up.
- ✔ **Extents:** Area where the first part of the file is located on the volume.
- ✔ **Forks:** Pointers to where the resource fork extents are located on the volume.

The HFS+ system refers to a logical segment of a physical storage device as a *volume* (not a *partition*). A volume can be all or part of a storage medium (except for a floppy disk, which is always one entire volume). Files are stored in 4-kilobyte logical blocks; any file bigger than 4 KB is stored in *allocation blocks* (a string of consecutive logical blocks). As with the FAT and NTFS file systems, if a file is smaller than its logical block, any data already written to the block but not overwritten is still there.

Even if you've never laid eyes on an Apple Macintosh computer running HFS+, you will undoubtedly run across an iPod or other mobile Apple device that uses HFS+. This file system has also been adapted for use in Linux and (to a lesser degree) Microsoft Windows; chances are you'll see more HFS+ file systems in the future. Meanwhile, just follow your basic forensic acquisition procedures. Computer forensic software programs such as FTK and EnCase can read the HFS+ file system and extract forensic data just as they do with Microsoft computer systems.

Since Mac OS X was first released in 1999, use of HFS and HFS+ is getting more remote, but with so many Macintosh computers still in existence (especially in public schools), the basic knowledge of how and where data is stored on these systems is still important — as is the ability to explain your results in court.

Linux/Unix

The Linux operating system mirrors many of the same file system techniques of the older Unix system. For the purposes of this discussion, the Linux operating system principles also apply to the Unix operating system because they share many of the same concepts.

In a Linux system, everything is considered a file by the operating system, including all hardware peripherals, such as monitors and memory. All files have properties and, even more useful, all files have attributes associated with them, which helps you work your case.

Just as in Microsoft and Apple file systems, the Linux file system uses units of storage space to save data in an organized fashion. In the case of Linux, the smallest unit of storage space is a *block*. Blocks start at 512 bytes, and their sizes can vary because of the size of the volumes being used.

The Linux system consists of four distinct components:

- **Boot block:** The location where the bootstrapping code is located to boot a Linux system.
- **Data block:** The logical addresses where data is stored on the storage device.
- **Inode:** A file that points to the block address of a file, links data blocks, and provides an index similar to a database of information regarding the file or directory. Every new file or directory that's created on a Linux system creates an associated inode that contains some of the following information:

  - Number of bytes in the file or directory
  - Time stamps
  - Block address for the file
  - Number of blocks used by the file or directory
  - Number of links to the file
  - User and group ID numbers

- **Superblock:** Manages the Linux file system in much the same way as the NTFS MFT or Apple HFS, by keeping track of inodes and the status of all blocks on the storage device in addition to many other technical aspects that are beyond the scope of this book.

Just as in other file systems, the block size determines how much data can be recovered because large block sizes tend to have more data left over from previous writes.

Linux keeps track of bad or damaged areas of the storage device in the Bad Block Inode (BBI). The BBI has a list of all bad sectors and blocks within the storage device and can be accessed if you're the root user or administrator. The BBI can be modified to include good areas of the storage device; someone trying to hide data can effectively hide data in those areas by making it appear that those good sectors are damaged.

Finding Digital Cavities Where Data Hides

To find digital evidence on a storage device, you first need to know what you're looking for. If the case involves e-mail containing sexual harassment, you want to look for e-mail; if you're looking into an embezzlement case, you know to look for spreadsheets or other documents that usually contain currency amounts. Rarely does an investigator tell you to "just look at the computer and see what you can find." This task is usually a huge waste of time because modern-day computers hold vast quantities of information — if you're working for law enforcement, it's often beyond the scope of the case you're working on.

For the most part, modern computer forensic software is very good at extracting all kinds of data and in copious amounts, which is a double-edged sword. You often end up with so much information that separating out the parts you truly need is a problem! Almost anyone can figure out how to use the software to extract data, but few forensic investigators truly understand the *art* of computer forensics in relation to the *science* of computer forensics.

Deleted files

When a file is deleted, the file system puts a marker in its file management system to let the system know that the file is no longer at that cluster or block. By doing this, the file system logically deletes the file from its records in an efficient manner, but hasn't physically worked its way through the storage device and wiped out the binary data. By saving itself from doing this task, the operating system has left behind a virtual binary archeological site that you can sift through. The irony here is that as storage devices get bigger, the amount of data left over from previous deletions stays intact longer because so much more storage space is available to work with.

Unallocated space is space that the file system considers empty and ready for use. Even though the operating system thinks the area is empty, you can find quite a bit of data there.

Older file systems, such as DOS, tend to have deleted data in unallocated space more so than modern Microsoft computers because newer operating systems essentially use a two-step process involving the Recycle Bin to delete files. In this case, check the Recycle Bin first and then check the unallocated space.

You can also find cached data in unallocated space. For example, when you're viewing your Yahoo! e-mail, the screen is cached to the storage device at certain times. This caching is used to speed up the viewing of your Web page, but has the unintended effect of saving the Web page you were viewing even after the cache file has been deleted.

Suppose that a secretary accidentally deletes an e-mail from a national hotel chain showing the cancellation of a room reservation for the next month. The hotel still charges the company credit card and refuses to honor the cancellation unless the secretary can prove that the e-mail existed. After a quick forensic examination, not only is that e-mail found, but also e-mail that had been sent from and received at the Yahoo! account from the previous two years. Needless to say, some data resides on the computer for a long time after it has been viewed.

Retrieving deleted files

Using computer forensic software, retrieving deleted files is quite easy. Figure 10-2 shows a typical forensic software list of deleted files. The list of files shows deleted JPEG files that still have entries on the system; in the case of the wedding rings image, the entire file still resides on the hard drive even though the operating system doesn't see it. All relevant metadata is still intact, including the time and date stamps.

Depending on the software you use, the process of listing deleted files can be as easy as letting the forensic software generate a list automatically for you when you search for deleted file markers. In Figure 10-2, all files found on the system are listed, and you only need to reorder the rows and columns to show the information you need. This scenario usually works when the file is still intact or was once listed in the FAT or MFT, but it doesn't work as well when file caching was used to write the file to the storage device.

Figure 10-2:
Typical
list of files
found on
the storage
device.

Retrieving cached files

If you know that you want to find files that are primarily the product of file caching, such as Web pages or temporary application cache files, you have to do a more detailed and manual search than when you're looking for deleted files.

If you're looking for a Web page that the suspect visited, you have to enter a search string found somewhere on the Web page to locate the relevant file. Several methods can help you accomplish this goal, and modern computer forensic software makes the process quite easy:

✔ **Let the computer forensic software find all references to the keywords you enter into the search.**

The software carves out the Web page for you. Figure 10-3 shows a typical dialog box for this task.

✔ **Use a keyword search on a unique aspect of the file, and manually carve out the information you need.**

This method gives you better control of your search in that you're not pulling out megabytes of data that you don't need. Figure 10-4 shows a typical keyword search dialog box. This method involves a little more manual labor, but allows you to skim over data and at times carve out data that a computer forensic software package may miss because of file garbage or incomplete file headers. A thorough knowledge of file structure helps tremendously in this search type!

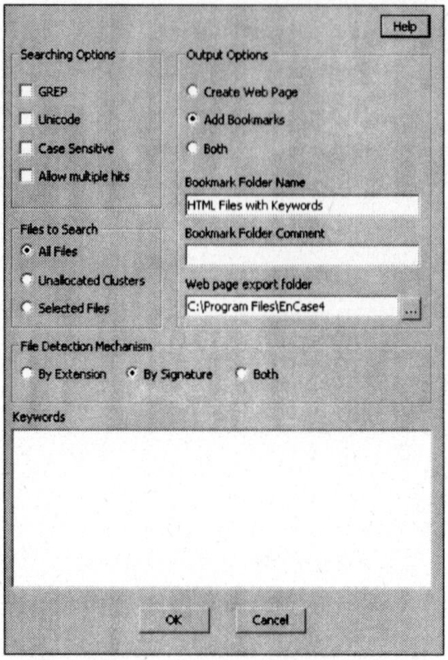

Figure 10-3:
Forensic
software
search
dialog box.

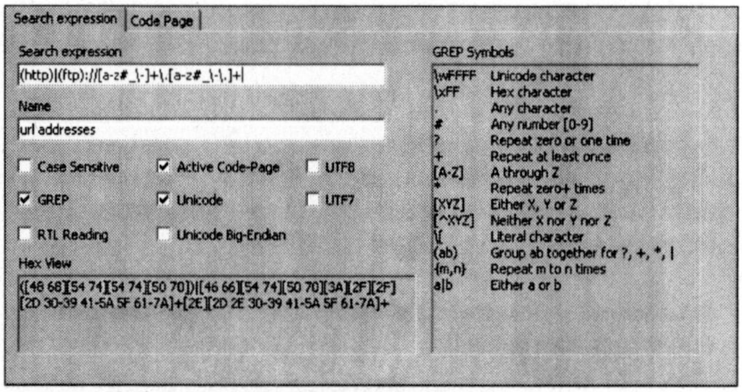

Figure 10-4:
Manual
search
method
using a
keyword
search
function.

Retrieving files in unallocated space

When you're dealing with files or file fragments in unallocated space, the files can be fragmented or damaged in some way that doesn't allow you to perform a regular search, such as for file headers or file extensions. Additionally, metadata is often lost in these areas because of the nature of how the application may cache the data. You sometimes get lucky, though, and find metadata embedded in the file itself, which is still intact.

Figure 10-5 shows a keyword search result for JPEG files in unallocated space. The metadata regarding the time and date stamps is missing and the file is truncated because part of the file was overwritten. This example is fairly typical of what you may find in unallocated space.

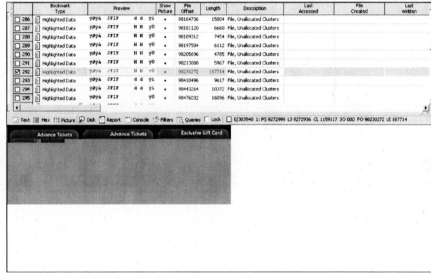

Figure 10-5: Searching for files using a keyword search in unallocated space.

In Figure 10-6, a keyword search using the sequence for a Microsoft Word header finds a Microsoft Word document in unallocated space. Although the file header is intact in this file, the subject of the document is known (which in this case deals with an express mail company). You can just as easily find the document using the company name. The metadata is also stripped from the document at the file system level but still may be intact at the application level.

Retrieving files in file slack areas

Old files may still be found in the file slack area on modern computers even though the beginning of the data block or cluster has been overwritten. Figure 10-7 shows a typical cluster that contains two distinct files. The upper half of the cluster contains a current HTML file, and the second half of the cluster contains an older setup file.

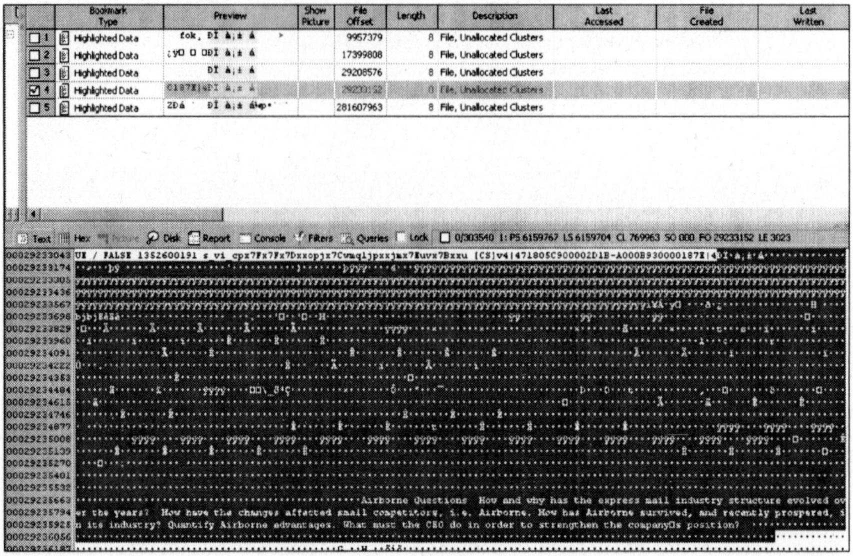

Figure 10-6:
Searching
for
Microsoft
Word
documents
in
unallocated
space.

Figure 10-7:
Unallocated
space
cluster with
two files.

You often can't open the files you find with this method using normal means
because the file header information has been overwritten. Because this situation occurs most often when dealing with file slack evidence, you can either
insert a header into a copied version of the file remnant and hope that it
works or just carve out the data and use it as is as part of your case.

Unless you have a pressing need to open the file remnant with the original application, you usually should just copy the information as is and bookmark it.

The procedure to insert a header into an existing file is simple in concept, but doesn't always work in the real world because of file damage or an application's tolerance of data that it may not recognize. The file header for a particular file format is always at the beginning of a file. If you know the file format you're dealing with, you can simply copy an existing file header and paste it into the damaged or deleted file. Some file formats are more forgiving than others, such as graphical files that display even partial information, whereas other formats, such as databases, often refuse to open if the file is even slightly damaged. Figure 10-8 shows the beginning of a file using a hex editor in the top pane and showing a damaged file on the bottom pane. The header is simply copied from the top pane and pasted into the file in the bottom pane.

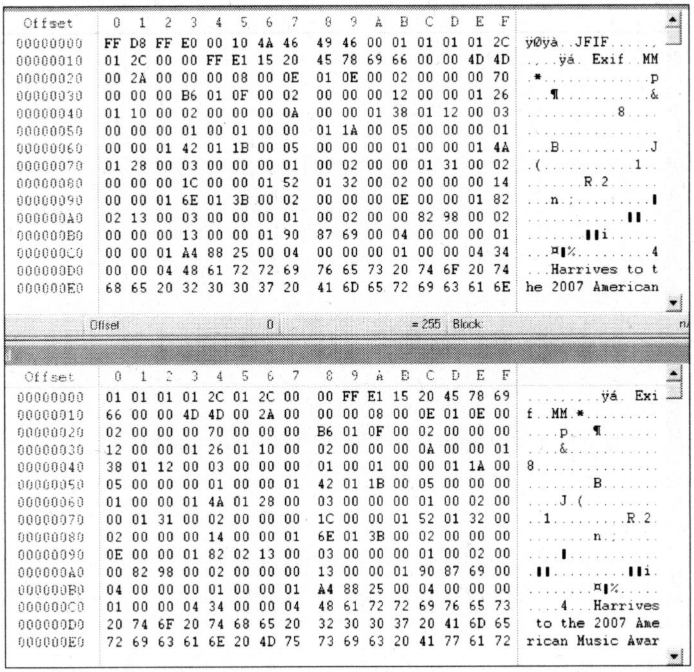

Figure 10-8: Hex editor comparison of a good file header and a missing file header.

Non-accessible space

An area where technically oriented suspects might hide data is in the areas not seen by the operating system. The operating system either classifies the areas as damaged or simply cannot access them because of file system limitations.

Because a file system can deem a storage area as bad or damaged, you can use a hex editor to modify the settings of the file system where this is controlled to mark those areas as bad and then copy information into them. This process isn't impossible, but it takes a little skill because you have to know how to modify the file system configuration files.

Another location where files may be hidden is in the area of a storage device an operating system does not recognize. Many storage devices have small areas of overhead measuring 1 gigabyte or smaller that are completely inaccessible by the operating system. This space is usually located at the physical end of the storage device and is accessible only by a hex editor.

Figure 10-9 shows a hex editor viewing the physical end of a storage device that the operating system doesn't recognize. A suspect only has to copy the information he wants to hide and use the hex editor to paste it into this area of the storage device to make the data invisible to anyone other than an experienced computer user.

Figure 10-9:
The volume slack at the end of a storage device.

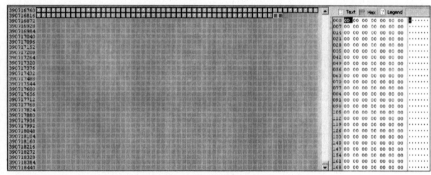

Although these techniques for data hiding are still used, they're not as effective as encrypting the data outright. With the ease and power of encryption software such as PGP, someone wanting to hide data will find it much easier to just encrypt the data, rather than modify the storage media and data.

RAM

Computer forensic technology, at its core, focuses on not changing a single bit when doing an investigation. In most investigations, this is a worthy goal, but in some circumstances you (or the person on the witness stand) have to justify making a change in data because of the investigator's actions. Data or evidence located in random access memory (RAM) is one of those circumstances.

The issue with RAM forensics is simply that if you don't already have a forensic agent or software client of some type running on the computer, adding one alters, and possibly overwrites, data. In cases where the RAM contents hold potential evidence that's critical to the case, using a program such as WinHex (a hex editor) may be the only option. Figure 10-10 shows the type of information you can pull from RAM. In this case, the computer had been used to access an e-mail account hours earlier, and the e-mail account information was still resident in RAM even though the program had been closed hours earlier.

Figure 10-10: Contents of RAM found after a RAM dump.

Linux and Unix are exceptional in that they can dump the entire contents of RAM with built-in utilities unlike Windows. You can use the dd command to copy the contents of RAM to a disk rather than install third-party software. Microsoft doesn't have a comparable system utility that can dump the entire contents of RAM to a storage device. Even with a system-level utility, you still run the risk of changing data in some form just by interacting with the computer, so this solution isn't perfect. Chapter 13 introduces the concept of network forensics, where forensic agents are usually preinstalled on the computer and you can use the computer forensic software client to copy the data from RAM. These systems tend to be the best solution to copying RAM forensically.

Windows Registry

Before Windows 3.11, configuration files for applications, utilities, and hardware were spread out in all corners of the operating system. Microsoft decided to centralize the scattered configuration files into one database called the *Registry*. The Registry has evolved over the course of 20 years into a complex database that tracks almost everything that's done on the computer *and* keeps all configuration settings up-to-date. The types of data you can find in the Registry are described in this list:

✔ **Password information:** Although most usernames and passwords are encrypted, using third-party software to read the information is possible. Depending on the version of Windows and the application, the username and password information are stored in different parts of the Registry. Some types of passwords (or usernames) you might encounter in the Registry include

- AutoComplete
- Computer
- Internet e-mail
- Internet Web sites

✔ **Startup application:** This Registry area contains the list of startup programs, and their configuration information, on the computer system.

✔ **Storage device hardware:** The Registry stores a list of currently connected, and any previously connected, storage devices. Figure 10-11 shows Paraben's Registry Analyzer, which displays a list of previously mounted devices on the computer system.

✔ **Wireless network:** The Registry records every wireless network that the computer system logs in to by logging the service set identifier (SSID).

✔ **Internet information:** The Registry stores information such as the typed URL history and download path information.

✔ **Unread e-mail:** The Registry tracks the number of unread e-mails in a user's Outlook account, and other accounts, on the system in addition to tracking the time stamp information.

Computer forensic software packages, such as FTK and Paraben, make short work of analyzing the Windows Registry settings and extracting information. The advantage of using one of the major computer forensic packages is that you can put all the analyzed data into one report with usually a few clicks rather than piece together the analysis from several different reports about several different software packages.

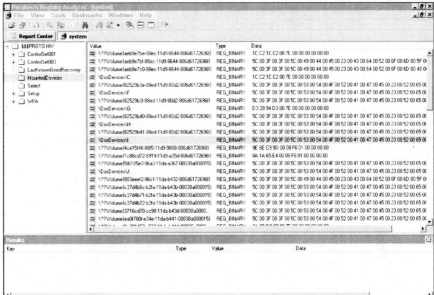

Figure 10-11:
List of
previously
mounted
storage
devices.

Search filtering

One of the problems with modern computer forensic investigations is data
overflow. The size of the typical storage device now hovers around 250GB,
and bigger storage devices are on the horizon. If a 250GB hard drive is filled
with nothing but regular text files, you have approximately 170 million pages
of text to sift through! To put this number into perspective, stacking all 170
million pages of text would create a structure that's 57,000 feet tall! And,
because storage devices now approach 500GB capacity, you can double
those figures. With this much storage capacity available, you must find out
how to filter searches for the information you're looking for while not being
so focused that you inadvertently miss vital information.

A unique circumstance where the sheer amount of data can often hamper
an investigation occurs when you're dealing with large organizational data
warehouses or databases. Some organizations have terabytes of storage
capacity, and examining this amount of data in a traditional computer forensic manner, where you image the entire data set, is often impossible. In this
scenario, your best option is to examine only the areas of the storage device
that the suspect was known to have access to. If during the investigation you
see tracks leading to other areas, you can also examine them. This piecemeal
approach runs the risk of your missing data; however, you must balance this
risk against analyzing terabytes of data that can lead to months of work —
and the possibility of taking down an organization's computer infrastructure
for that length of time.

Forensic software such as EnCase can filter searches in various ways, such as using a GREP search to find and extract a variety of specific data or using internal filters on bookmarked data to eliminate data hits that don't pertain to your specific search. Paraben software has much the same capabilities to filter searches for specific criteria by using a search interface, as shown in Figure 10-12.

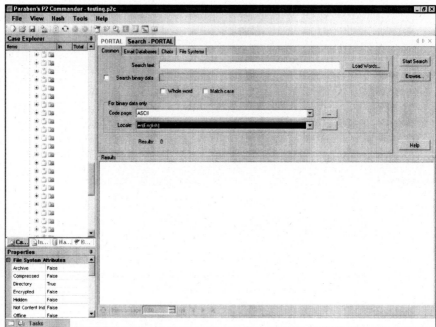

Figure 10-12: The Paraben search dialog box.

Extracting Data

Because of modern computer forensic software, the extraction of computer forensic data is a relatively simple operation, for several reasons:

- The software has automated much of the task of finding and extracting data.

- Average users have no true understanding of how computers work and have even less understanding of how data is stored on storage devices.

✔ Users who are technically proficient may not have access to all parts of the computer or network in which they're leaving digital tracks and may leave behind some form of digital footprint.

✔ Because computer forensic professionals are getting better at finding digital tracks, criminals are resorting to hiding in plain sight by using encryption or other methods, such as steganography. In other words, you can find a file, but you cannot open it!

Basic data extraction using computer forensic software such as FTK, EnCase, or Paraben is a relatively simple operation after you forensically acquire the image from the original storage media into your forensic workstation. Then you can use the automated tools to extract data and generate a report. The following simple steps show how to extract a deleted file:

1. **Acquire the image and list the entire contents of the storage device, and then sort the data by those files that have been deleted.**

   Figure 10-13 shows the files that EnCase found, sorted by the Is Deleted column.

Is Deleted column

Figure 10-13: Files sorted by the Is Deleted column.

		Name	File Ext	Is Deleted	File Type	Description	Last Accessed	File Created	Last Written	Entry Modified
☐	1335	✗ EN00902_.WMF	WMF	•	Windows Metafile	File, Deleted, Overwritten,	05/06/08 07:49:06PM	05/06/08 07:49:06PM	03/10/98 11:43:34AM	05/06/08 07:49:0
☐	1336	✗ FD00074_.WMF	WMF	•	Windows Metafile	File, Deleted, Overwritten,	05/06/08 07:49:06PM	05/06/08 07:49:06PM	03/09/98 04:33:42PM	05/06/08 07:49:0
☐	1337	✗ FD00076_.WMF	WMF	•	Windows Metafile	File, Deleted, Overwritten,	05/06/08 07:49:06PM	05/06/08 07:49:06PM	03/09/98 04:33:38PM	05/06/08 07:49:0
☐	1338	✗ FD00077_.WMF	WMF	•	Windows Metafile	File, Deleted, Overwritten,	05/06/08 07:49:06PM	05/06/08 07:49:06PM	03/09/98 07:44:12AM	05/06/08 07:49:0
☐	1339	✗ FD00086_.WMF	WMF	•	Windows Metafile	File, Deleted, Overwritten,	05/06/08 07:49:06PM	05/06/08 07:49:06PM	03/09/98 07:44:10AM	05/06/08 07:49:0
☐	1340	✗ FD00090_.WMF	WMF	•	Windows Metafile	File, Deleted, Overwritten,	05/06/08 07:49:06PM	05/06/08 07:49:06PM	03/09/98 04:32:40PM	05/06/08 07:49:0
☐	1341	✗ FD00096_.WMF	WMF	•	Windows Metafile	File, Deleted, Overwritten,	05/06/08 07:49:06PM	05/06/08 07:49:06PM	03/09/98 07:44:08AM	05/06/08 07:49:0
☐	1342	✗ MSO.ACL	ACL	•		File, Deleted, Overwritten,	05/06/08 07:56:45PM	05/06/08 07:50:28PM	09/15/04 01:23:28PM	05/06/08 07:50:2
☐	1343	⊘ MSO.ACL	ACL	•		File, Deleted, Archive	05/06/08 07:56:45PM	05/06/08 07:50:07PM	05/17/00 01:05:34AM	05/06/08 07:50:0
☐	1344	✗ FD00296_.WMF	WMF	•	Windows Metafile	File, Deleted, Overwritten,	05/06/08 07:49:06PM	05/06/08 07:49:06PM	03/09/98 07:44:06AM	05/06/08 07:49:0
☐	1345	✗ FD00297_.WMF	WMF	•	Windows Metafile	File, Deleted, Overwritten,	05/06/08 07:49:06PM	05/06/08 07:49:06PM	03/09/98 09:00:14AM	05/06/08 07:49:0
☐	1346	⊘ FD00306_.WMF	WMF	•	Windows Metafile	File, Deleted, Archive	05/06/08 07:49:06PM	05/06/08 07:49:06PM	03/09/98 07:44:04AM	05/06/08 07:49:0
☐	1347	✗ MSO.ACL	ACL	•		File, Deleted, Overwritten,	05/06/08 07:56:45PM	05/06/08 07:50:28PM	11/11/02 12:15:48PM	05/06/08 07:50:2
☐	1348	✗ FD00336_.WMF	WMF	•	Windows Metafile	File, Deleted, Overwritten,	05/06/08 07:49:07PM	05/06/08 07:49:06PM	03/09/98 04:57:04PM	05/06/08 07:49:0
☐	1349	✗ FD00361_.WMF	WMF	•	Windows Metafile	File, Deleted, Overwritten,	05/06/08 07:49:07PM	05/06/08 07:49:07PM	03/09/98 07:44:02AM	05/06/08 07:49:0
☐	1350	✗ FD00369_.WMF	WMF	•	Windows Metafile	File, Deleted, Overwritten,	05/06/08 07:49:07PM	05/06/08 07:49:07PM	03/09/98 04:35:52PM	05/06/08 07:49:0

2. **Identify a deleted file that pertains to your investigation and then analyze the file for metadata, such as time stamps and file headers and any links to the suspect.**

   Figure 10-14 shows the deleted file with a hex view to double-check the file header (to make sure that the file is truly what you think it is) and internal structure of the file. Notice that the file lists all the time stamp information in the top pane.

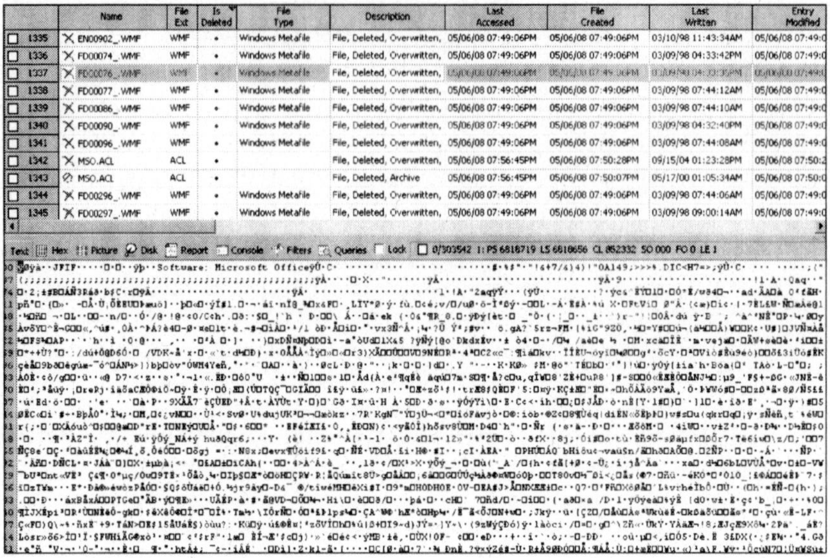

Figure 10-14:
The deleted
file in Hex
view.

3. **Test the internal file structure.**

   Because this file appears to be a graphics file, a good way to test its
   internal file structure is to view the file graphically. In Figure 10-15, the
   EnCase internal graphics viewer is used to view the file — and it appears
   that the internal structure of the file matches the header.

4. **Bookmark or include this piece of evidence in your report.**

   This step varies according to your forensic software. Use as much detail
   as possible when including this file as evidence in your report, and
   include *all* metadata in your report. When you put graphical files in a
   report, make sure that you scrutinize any explicit images so that they're
   not offensive to potential jurors or illegal, as is the case with child pornography images.

5. **Extract the file and analyze the file for hidden data, metadata, or
   information particular to the case.**

   How you extract or copy the file to your workstation varies depending
   on which forensic software you use, but they all can copy files.

6. **Make a copy and use it for the analysis.**

   That way, if you accidentally destroy the file, you have a backup.

		Name	File Ext	Is Deleted	File Type	Description	Last Accessed	File Created	Last Written	Entry Modified
☐	1335	EN00902_.WMF	WMF	•	Windows Metafile	File, Deleted, Overwritten,	05/06/08 07:49:06PM	05/06/08 07:49:06PM	03/10/98 11:43:34AM	05/06/08 07:49:0
☐	1336	FD000074_.WMF	WMF	•	Windows Metafile	File, Deleted, Overwritten,	05/06/08 07:49:06PM	05/06/08 07:49:06PM	03/09/98 04:33:42PM	05/06/08 07:49:0
☐	1337	FD000076_.WMF	WMF	•	Windows Metafile	File, Deleted, Overwritten,	05/06/08 07:49:06PM	05/06/08 07:49:06PM	03/09/98 04:33:36PM	05/06/08 07:49:0
☐	1338	FD000077_.WMF	WMF	•	Windows Metafile	File, Deleted, Overwritten,	05/06/08 07:49:06PM	05/06/08 07:49:06PM	03/09/98 07:44:12AM	05/06/08 07:49:0
☐	1339	FD00086_.WMF	WMF	•	Windows Metafile	File, Deleted, Overwritten,	05/06/08 07:49:06PM	05/06/08 07:49:06PM	03/09/98 07:44:10AM	05/06/08 07:49:0
☐	1340	FD00090_.WMF	WMF	•	Windows Metafile	File, Deleted, Overwritten,	05/06/08 07:49:06PM	05/06/08 07:49:06PM	03/09/98 04:32:40PM	05/06/08 07:49:0
☐	1341	FD00096_.WMF	WMF	•	Windows Metafile	File, Deleted, Overwritten,	05/06/08 07:49:06PM	05/06/08 07:49:06PM	03/09/98 07:44:08AM	05/06/08 07:49:0
☐	1342	MSO.ACL	ACL	•		File, Deleted, Overwritten,	05/06/08 07:56:45PM	05/06/08 07:50:28PM	09/15/04 01:23:28PM	05/06/08 07:50:2
☐	1343	MSO.ACL	ACL	•		File, Deleted, Archive	05/06/08 07:56:45PM	05/06/08 07:50:07PM	05/17/00 01:05:34AM	05/06/08 07:50:0
☐	1344	FD00296_.WMF	WMF	•	Windows Metafile	File, Deleted, Overwritten,	05/06/08 07:49:06PM	05/06/08 07:49:06PM	03/09/98 07:44:06AM	05/06/08 07:49:0
☐	1345	FD00297_.WMF	WMF	•	Windows Metafile	File, Deleted, Overwritten,	05/06/08 07:49:06PM	05/06/08 07:49:06PM	03/09/98 09:00:14AM	05/06/08 07:49:0

Text ▦ Hex ▦ Picture 🔍 Disk ▤ Report ▢ Console ⚡ Filters 🔍 Queries ☐ Lock ☐ 0/303542 1: PS 6818719 LS 6818656 CL 852332 SO 000 FO 0 LE 1

Figure 10-15:
The EnCase internal graphics file viewer.

This extraction process is the same for all files or evidence you find that can be extracted using standard techniques or software. Computer forensic software has standardized the way evidence is extracted from storage devices and presented in courts of law throughout the world. The issue now becomes how to extract data that isn't standard or easily found. How do you extract — or even find — evidence that has been hidden by technically savvy criminals? The short answer is that it's difficult to find and extract evidence that's truly well hidden. The simplest example is trying to find a hidden steganographic file among tens of thousands of other files with no hint about which one holds the hidden data. Another example is extracting an encrypted file and not being able to view its contents.

Rebuilding Extracted Data

After the data is extracted, your next step is to figure out exactly what the data means to your case. (At this point, computer geeks tend to fall off the investigative wagon and get lost because you're now moving from the *science* to the *art* of the investigation.) The technological part of a forensic investigation is usually the easier part because the tools that are used to find raw data are quite efficient. However, the real challenge lies in using your investigative skills to piece together the evidence.

Here are some questions you may need to ask yourself when looking at different areas of digital evidence:

- ✔ **Timeline:** How does this evidence fit into a case timeline?

- ✔ **Suspect link:** How is the evidence linked to the suspect? Are the links corroborated by other factors or evidence?

- ✔ **Evidence trail:** Does the digital evidence have a history or digital trail that I can fit into the timeline? How did this evidence get to where it is?

- ✔ **Evidence integrity:** Is the file or evidence what it appears to be? Does the file have hidden data? Could the file have been faked or put into the computer as a red herring?

- ✔ **Why:** Why is the data located where it is? Why is the evidence in the format it's in?

You probably need to ask yourself *dozens* of questions, but these basic questions can get you started in looking at how the data or evidence fits into a case. If you have any doubts, use the old standards: who, what, when, why, where, and how.

Chapter 11

Document Forensics

. . . .

In This Chapter

▸ Finding data about data

▸ Finding the CAM

▸ Where documents are found

. . . .

*W*hat a document says about the person who created it is almost as important as what the document's intended purpose appears to be. You have a document that has smoking gun evidence, but how do you *really* know that the suspect wrote the document and when it was written? Just extracting a document and intending to use it as evidence of a crime aren't enough to do a complete analysis. You must link the evidence to the suspect in some way, and that's where document forensics and the use of metadata come into play.

Metadata is simply data about data. Because the computer field is huge, metadata is necessarily different for many individual computer fields or domains. For example, document metadata is much different from Web page metadata, but they both describe in some form the characteristics of the data they represent. For example, one piece of metadata for a digital photo is the time stamp indicating when the photo was taken.

When you're doing an investigation, one of the classic questions any television investigator would ask is, "Where were you on January 2, 2008, and can you prove it?" Computer forensics and, by association, document forensics have the same goal as your regular physical forensic counterpart — computer forensics wants the truth, but needs hard digital evidence to prove that truth. The key with computers is not only knowing the right question to ask, but how a computer answers the question. Although a computer-generated document or file cannot literally speak, what the document or file has to say about who, what, when, where, why, and how is often much more credible than any human witness testimony. This chapter is all about finding the clues that a document might be hiding that can tell you whether the human and computer versions of the story are the same.

Finding Evidential Material in Documents: Metadata

Documents are arguably one of the most important areas where metadata is found. The rapidly growing field of e-discovery has figuratively found a goldmine with metadata and the use of it to win court cases. It is no understatement to say that in addition to attorneys wanting to find the memorandum, they want to also find the metadata to prove who wrote the memorandum and when.

The following list describes the basic types of metadata found in a typical word processing document:

- **Author:** Regardless of whether this information comes from the operating system or from the installation of the word processing software, a name is embedded as part of the document for all to see.

- **Organization:** This information is usually acquired by the word processing software from the same sources as the author information. If information is listed during the installation of the operating system or the word processing software, chances are good that it's embedded in the document.

- **Revisions:** As part of creating the revision log, the previous authors can be listed as well as the path where the file was stored.

- **Previous authors:** Documents often have a history of users who worked on the document.

- **Template:** This piece of data shows which template is embedded within the document.

- **Computer name:** This name connects the document with the computer on which it was typed.

- **Hard disk:** This data often includes the hard drive name and the path where the file was located.

- **Network server:** An extension of the hard drive information — if a file is stored on a network server, the metadata reflects the network path name.

- **Time:** This type of metadata often indicates how long the document was open for editing.

- **Deleted text:** Some metadata logs text that has been deleted.

- **Visual basic objects:** Objects used and created by Visual Basic are often part of a macro execution and are saved and hidden from the user.

✔ **Time stamps:** This type of data is usually based on the operating system time stamp and covers the created, accessed, and modified time stamps (CAM). We discuss CAM facts in more detail later in this chapter, in the section "Honing In on CAM (Create, Access, Modify) Facts."

✔ **Printed:** Metadata often tells you when the document was last printed.

Although Microsoft is the focus of much of the metadata extraction, metadata can be found in almost all application software. You can find metadata in Adobe PDF files, multimedia files, Web pages, databases, and even geographic software applications. The type and amount of metadata you find varies depending on the application and on how thorough the user is at either entering his life story metadata on a form (by filling in every empty box with personal information) which gives you the first link between the document and the user.

As attorneys request more and more data as part of the e-discovery process, organizations have begun to clean their documents of any metadata that could possibly prove embarrassing. The issue has reached such proportions that Microsoft has published methods to remove metadata from its documents for organizations that feel they need to wipe their documents clean.

Metadata located within the document falls into two distinct areas: viewable by the user and not viewable by the user. If you can't view information, you have to extract it.

Viewing metadata

This list describes the information you can find when you're looking at user viewable metadata:

✔ **Basic user information:** A typical Microsoft Word document populates various fields in the Properties section that generally show basic user information as it relates to the document. Figure 11-1 shows general information about a document.

✔ **Document statistics:** Statistical information that's often useful to determine timelines and corroborate whereabouts is also often found in the Properties dialog box depending on which tab (General, Summary, Statistics) you choose. Figure 11-2 shows the statistics of the document itself, such as how many pages or paragraphs the document has, although you're often seeking the other information, such as time stamps and path information.

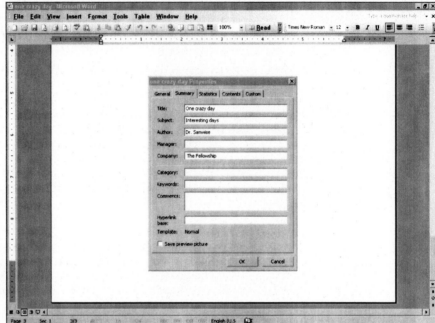

Figure 11-1:
The
Microsoft
Word
Properties
dialog box.

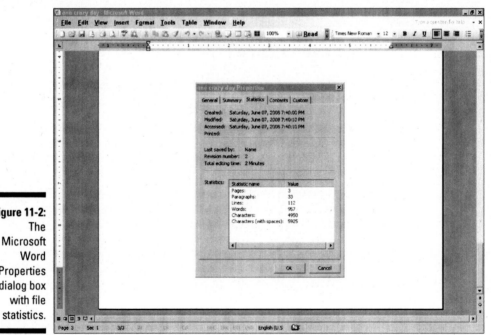

Figure 11-2:
The
Microsoft
Word
Properties
dialog box
with file
statistics.

Delving into revision logs

You might be wondering why it matters whether you know who the previous author is or even whether various people have modified the document. Tony Blair and the British government learned the hard way just how much information metadata can provide and why this information can be important. A dossier on the military status of Iraq in 2003 compiled by the British government was in fact plagiarized from a postgraduate student's research analysis report on Iraq. Richard M. Smith of ComputerBytesMan.com extracted the following revision log, which showed the progression of revisions to or copies of the document, including the purported copy made for Colin Powell (see Revision 5) for his presentation to the United Nations. The revision log had such detailed information that Internet users were able to identify the authors and which part of the British government they worked for at the time when the story first hit the Internet — in addition to where the file was copied or saved. Here's the revision log:

Rev. 1: `"cic22" edited file "C:\DOCUME~1\phamill\LOCALS~1\Temp\AutoRecovery save of Iraq - security.asd"`

Rev. 2: `"cic22" edited file "C:\DOCUME~1\phamill\LOCALS~1\Temp\AutoRecovery save of Iraq - security.asd"`

Rev. 3: `"cic22" edited file "C:\DOCUME~1\phamill\LOCALS~1\Temp\AutoRecovery save of Iraq - security.asd"`

Rev. 4: `"JPratt" edited file "C:\TEMP\Iraq - security.doc"`

Rev. 5: `"JPratt" edited file "A:\Iraq - security.doc"`

Rev. 6: `"ablackshaw" edited file "C:\ABlackshaw\Iraq - security.doc"`

Rev. 7: `"ablackshaw" edited file "C:\ABlackshaw\A;Iraq - security.doc"`

Rev. 8: `"ablackshaw" edited file "A:\Iraq - security.doc"`

Rev. 9: `"MKhan" edited file "C:\TEMP\Iraq - security.doc"`

Rev. 10: `"MKhan" edited file "C:\WINNT\Profiles\mkhan\Desktop\Iraq.doc"`

Based on metadata, the British document was shown to be plagiarized and then edited for dramatic effect, and the visual chain showing who made which revisions to the document was followed all the way back to the postgraduate researcher. For a thorough analysis of the document, see `www.casi.org.uk/discuss/2003/msg00457.html`.

Extracting metadata

When you're extracting metadata, you have to use special software tools, such as Metadata Analyzer (www.smartpctools.com) or iScrub (www.esqinc.com), to extract the data that you can't easily see. These tools can analyze the document at a binary level for revision logs, Visual Basic objects, or deleted text that might still be present in the document. Figure 11-3 shows the information that Metadata Analyzer can extract. Esquire's iScrub is a bit more powerful and can even find drafting history to see changes made to a document.

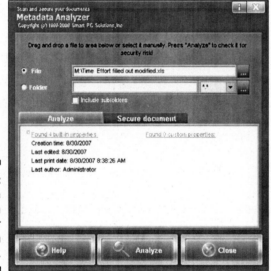

Figure 11-3: The Metadata Analyzer main screen.

The highly publicized arrest of Dennis Rader, also known as the BTK Killer, is a classic use of metadata to find evidence or information in documents. Beginning in 1974, the self-nicknamed serial killer began taunting police and the media with a series of letters detailing his murders. Over the course of 30 years and numerous letters, Rader gave the police their first major break in the case when he mailed a purple floppy disk along with several other articles to a local television station in 2005. Unbeknownst to him, a document he had deleted had the name Dennis embedded in the metadata, and in another area of metadata, the church where he was president of the congregation council was listed. The police quickly put together the pieces of this circumstantial evidence to gather hard DNA evidence linking Rader to several BTK murders.

Honing In on CAM (Create, Access, Modify) Facts

The use of the *c*reate, *a*ccess, and *m*odify (CAM) time stamps often helps to track a document and determine timelines. The location of CAM information is logged in different areas, such as directory entries or inodes, depending on the operating system. The importance of creating a timeline of a suspect's whereabouts, the file history, or even tracking a file across a network is possible by using CAM metadata and is often part of the circumstantial evidence that helps support other aspects of a case.

You need to understand exactly what these time stamps really mean:

- ✔ **Create:** Shows the date and time that the file was created on that particular storage media. Keep in mind that this time stamp changes whenever a file is copied to new media — even within the same storage device.

- ✔ **Access:** Specifies the last time the file was opened or accessed, but not changed in any form.

- ✔ **Modify:** Indicates the date and time that a file was modified or changed. On files that have been copied to new media, the modified time stamps might be older than the created time stamps. The reason is that the file in its original location had been modified before it was copied to the new location and thus created at a later date in the new location.

Figure 11-4 shows the CAM information for a word processing file. This application also noted the last time the file was printed, which can also be very helpful.

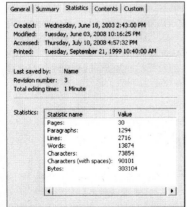

General | Summary | Statistics | Contents | Custom |

Created: Wednesday, June 18, 2003 2:43:00 PM
Modified: Tuesday, June 03, 2008 10:16:25 PM
Accessed: Thursday, July 10, 2008 4:57:32 PM
Printed: Tuesday, September 21, 1999 10:40:00 AM

Last saved by: Name
Revision number: 3
Total editing time: 1 Minute

Statistics:	Statistic name	Value
	Pages:	30
	Paragraphs:	1294
	Lines:	2716
	Words:	13874
	Characters:	73854
	Characters (with spaces):	90101
	Bytes:	303104

Figure 11-4:
CAM entries
for a
document.

The dates and times associated with the CAM information are from the operating system clock, so if the clock is wrong, your time stamps are wrong too. A wide-ranging debate on the issue of time and date settings for computers takes place in the forensic community because crimes don't occur in just one time zone. The central issue isn't whether the time and date are accurate on the computer but, rather, whether the date and time are local or Zulu based, for example.

The world is divided into 24 different time zones denoted by letters of the English alphabet; time zone Z (Zulu) indicates the clock at Greenwich, England. Aviation has long used Zulu time as the standard so that no matter which time zone you're in, you know what time it is. The issue you run into is that a file might be created in Hong Kong, and then transmitted to London, and then copied to New York — all within a one-second period. This range of local time zones tends to be confusing unless you know exactly what you're looking at; if you're using Zulu time, it's extremely easy to figure out the time-line of the file copy.

For most people, using local or Zulu time is a semantic argument. For investigators, however, the issue is one of accuracy and reliability of the time and date stamps. Essentially, if your case is a local case with no crossing of time zones, using a third-party clock to check the accuracy of your suspect computer will usually suffice. If, on the other hand, you have an international case, using Zulu time might be the best strategy because you can track the file times more easily by using time zone Z as your baseline.

In all cases, choose a method that standardizes your procedures for time and date checking, and stick to that method for the duration of your case.

Because the CAM information has become critical to computer forensic cases, criminals have begun to scramble this data to hide or camouflage their digital footprints. Several software packages scramble the CAM data fields with random numbers or with random dates and times, or they just plain eliminate them. This turn of events has made the computer forensic field a bit more challenging because you have to rely not on the time-and-date stamps of the files themselves but, rather, on the time-and-date stamps of secondary sources, such as e-mail servers or other trusted points, that a file might have passed. The Metasploit project (www.metasploit.com) has some helpful information on the subject of antiforensics and a test project in the works.

Discovering Documents

For most users, the place to save documents from day to day is usually in the My Documents folder on their local computers. Most people don't even give a second thought to where they save their files — as long as they can find them. Unfortunately for forensic investigators, documents can be stored in an endless number of places, and even hidden in plain sight. Even experienced investigators can miss these clever hiding places from time to time.

Luring documents out of local storage

The first place to look for documents is the application in which they were created. Most application software keeps a list of recent documents that tells you in which folder or directory these recent files were last saved. Figure 11-5 shows a Microsoft Word menu that lists the most recent files used in this application. The files' paths are listed, which makes it much easier for you to find the place where the files are saved. You don't have to hunt for the files over an entire storage device, and you gain a good idea of where other files might be located. This method also has the advantage of rapidly pointing out whether you also need to look at external storage devices.

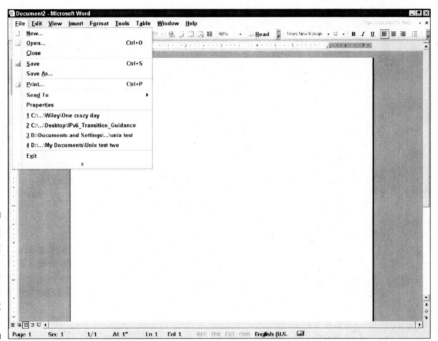

Figure 11-5:
Microsoft Word drop-down menu with the most recent file entries.

If you're matching wits with a computer user who has some fairly good technical knowledge, the file history most likely is erased. In this case, your next step is to use a forensic software suite to open on the local machine all the files that match the type you're looking for. Forensic software, such as FTK and EnCase, has features that allow you to rapidly sort files by type and make your work much easier when dealing with large numbers of files. Figure 11-6 shows a typical list of files sorted by file type.

Sorting by file type

		Name	Filter	In Report	File Ext	File Type	File Category	Signature	Desc
☐	204951	Cast of Characters ...			wpd	WordPerfect Demo	Document\Education		File, Archive
☐	204952	black codes.wpd			wpd	WordPerfect Demo	Document\Education		File, Archive
☐	204953	Background.wpd			wpd	WordPerfect Demo	Document\Education		File, Archive
☐	204954	Background2.wpd			wpd	WordPerfect Demo	Document\Education		File, Archive
☐	204955	wordpfct.wpg			wpg	WordPerfect Graphic	Picture		File, Archive
☐	204956	WORDPFCT.WPG			WPG	WordPerfect Graphic	Picture		File
☐	204957	wordpfct.wpg			wpg	WordPerfect Graphic	Picture		File, Archive
☐	204958	MS.WPG			WPG	WordPerfect Graphic	Picture		File, Archive
☐	204959	wordpfct.wpg			wpg	WordPerfect Graphic	Picture		File, Archive
☐	204960	wordpfct.wpg			wpg	WordPerfect Graphic	Picture		File, Archive
☐	204961	wordpfct.wpg			wpg	WordPerfect Graphic	Picture		File, Archive
☐	204962	MS.WPG			WPG	WordPerfect Graphic	Picture		File, Archive
☐	204963	wordpfct.wpg			wpg	WordPerfect Graphic	Picture		File, Archive
☐	204964	Default.rul			rul	WordPerfect Rule	Code\Application		File, Archive
☐	204965	Normal.wpt			wpt	WordPerfect Template	Document		File, Archive
☐	204966	Normal.wpt			wpt	WordPerfect Template	Document		File, Archive
☐	204967	CA9CE1E52B76875...			bm	X Window Bitmap	Picture		File, Archive
☐	204968	flower.xpm			xpm	X-Pixelmap Graphic	Picture		File, Archive
☐	204969	foliage.xpm			xpm	X-Pixelmap Graphic	Picture		File, Archive
☐	204970	waffle.xpm			xpm	X-Pixelmap Graphic	Picture		File, Archive
☐	204971	marker.xpm			xpm	X-Pixelmap Graphic	Picture		File, Archive

Figure 11-6: Forensic software grouping files by type.

If you're looking for files of a certain type, this search is easy for you to per-form. You see Microsoft Word files in the My Documents folder, and your first assumption is that they're Microsoft Word files. But, unfortunately, when you're dealing with savvy computer criminals, that assumption can often lead to overlooking evidence that might be in plain sight. If you're looking for JPEG files and you find only Word files, you pass up any Word files. That's not a good thing if the suspect changed the extension or the file header. You need to take the additional step of matching file headers to their file extensions. If they match but you can't open the file, you have to modify the file header.

Matching file headers to extensions

To figure out whether a file's extension has been tampered with, you have to understand the way files are recognized by operating systems and applica-tion software. An application program generally recognizes a file by either its file header or file extension, whereas operating systems tend to rely mostly on the file extension to determine file type.

A *file header* is usually a sequence of characters at the beginning of a file that signifies what type of file it really is. Literally thousands of different file types now exist, so finding file headers can be a challenge if the file is created by an obscure program. Fortunately, most files fall into popular software packages such as Microsoft, Novell, Adobe, or Sun. If you do happen to be working with an oddball file and need to know which headers go with that file, a good to place to start your search is `www.fileinfo.net`.

Figure 11-7 shows a file header from Microsoft Word. The character sequence for this file is always the same even if the file extension changes! Look care-fully at the beginning of the file and you can see a character sequence that looks like a funny-looking *D* followed by a strange-looking *I*. That's your file header character sequence.

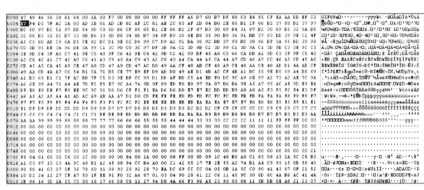

Figure 11-7:
Microsoft
Word file
header.

Figure 11-8 shows the file header for a picture file with a file header that has the character sequence GIF89.

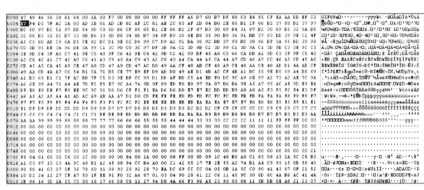

Figure 11-8:
File header
for a GIF
picture file.

If a user changes a file extension to fool the operating system, the application software still opens the file because the file header is still intact. Changing the file extension makes no difference to the software application.

Most forensic software programs perform a signature analysis to determine whether the file header and the file extension match. If the extension and header match, the file is exactly what it claims to be; if you have a mismatch between the header and the extension, the file might have been changed to conceal its true identity. The trick is to let the forensic software do the heavy lifting and identify which files are suspect. You can study those files further to determine whether the extensions have been changed. When dealing with hundreds of thousands of files at a time, you begin to appreciate the power of forensic software.

Modifying the file header

Just because the extension and the file header match doesn't mean that the file is exactly what it seems to be. A user can also modify the file header to hide the file in plain sight.

If a user changes the file header, file extension, and filename to look like a Windows system file, a signature analysis only confirms that the extension and header match, so the software doesn't flag the file as suspicious. If you run the file — if it's an executable file, for example — an error message says that the file doesn't work or cannot be used. This message doesn't normally set off any red flags because many executable files don't work correctly if they're run by themselves.

To determine whether this hiding technique has been used

> ✔ **See whether you can open the file.**
>
> If you try to open the file from an application, an error message states that the file cannot be opened because it is an unknown file type. The only way you can open the file at this point is to know which file header to insert at the beginning of the file to make it work again. Use the header of a file you know that works and insert it at the beginning of the suspect file.
>
> ✔ **Use hash values of known files to eliminate them from consideration.**
>
> Libraries of hash values exist for almost every operating system and the support files they use. Most popular application software (and their support files), such as Microsoft Word or Excel, is also included in many hash libraries to eliminate them as potential hidden files.
>
> If a user tries to hide a file by disguising it in this fashion, it stands out as a file with a hash value that doesn't match any standard files for that operating system or application. The National Software Reference Library (NSRL) is a helpful source of information regarding hash values of known files and how to use these hashes. You can download the hash libraries directly from NSRL (www.nsrl.nist.gov) and incorporate them into your forensic software to filter out known files. Keep in mind that the NSRL doesn't contain hash values for anything other than known files! If you need hashes for illicit files, you might have to contact your local law enforcement representative for a source of these types of hashes.
>
> ✔ **Look for files that have been modified recently or quite often.**
>
> The user has to modify the file to open it and then modify it again to hide it. Keep in mind that literally thousands of files are modified on modern computers every day, so this option is a last resort.

If the suspect is capable of modifying file headers and extensions, clues such as hex editors and viewers are often tip-offs that you might have to look closely at file headers.

Finding links and external storage

When a file is stored or copied externally to the local computer, a link file is generated so that the operating system knows where the file is located. Quite often, link files are your only clue that an external storage device was connected to the computer. Figure 11-9 shows a typical link file that shows the path where a file might be found; in this case, it's the G volume.

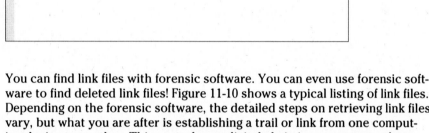

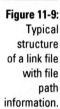

Figure 11-9: Typical structure of a link file with file path information.

You can find link files with forensic software. You can even use forensic software to find deleted link files! Figure 11-10 shows a typical listing of link files. Depending on the forensic software, the detailed steps on retrieving link files vary, but what you are after is establishing a trail or link from one computing device to another. This part of your digital chain is necessary to show the connection between where the evidence was found in relation to where it resided before. If your suspect had or has access to one or both locations, you can reason the suspect has access to the evidence in question. Very few cases have a black and white smoking gun, but rather have an accumulation of evidence of which link files can be a part.

	Name	Filter	In Report	File Ext	File Type	File Category	Signature	Description	Is Deleted	Last Accessed
☐ 194621	⊘ A0096975.lnk			lnk	Link	Windows		File, Deleted, Archive, Com	•	05/07/08 10:48
☐ 194622	Smart Pix Manager.lnk			lnk	Link	Windows		File, Archive		05/07/08 08:43
☐ 194623	MUSICMATCH Burner Plus.lnk			lnk	Link	Windows		File, Archive		05/07/08 08:43
☐ 194624	✗ A0097021.lnk			lnk	Link	Windows		File, Deleted, Overwritten,	•	05/07/08 10:48
☐ 194625	⊘ A0096985.lnk			lnk	Link	Windows		File, Deleted, Archive, Com	•	05/07/08 10:48
☐ 194626	New Volume (G).lnk			lnk	Link	Windows		File, Archive		05/07/08 01:07
☐ 194627	⊘ A0096778.lnk			lnk	Link	Windows		File, Deleted, Archive, Com	•	05/07/08 10:48
☐ 194628	⊘ A0096785.lnk			lnk	Link	Windows		File, Deleted, Archive, Com	•	05/07/08 10:48
☐ 194629	Cases.rar.lnk			lnk	Link	Windows		File, Archive		05/07/08 01:07
☐ 194630	Sample Pictures.lnk			lnk	Link	Windows		File, Archive		05/07/08 08:40
☐ 194631	✗ A0100276.lnk			lnk	Link	Windows		File, Deleted, Overwritten,	•	05/07/08 10:49
☐ 194632	msoffice2003.zip.lnk			lnk	Link	Windows		File, Archive		05/07/08 08:43
☐ 194633	⊘ A0096788.lnk			lnk	Link	Windows		File, Deleted, Archive, Com	•	05/07/08 10:48
☐ 194634	Mozilla Thunderbird (No Extensi...			lnk	Link	Windows		File, Archive		05/07/08 10:31
☐ 194635	default.lnk			lnk	Link	Windows		File, Archive		05/07/08 08:43
☐ 194636	⊘ A0096944.lnk			lnk	Link	Windows		File, Deleted, Archive, Com	•	05/07/08 10:48
☐ 194637	✗ A0100275.lnk			lnk	Link	Windows		File, Deleted, Overwritten,	•	05/07/08 10:49
☐ 194638	⊘ A0096789.lnk			lnk	Link	Windows		File, Deleted, Archive, Com	•	05/07/08 10:48

Figure 11-10: List of link files and related information found by forensic software.

Finding external storage options

When you find a link file, the first thing to do is determine whether any external storage devices are within arm's length of the computer you're working on. If you're in the lab, refer to your documentation of the original scene; if you're still on scene, double-check the area for any type of storage device, such as

- ✔ A thumb drive
- ✔ An external hard drive
- ✔ A camera
- ✔ An audio recorder
- ✔ An answering machine
- ✔ A digital copier

Any of these electronic devices has the potential to be a storage device. We talk more about retrieving forensic evidence from these devices in Chapter 14. On a Microsoft Windows computer, the best place to look for previously connected external devices and correlate them with link files is in the Windows Registry. Chapter 10 covers that little known area in more detail.

Finding external networks

If your link file points to a network path (for example, \\server\test.doc), your job becomes a bit more complicated because you now have to track down a computer that may or may not be on the premises. If the computer resides within your local jurisdiction or control, obtaining the permissions or warrants should be fairly easy. If the files are stored on a computer located a couple of continents away, you might have some trouble getting the local Russian or Chinese law enforcement officials to see things your way.

Network leads tend to fade quickly on the Internet. Always pursue files and their associated digital footprints on a network or the Internet with all due haste lest the trail goes cold!

If you see a wireless system or router, assume that a wireless computer is nearby that may have files saved on it that you might be interested in — even if you don't find any link files on the computer you're working on. Remember that newer smart phones have WiFi capability, so they also count as wireless network devices!

In any case, link files provide almost as much information as the file itself with regard to time and date stamps. The link files are literally linked to the suspect file so that whenever the suspect uses the file in question, the link file mirrors this action as well. Figure 11-11 shows that the type of CAM information you can find in a link file is just as detailed as it is from the actual file.

		Name	In Report	File Ext	File Type	Last Accessed	File Created	Last Written	Entry Modified
☐	82336	Notepad.lnk	lnk	Link	05/25/08 02:01:22PM	05/07/08 01:59:49PM	05/08/08 12:04:41PM	06/09/08 12:15:52PM
☐	82337	Program Compatibility…	lnk	Link	05/25/08 02:01:22PM	05/07/08 01:59:49PM	05/07/08 01:55:02PM	06/09/08 12:15:52PM
☐	82338	Synchronize.lnk	lnk	Link	05/25/08 02:01:22PM	05/07/08 01:59:49PM	05/07/08 01:55:02PM	06/09/08 12:15:52PM
☐	82339	Tour Windows XP.lnk	lnk	Link	05/25/08 02:01:22PM	05/07/08 01:59:49PM	05/07/08 01:55:02PM	06/09/08 12:15:53PM
☐	82340	Windows Explorer.lnk	lnk	Link	05/25/08 02:01:22PM	05/07/08 01:59:49PM	05/07/08 01:53:41PM	06/09/08 12:15:53PM
☐	82341	Internet Explorer (No…	lnk	Link	05/26/08 09:54:44PM	05/07/08 10:23:18PM	05/07/08 10:23:18PM	06/09/08 12:15:53PM
☐	82342	Magnifier.lnk	lnk	Link	05/26/08 09:54:44PM	05/07/08 01:59:49PM	05/07/08 01:55:02PM	06/09/08 12:15:52PM
☐	82343	Narrator.lnk	lnk	Link	05/26/08 09:54:44PM	05/07/08 01:59:49PM	05/07/08 01:55:02PM	06/09/08 12:15:52PM
☐	82344	On-Screen Keyboard.lnk	lnk	Link	05/26/08 09:54:44PM	05/07/08 01:59:49PM	05/07/08 01:55:02PM	06/09/08 12:15:52PM
☐	82345	Utility Manager.lnk	lnk	Link	05/26/08 09:54:44PM	05/07/08 01:59:49PM	05/07/08 01:55:02PM	06/09/08 12:15:52PM
☐	82346	Bluetooth File Transfe…	LNK	Link	06/06/08 09:23:36PM	05/10/08 07:25:27PM	05/10/08 07:25:27PM	06/09/08 12:15:52PM
☐	82347	WM_Me My Documen…	LNK	Link	06/06/08 09:23:36PM	05/22/08 03:15:53PM	05/22/08 03:15:53PM	06/09/08 12:15:52PM
☐	82348	One crazy day.lnk	lnk	Link	06/09/08 07:02:13AM	06/08/08 12:44:03AM	06/09/08 07:02:13AM	06/09/08 12:15:50PM
☐	82349	chap 11 link file table.lnk	lnk	Link	06/08/08 11:09:23PM	06/08/08 11:09:23PM	06/08/08 11:09:23PM	06/09/08 12:15:49PM
☐	82350	chap 11 link file.lnk	lnk	Link	06/08/08 11:00:02PM	06/08/08 10:50:25PM	06/08/08 11:00:02PM	06/09/08 12:15:49PM
☐	82351	chap 11 gif file heade…	lnk	Link	06/08/08 10:24:35PM	06/08/08 10:24:35PM	06/08/08 10:24:35PM	06/09/08 12:15:49PM
☐	82352	chap 11 recent file sc…	lnk	Link	06/08/08 11:00:52PM	06/08/08 03:48:34PM	06/08/08 03:48:34PM	06/09/08 12:15:49PM
☐	82353	chap 11 figure 4.lnk	lnk	Link	06/08/08 10:02:22PM	06/08/08 10:02:22PM	06/08/08 10:02:22PM	06/09/08 12:15:49PM
☐	82354	word file header for c…	lnk	Link	06/08/08 10:22:08PM	06/08/08 10:18:31PM	06/08/08 10:22:08PM	06/09/08 12:15:52PM
☐	82355	cornish hydrogen.lnk	lnk	Link	06/08/08 11:00:52PM	06/08/08 09:12:16AM	06/08/08 09:12:16AM	06/09/08 12:15:50PM
☐	82356	reaction paper two.lnk	lnk	Link	06/07/08 02:34:33PM	06/07/08 02:34:33PM	06/07/08 02:34:33PM	06/09/08 12:15:50PM

Figure 11-11:
Link file
CAM
details.

Rounding up backups

In organizations of any substantial size, you tend to find a data backup system of some type. Most organizational users have no idea how the backup system works until they lose a file or storage device and even then forget rather quickly about the backup systems that are in place. For computer forensics, backup systems can be a bonanza of information because they tend to be snapshots in time of the computer systems and are often kept long after the physical computers are discarded.

For criminals who are quite tech savvy and know how to hide their digital tracks on computers they control, analysis of backup media is often quite productive because they usually have little control over the backup systems — if they even know of their existence.

Data can be backed up in several ways, and each one has pros and cons with regard to computer forensic analysis. You can back up information on duplicate storage devices, tape drives, and even network storage services. Here are the points to consider:

✔ **Backups done on duplicate storage devices and network storage devices usually follow the same file system formats as the original versions.**

Your job becomes much easier because the file system formats are fairly standardized.

The problem with these methods of backing up data is that they tend to be expensive and have the same failure points as the storage media they're backing up.

✔ **Using tape for backups is by far the most popular and cost effective method.**

Tape backups cost pennies per linear foot, are relatively stable, have been around for decades, and are portable, so you can take them offsite to further protect your data, if necessary.

The disadvantage is that many different standards exist for tape backup systems. Another issue to consider is that quite a number of legacy tape backup solutions exist. The problem with these systems is twofold:

- The company that made the equipment may no longer be around, leaving you with no fallback support.

- You might not be able to find the equipment to read the tapes easily.

Because literally dozens of tape drive types have differing standards and a multitude of software applications to run the tape backup drives, you have to know exactly what type of tape backup system you're working with. Otherwise, extracting data from a tape backup is extremely challenging.

The best-case scenario is to use the same tape drive and tape software to extract a list of files from the tape to create an index of the files that reside on that tape. By using the same equipment that saved the data, you eliminate any problems with different data archiving standards. And, by creating an index, you can scan terabytes of data rather quickly to make a list of the files you really want. By a happy coincidence, the best way to create an index of files on a tape is to scan the metadata for items such as file type, CAM, and any particular file attributes you're looking for. After you figure out which files you need to extract, restoring them from the tape is just a matter of pulling the right tape and extracting the file or files.

If you happen to be the unlucky computer forensic analyst who is tasked with finding data on a tape backup set that has an unknown history, your job becomes a little more difficult.

Before you start, make a duplicate of the tape you're testing, or at least make sure that the write protection is enabled on the tape!

If a tape backup is handed to you and you don't know its history, you need to follow several basic steps to determine its format:

1. **Determine which tape drive was used.**

   Most tape backup systems use standard tapes that are compatible with particular tape drives. You must first match the tape to the tape drive. The number one problem that trips up most investigators in this step is that certain tape drives accept tapes that are incompatible even though they fit physically. This is usually because tapes are available in various storage capacities, which leads to different physical densities even though they look identical on the outside. The best example is the old-fashioned 3½ floppy disk, which was either high density or low density. Both types of floppy disk looked identical externally, but their internal structures were so different that mixing up the two disks often led to confusion and lost data.

2. **Determine which tape backup software was used.**

   After you know the physical components of the tape backup system, you must determine exactly which type of tape backup software was used to archive this data. This step might not be as easy as it sounds because many tape backup drives are designed to work with almost any type of tape backup software. The most logical approach is to find the most popular software used with that particular tape drive and work your way down the list by popularity until you find a software package that recognizes the tape in the drive. The issue with tape backup software and why it's often difficult to identify which software program wrote the archive is that no real standards exist for writing tape backup software to the tape. Each tape software vendor is free to create its own file backup structure that only its software can read or write.

3. **Determine the structure of the file system.**

   Because tape archival is a specialized area of computer forensics, few computer forensic professionals dig down to this level. At this point, you're essentially creating your own software to read and analyze the contents of the tape — you're essentially creating your own tape restoration software. If you're in this situation, seek out a computer forensic firm that handles this area of computer forensics. Chances are good that you aren't the first person to have this problem, and reinventing the wheel usually isn't necessary or even advisable.

Chapter 12

Mobile Forensics

A computer forensic case in which a mobile computing device is the center of your case is a guaranteed certainty as the computing world progresses. Most people don't realize the capabilities of an iPod, an MP3 player, a BlackBerry, or a personal digital assistant (PDA). To put the use of these popular devices in perspective, a mobile phone or a PDA now has roughly the computing power of a computer manufactured within the past five years. A present-day mobile device commonly comes supplied with a 1 gigahertz (GHz) processor, 128 megabytes (MB) of RAM, and 80 gigabytes (GB) of storage. The secondary factor associated with mobile devices is their steady march toward complete wireless functionality by way of Bluetooth, 802.11, and infrared technology.

If you think that the desktop computer industry changes rapidly, the mobile computing world changes even faster — and offers you challenges because of that rapid change. If you like challenges, this chapter is a helpful primer into the world of mobile computer forensics, where challenges happen daily.

The definition of a mobile device is somewhat blurry because many devices, such as iPods and video cameras, are becoming smaller and more mobile. The majority of mobile forensics is concerned with the mobile phone and PDA device. Although iPods, audio recorders, and other devices of this type are covered in this chapter, the real focus of this chapter is the mobile phone/PDA device and how to forensically extract data because these devices are truly wireless by design.

Keeping Up with Data on the Move

If you're one of the millions of people around the world who owns a little device the size of a deck of cards that holds thousands of favorite songs, you know how fast technology can change. Not too long ago, we were all using cassette tapes on portable players to listen to maybe 15 songs per tape! Fast-forward (no pun intended) 20 years, and you can carry around not only audio but also video of your favorite music limited only by the amount of memory on your device. In some cases, people can store tens of thousands of songs on their devices!

If consumers sometimes find it hard to keep up with the changes in technology, how do you as an investigator keep track of all the emerging technologies, especially when criminals often adopt them before they're completely understood by investigators and courts of law? In most computer fields, this problem is real, but it's especially difficult in the mobile arena simply because the rate of change is so rapid. The answer to this conundrum is exactly what you are doing right now, reading up on new techniques, studying, and training as often as possible.

Even though computer users often increase the amount of RAM or hard drive space on their computers, computers essentially use the same technology year after year. When you're investigating mobile devices, you must remember that they differ from computers in three ways. Mobile devices

- ✔ **Change operating systems, interface methods, hardware standards, and storage technologies quite often:** They can change several times within a span of just one product year. Computer software, on the other hand, tends to be updated every year or two.

- ✔ **Have many different mobile device platforms:** To pry open the potential secrets of mobile devices for your investigation, you must use several tools. For example, if you've been using mobile phones for several years, chances are good that you have several old chargers lying around that work on only those particular mobile phone models. Computers on the other hand still use the same power source, connect to the network in the same fashion as they always have, and even keep the same interfaces, such as USB, constant for years at a time.

- ✔ **Use wireless technologies to communicate:** Because mobile devices are on the move, using a method that eliminates wires is the only method quite a number of them use as their exclusive means of communication, unlike desktop computers that can use a wired communication setup.

There are three basic means of communication for mobile devices in addition to the mobile phone radio used by all mobile phone companies:

- *802.11:* This standard is used by all wireless networks in existence today. Your wireless router sitting at home uses the 802.11 to communicate wirelessly with your office laptop, for example. The range of a mobile device using 802.11 varies considerably due to power constraints on the device, but you can count on around 100 yard diameter at any one time.

- *Bluetooth:* A fairly new standard used for extremely small distances, such as a regular sized room. The original Bluetooth standards conflicted with some 802.11 devices, but changes on both standards have largely eliminated this problem. A distance of 10 meters is considered average for a Bluetooth device.

- *Infrared:* Using the older method of communication, mobile devices can exchange information using the infrared part of the light spectrum. This method is more directional in nature in that you aim the infrared port of the mobile device to the other device's infrared port to communicate. A good number of television remote controls work with infrared.

Shifting from desktop to handhelds

The progression from desktop computer to handheld device has brought so many changes to the worlds of business, consumers, and criminals that entire books can be written about the fundamental changes brought on by these new technologies. Think of it this way: When was the last time you received a Polaroid picture by way of the US Postal Service? The answer is, most likely, not lately. Most people send digital photos from their desktop computers by e-mail.

The transition to mobile e-mail is occurring in much the same way, where rather than be tied to a computer in your home or office, you can send and receive electronic mail from your villa in the south of France during your vacation. In fact, you can now take digital photographs with most mobile phones and send them by way of mobile e-mail to anyone in the world without even being near a desktop personal computer.

For the most part, when people think of mobile forensics, they picture mobile phones; however, the convergence of personal digital assistants with mobile phone technology has essentially created low-end portable computers that have a myriad of different interfaces, operating systems, and application programs. Where nonmobile computer forensics has been virtually standardized in its approach, mobile forensics is still feeling its way around the different standards that are being used and rapidly created.

Mobile forensics cannot be treated in the same way as static computer forensics, even though a person without a technical background may see the concepts as the same!

Because this part of the computer forensic field is still very new, you have to shift the way you think. The classic rules (such as not writing to the suspect media) sometimes may not apply in mobile forensics because the technology doesn't allow that type of investigation. Your mobile forensic investigations therefore relies less on the technology and more on your skills, procedures, and problem-solving abilities.

Considering mobile devices forensically

When looking at potential evidence in any investigation, you almost always have a general idea of what type of evidence you're looking for. The same concept applies to mobile forensics, but you have to know what evidence is available on that particular mobile device. Depending on the type of device you're handling, you might find these types of evidence:

- **Subscriber identifiers:** On mobile phones, this information is used by the mobile phone network to authenticate the user to the network and also verify the services tied to the account. In other words, you can tie the mobile phone identity to the records kept by the mobile phone provider. Subscriber Identity Modules (SIM) have this information embedded in them; if the phone doesn't support SIM cards, the information is hard coded into the phone itself.

- **Logs:** Mobile phones often have logs of calls that were placed, missed, and received that can often form crucial timelines. Other logs that are often kept in the background contain GPS, network cell connection, and network cell termination information. These logs may or may not exist, but if they are, you can track the locations of mobile phones quite easily.

- **Phone books/contact lists:** This listing of other names and numbers often yields investigative leads as well as potential witnesses and victims. You may find, in a typical phone book, information such as e-mail addresses, physical addresses, photographs, and even alternative phone numbers.

- **Text messages:** These concise messages often contain bits of evidence, as well as date and time stamps, that are invaluable to investigators. Most users believe that, after these messages are deleted, they're gone forever. That's often not the case, however, because they can be recovered by using the right software (and having a certain amount of luck).

- **Calendars:** With the prevalence of personal digital assistants on the market, looking at calendar and appointment data can often yield clues or leads.

- **Electronic mail:** Just as in regular computer forensics, e-mail on mobile devices can often yield extremely valuable bits of evidence.

- ✔ **Instant messages:** The live version of text message communication often retains entire conversations that have important evidentiary value, in both their content and their time-and-date information.

- ✔ **Photos:** Almost all mobile phones and PDAs have cameras embedded in them. Still photos and video recordings are all potential bits of evidence.

- ✔ **Audio recordings:** Devices often double as digital audio recorders, and it's often worth your time to investigate what has been recorded and why.

- ✔ **Multimedia messages:** On newer mobile devices, users can now send not only text messages but also audio and video messages.

- ✔ **Application files:** With newer mobile devices using productivity software to view and produce documents, spreadsheets, presentations, and many other file formats, you're quite likely to find evidence in these areas.

Most mobile devices have the capability to use external media such as SD cards. You often find data has been transferred from a desktop computer to the mobile device via this vector. These are often great sources of forensic information.

Devices vary, even among the same models, in the type of information they hold, depending on which services the subscriber has activated. To get a good handle on the device evidence options you have to work with, be sure to fully investigate these items:

- ✔ Model type
- ✔ Services used on the device
- ✔ Hardware version numbers

Recognizing the imperfect understanding of the technology

In the current state of mobile forensics, your skills as an investigator are more important than the technology used to extract the evidence. The primary reason for this state of affairs is simply that many manufacturers are pushing different standards in hardware, interfaces, software, and protocols. The computer industry experienced the same issues in the early 1980s until industry standards were codified by various organizations in an attempt to standardize equipment and make everyone's computer life relatively simple. The mobile computer industry is still coping with emerging technology, so the adoption of a standardized platform, or platforms, is still in the future. Even so, many manufacturers are beginning to recognize the advantages of working together to introduce mobile devices that have standardized components.

Against this backdrop, mobile forensic software is continually changing to keep up with the avalanche of changes in the mobile computer industry. Mobile forensic software is always slightly behind the curve with regard to the new mobile technology, and you often need to use various tools, both forensic and nonforensic, to complete an investigation.

The preferred method of using mobile forensic tools is your first option, but you may not always have a tool that works with the mobile device you're investigating. The purpose of forensic software is always twofold:

- ✔ **Protect the existing data on the original device by not allowing writes to the original data.**

    Write protection ensures that the data isn't changed on the original and hash values ensure that the integrity can be checked on the copies.

- ✔ **Have in place a mechanism that proves the integrity of the forensically copied data.**

    The hashing functions and write protection schemes accomplish this goal with all forensic tools.

Sometimes you have to write to a mobile device to retrieve information you need for an investigation. The goal in this situation, where you must write to original media, is to write as little as possible using the smallest possible digital footprint. The best example of nonforensic acquisition is the use of synchronization software to access data on the mobile device: You essentially copy the data from the original device, but you also alter files that change the date and time stamps and log files. You have to ask yourself whether the data being acquired is worth the result of making these changes. If the answer is Yes, you have to explain to someone (often a judge) why you decided to extract the evidence in this form and how your expertise combined with your policies and procedures ensure that the integrity of the evidence hasn't been compromised.

Because the mobile computer forensic field is changing so rapidly, you must test the mobile forensic software and hardware tools you use before you take on a live case. Establishing a baseline of how your tools work on a particular type of mobile device ensures that you endure no major surprises. In a parallel concept, different tools often produce different results on the same device! Know how each of your tools works regarding each mobile device, and, more importantly, know whether the tools you're using are working properly on that device. If you're working on a case in which the mobile device is so new that you have never developed a baseline for it, check with the manufacturer of the mobile forensic tool to see whether someone there has worked with it. If so, request a recommended course of action. If your investigation is breaking new ground, take every opportunity to safeguard the original data and document your procedures in extreme detail.

Test your computer forensic tools at least once a month to ensure that your write protection and integrity hashes are working properly.

The bottom line: Mobile forensic technology is still relatively young and isn't as stable as computer forensics for regular computer environments. You need a higher level of skill in this new forensic field, so be prepared!

Making a Device Seizure

The process of acquiring data from mobile devices varies among device types. Some mobile devices, such as cameras, are treated as storage devices in much the same way as USB drives. Mobile phones, on the other hand, require specific forensic software to extract data in a forensic manner. This section lists broad guidelines for how to extract information from different devices, but as always, check your local guidelines and always test your forensic tools before using them in a live case.

This area of mobile forensics is arguably the most fun — and often the most frustrating. Even though the field is relatively new, you have to follow basic guidelines in almost all situations when handling digital forensic data:

✔ Avoid changing data on the original media.

✔ Be competent and trained.

✔ Document all aspects of the investigation.

✔ Designate one person or organization responsible for all aspects of the investigation.

Mobile phones and SIM cards

The area of mobile phone forensic acquisitions and extractions is one of the most difficult to stay trained in simply because of the rapidly changing nature of the industry and the wide array of nonstandard devices on the market. Constant training and studying keeps you up to date on the new technologies that are constantly coming out in the marketplace.

Despite all their differences, all mobile phones have three fundamental components:

✔ **Read Only Memory (ROM):** This area of memory on a mobile phone houses the operating system and, often, troubleshooting software to diagnose the device.

✔ **Random Access Memory (RAM):** This area of memory is often used to store data temporarily; if the mobile phone is turned off, all data is lost.

✔ **Data storage:** Although most mobile phones have internal storage capacity that's usually based on flash memory technology, most advanced mobile phone models come supplied with external memory card slots that expands the storage capacity of the device.

External storage often takes the form of MiniSD or MMC mobile cards that require special card readers. Most computer forensic tools treat these cards as regular personal computer storage devices and are accessed in much the same way.

Write-protect the USB port if the mobile phone includes a card reader that uses a USB interface.

The guidelines in this chapter are necessarily generic. Always follow your unique policies and procedures and test your forensic software before starting any investigation.

The cellular network

One of the first things you need to know is which type of cellular phone network system the mobile phone connects to:

✔ **Code Division Multiple Access (CDMA):** Designed by Qualcomm, this technology is in use primarily in the United States. The two primary cellular phone carriers in the United States are Sprint and Verizon.

The CDMA system doesn't have a separate Subscriber Identity Module (SIM) in the mobile device, which means all your data is stored on the mobile device.

✔ **Global System for Mobile Communication (GSM):** Designed by Ericsson and Nokia, this technology is in use primarily in Europe, but is also used in the United States by two major cellular phone carriers, Cingular and T-Mobile.

GSM systems have the SIM as a separate component designed to be portable from one mobile device to another. For the purposes of an investigator, this mean you have to analyze both the mobile device and the SIM card to get all the data.

✔ **Integrated Digital Enhanced Network (iDEN):** A proprietary system, developed by Motorola, that uses advanced SIM cards (USIMs) and is slated to replace both CDMA and GSM.

iDEN systems have the SIM as a separate component designed to be portable from one mobile device to another. As with a GSM system, you need to analyze both the USIM and the mobile device to find all data.

Always make finding the network the first step you take. The type of network determines which forensic tools you need in order to examine the mobile phone.

One aspect of mobile forensic investigations that's beyond the scope of this chapter is the investigation of the cellular network. Depending on which phone carrier you're working with, the amount and type of network data, such as cell site vectors, handoff information, and other timeline data, can be extremely helpful to your investigation. Check with your cellular network liaison to see what data is available and how the carrier can help you extract the data on its system.

The device you're investigating

After you determine which system the mobile phone works with, your next step is to determine which specific type of mobile phone you're working with. Your purpose isn't simply to know which type of mobile phone you're investigating, but rather the characteristics of that particular phone.

You can identify the mobile phone in a number of different ways:

- ✔ **Logos:** Manufacturing logos are often prominently displayed along with model numbers. Check the manufacturer's Web site for up-to-date information about the model you're working with.

- ✔ **Serial numbers:** Even within the same mobile phone model, changes affect the way you approach the investigation. Checking with the manufacturer about the characteristics of the mobile phone by way of a serial number often yields surprising results. You can find most serial numbers under the battery or somewhere around the battery compartment. You normally have to take the battery cover off to even begin looking for serial numbers. Unfortunately, some mobile devices don't have a serial number and you have to fall back on other methods of identification such as manufacturing codes.

- ✔ **Synchronization software:** You often see mobile phones paired with a suspect's personal computer. After you forensically extract the data from the personal computer, you can often find device information that gives you clues to which type of mobile phone you're investigating.

- ✔ **Manufacturing codes:** The following types of coded numbers can identify a phone's manufacturer, model, country code, and even serial number. As with the mobile device serial number, you often find these numbers in or around the battery compartment. Other places you find this information is in the operating system software of the mobile device.

  - *ESN:* Electronic Serial Number

  - *ICCID:* Integrated Circuit Card Identification

  - *IMEI:* International Mobile Equipment Identifier

  Check the Internet for online databases where you can look for detailed code information or contact the manufacturers.

Phone characteristics

After you know which type of mobile phone you're investigating, the important characteristics of the device are essentially listed by manufacturer, and you can see a list of areas in which to begin your search for evidence. The list of features the manufacturer has for the mobile device may differ radically from the reality of what is on the mobile device (due to user customization), but at least you can get a good idea of what to expect:

- ✔ **Wireless access methods:** Determine whether the device uses only cellular technology to communicate or can use Bluetooth, WiFi, or infrared technology.

- ✔ **Internet access:** Find out whether the device can be used to surf the Web, check e-mail, or participate in chat sessions.

- ✔ **Camera:** See whether the device has a camera, and then whether it takes still photos or videos.

- ✔ **Operating system:** Look to see whether the operating system is proprietary to the mobile phone.

- ✔ **Personal information manager (PIM):** PIMs vary in their components, but most have a calendar, address book, and full business productivity software.

- ✔ **Applications:** Find out which types of applications the mobile phone was supplied with, such as audio, video, word processing, spreadsheet, or financial.

- ✔ **Messaging:** Determine whether the device can send and receive text messages, multimedia, or e-mail messages.

- ✔ **Interface or cable:** Find out which type of cable is required in order to connect the mobile phone. Determine which kind of power connector you need in order to keep the device working, and whether a wireless interface is an option.

The areas where you actually find this information on the mobile device vary tremendously due to so many different standards (an oxymoron if there ever was one). For example, where you find messaging data on a Windows based mobile device differs from where you find messaging data on a regular proprietary Nokia phone.

The purpose of knowing which type of mobile phone you're investigating, and the characteristics that the mobile phone comes supplied with, is so that you can use the right mobile forensic tool for the right job.

If you're investigating a particularly sophisticated criminal, the mobile device may have been altered to hide data or increase security. In this situation, all your research on the device doesn't matter much because alterations essentially mean that you're working on a custom device. Your skill and resources dictate how well you extract the evidence you need. In some extreme cases, mobile forensic investigators have drilled down to the chip level to extract data from nonstandard mobile phones.

The SIM card

The Subscriber Identity Module (SIM),which works with GSM and iDEN networks, allows the user to move data and user authentication (proving to the phone network who you are) between mobile phone hardware as well as address book info and messaging. In other words, users can move from mobile phone to mobile phone by simply transferring SIM cards. What this means for you as the investigator is that a user may change phones, but they can still be tracked via the SIM. SIMs are 15 millimeters tall, 25 millimeters wide, and.76 millimeters thick. A typical SIM is shown in Figure 12-1.

Figure 12-1:
Typical SIM
card.

SIM cards have memory for addresses, messaging, and user settings along with proving who the user is to the physical mobile phone device.

Do not access the device using another SIM in order to avoid tainting evidence. Putting a different SIM into a suspect's mobile phone may change or even replace data automatically. Instead, clone the SIM or use forensic software to access the mobile device.

A SIM card often has a personal identification number (PIN) to protect the data on the cards as well as on the physical device. The PIN is usually between four and eight characters long and has a lockout feature that forces you to enter the correct PIN in a certain number of attempts. The usual number of attempts is set to three, but can vary depending on user settings. If you're locked out, the service provider can supply the PIN Unblocking Key (PUK) to help you gain access to the mobile phone.

If by some stroke of bad luck you mistype the PUK several times, the mobile device blocks you out *permanently*.

Personal digital assistants

Until recently, personal digital assistants (PDAs) were used as stand-alone devices by consumers to increase their productivity with scheduling, note taking, and other time-saving tools for their busy lives. Because most people don't want to look as though they're using Batman's utility belt (with its numerous separate devices — such as a PDA, mobile phone, or pager), these technologies have essentially merged into what are now termed *smart phones*. You're not going to encounter PDAs any more. When you run across a PDA, it's more likely a Palm OS, which is the most popular PDA platform still in existence without any major mobile phone support.

The considerations you take into account, such as isolating the device or using proper forensic software, for mobile phone devices also apply to PDA platforms. In reality, the only major difference now is that you cannot make a phone call on the Palm. All other functions (such as calendars, e-mail, wireless network functionality, and productivity software), however, are all the same as on high-end smart phones.

Digital cameras

Certain types of cases (such as child pornography) tend to involve photographic equipment in higher proportions than in other types of cases, such as bank fraud or drug trafficking. In cases where digital cameras are used, you *must* realize how these devices work in a forensic setting.

Modern-day digital cameras and video recorders are essentially the same device, whereas several years ago, still cameras and video cameras were separate technologies. The single biggest factor to keep in mind is that storage is the key when looking at digital cameras. Digital cameras that have small amounts of storage space tend to be still cameras, whereas digital cameras that have large amounts of storage space can do double duty as either still cameras or video cameras.

The sheer number of camera manufacturers now in the marketplace is astounding, but luckily for forensic investigators, the digital camera market has more or less standardized the way its equipment communicates. Most digital camera models use a standard or mini USB connection to interface with a computer to facilitate photo downloads, and digital cameras also use standard memory cards, such as MiniSD, or Compact Flash, to expand the storage capabilities on the digital camera.

The majority of current digital camera systems are viewed as just another storage device by both personal computers and forensic tools. In other words, when you plug in the camera, the computer treats the digital camera as just another drive where files can be accessed. This arrangement simplifies the situation dramatically for most investigators because they're now essentially working with regular computer forensic technology that's stable and well understood — unlike doing forensics on mobile phone models that tend to change rapidly.

Because you're investigating USB interfaces, you must enable the write-protect feature on your forensic computer operating system to keep from performing any writes that may potentially alter the data on the digital camera. This also applies if you're extracting data from either the internal memory or trying to access the digital camera external card storage by way of the USB port. If you're using a card reader to work on the storage memory cards directly, you must also use the USB write protection to keep to zero the number of writes to the memory card.

Digital audio recorders

Just like everything else in this fast-changing world, audio equipment has gone digital. Not only have tape recorders gone by the wayside, but personal audio players, such as iPods and MP3 players, have replaced anything that even resembles magnetic tape.

As with digital cameras, most digital audio devices are seen as storage devices by computers and forensic tools. You can upload and download not only music files but also any file that fits on the device. Modern-day audio players can often hold as much as 60GB of information, making them very large storage devices that often have hidden evidence stored there simply because most nontechnical-minded investigators don't check them for evidence.

You can treat digital audio recorders the same as any other static forensic storage device even though they are considered mobile devices.

Cutting-Edge Cellular Extractions

After you identify the phone and know with some certainty what evidence you're looking for and where it can be found, you have to choose which type of forensic tool can do the job you require. As in standard computer forensic acquisitions, the choice of whether to do your extractions in the field or in a lab environment also dictates the type of forensic tool you need.

Equipping for mobile forensics

Because the mobile forensic field is still fairly new, one forensic tool doesn't cover all situations. You need to have multiple tools handy to cover any areas where one tool is lacking. In certain cases, forensic tools cannot extract data and you have to rely on nonforensic software. If at all possible in those situations, understand thoroughly the implications and consequences of how nonforensic software may change the data you're working on.

Computer forensics generally falls into two types of acquisition types: physical and logical. Mobile forensic techniques follow the same format, but because a multitude of different mobile platforms exist, logical forensic acquisitions are by far the type most commonly performed. The obvious reason for this state of affairs is that the forensic software is using the operating system of the mobile device to help extract data. As the field matures, more and more physical acquisitions will take place. In fact, a physical acquisition is the preferred method because it extracts data not normally seen by the operating system.

The role of the forensic software is twofold:

- ✔ Keep the data from changing on the device you're extracting data from.
- ✔ Provide a mechanism to verify the integrity of the data you extract to mathematically prove that nothing has changed.

The mobile forensic field is primarily concerned with mobile phone data acquisition, and the tools described in the following sections reflect this trend. PDA tools are listed, but as time goes by the merging of mobile phone and PDA technologies virtually guarantees that forensic tools will work on both types of devices as they merge into one.

To further complicate matters, mobile phone technology now separates tools into GSM and CDMA acquisition types. In other words, some forensic tools work with only the handset or the SIM, whereas others can work with both handset and SIM investigations.

Integrated forensic tools that work with both handset and SIM are ideal; however, some forensic tools are specialized to handle either SIM or handset acquisitions. In fact, some forensic tools are so specialized that they work only with certain mobile devices or operating systems.

The tools in the following list work with both handset and SIM:

- ✔ **Paraben (www.paraben.com):** Paraben's mobile device suite of tools covers everything from Palm devices to Garmin GPS units. The primary Paraben workhorse in the mobile device area is its Device Seizure. Depending on the mobile unit, Device Seizure can extract data logically or physically, or both. The kit provides cables and a SIM card reader; it also gives you the ability to work with CDMA and GSM systems, and it has hash value capabilities.

- ✔ **Logicube (www.logicube.com):** CellDEK kit has the same capabilities as the Paraben system, with the addition of a rugged case to help facilitate field examinations and acquisitions. The cool thing about the CellDEK is that inside the case is a portable touch screen field computer that guides you according to which type of device you're working with.

- ✔ **Oxygen software (www.oxygensoftware.com):** Oxygen Forensic Suite 2, an outgrowth of PDA management software, has now grown into a complete mobile forensic investigative software suite. At last count, more than 500 mobile devices and operating systems were supported by Oxygen Forensic Suite 2.

The following list describes a couple of SIM mobile forensic tools:

- ✔ **Crownhill (www.crownhillmobile.com):** SIMIS has been used for several years (and has a good track record) to extract data from SIM cards and can extract data from newer USIMs. SIMIS can also extract information from satellite SIM cards from Irridium and Inmarsat.

- ✔ **InsideOut Forensics (www.simcon.no):** SIMCon extracts data from SIMs and USIMs forensically and also uses either MD5 or SHA1 hashing functions. All you need is a card reader, and the software does the rest. The interface and software are fairly easy to use and work in conjunction with Paraben's equipment.

Mobile forensic hardware

The type of forensic hardware you need varies slightly from the standard computer forensic tools you're used to. The reason is that you're working with wireless functionality and a wide range of device types.

Although this list describes the basic hardware you need, keep in mind that as your experience grows, so does your toolkit:

✔ **Faraday bag:** A Faraday bag keeps a mobile device from communicating with an external wireless device, by intercepting radio waves and effectively acting as a large, external antenna that redirects the radio energy away from the device. Faraday bags work to keep data from reaching the mobile device and keep the mobile device from transmitting any data outward. A Faraday bag can be as small as the device you're isolating to as large as a tent when you need to do field work and need to isolate the device and your acquisition equipment at the same time.

In the mobile forensic environment, isolating the device is of prime importance when you arrive on-scene. The last thing you need is the device synchronizing on its own by way of a wireless link and changing all kinds of data.

✔ **SIM card reader:** Found in any computer supply store, a card reader is used to read SIM and USIM cards without having to use the handset. Some card readers are built into the computer platform, and other card readers use a USB interface.

✔ **Cable connections:** With the multitude of mobile devices now on the market, having just one mobile device connector seriously hampers your ability to do an investigation. Different mobile device manufacturers have not only different data cable connections but also different power connection interfaces. At the top of your list should reside the standard USB cable followed by the USB cable with a mini-USB connection.

Securing the mobile device

In addition to following all other policies and procedures that you normally follow in the course of a regular computer forensic crime scene investigation (see Chapter 5), your first priority when investigating a mobile device is to isolate the mobile device from its wireless network. You want to isolate not only the device from its cellular phone service (if it's a mobile phone) but also the device from Bluetooth devices, WiFi networks, and infrared devices. At all costs, you must keep new data from contaminating the mobile device after it has been seized, for a couple of reasons:

✔ **For practicality:** You don't want the new information to overwrite or eliminate the evidence already on the device.

✔ **For security:** Mechanisms in the wild allow users to remotely lock or destroy mobile device data.

✔ **For legality:** The courts may not view as admissible evidence the evidence added to the mobile device after you seized it.

You can isolate the mobile device in several ways:

- ✔ **Isolate its wireless features:** By using a Faraday bag or jamming device, you can isolate the device until the moment the battery dies.

  Most devices increase their signal strength in an attempt to connect, so this process shortens battery life considerably.

- ✔ **Power off the device:** This method definitely isolates the phone, but isn't recommended, because a security protocol on the phone may be enabled when you turn it back on.

- ✔ **Put the device in Airplane mode:** This feature on some smart phones is designed to turn off the radio within wireless devices. Users can use their devices in aircraft without violating FAA rules. The drawback is that you have to interact with the device before doing your forensic work, and you may accidentally change data.

After you isolate the mobile device, you must keep its batteries charged so that you don't lose any data in its RAM. You can charge the device with a regular 120V charger, but you should use a mobile charger, just to be sure. Keep in mind that you're also keeping the mobile device isolated, so using a charger may increase the risk of defeating your isolation protocol.

Keep seized mobile devices powered on if they're already on, and keep seized devices turned off if they're powered down. The policies and procedures you follow depend heavily on your organization's needs, but you can follow several guides from either the National Institute of Standards and Technology (NIST) at www.nist.gov or the Association of Chief Police Officers (ACPO) at www.acpo.police.uk. Both organizations have basic policies and procedures on which you can model yours.

Finding mobile data

After you isolate the mobile device and the batteries are fully charged, your next step is to find the data you're looking for. Depending on whether you're working with a SIM or a handset, the procedures to extract data or create an image vary slightly.

If you're working with a SIM card, first clone the card. If you can't, you can still use forensic software to image or extract data using a card reader, as long as you use mobile forensic software to ensure that no writes to the SIM card take place. If you can clone the SIM, your option to use nonforensic software to view the SIM contents poses no risk of changing the original data.

After you image or extract the data for analysis, the forensic software usually has an automated search-and-retrieve function to extract the data you're looking for. The functions to do the search vary by software program, but the concepts and reporting are the same among all major mobile forensic software packages.

When you extract or image the data from a handset, the procedures are the same as in the SIM extraction; however, you're adding the extra step of figuring out how to connect the mobile device to your forensic equipment. Using either a docking station that comes with the device or cables is usually the quickest and most reliable method. Using Bluetooth or infrared wireless communication is also an option but can be problematic because of interference or protocol issues such as accidentally changing data on the suspect media. Whichever manner you choose, make sure that your write protection protocols are in place to minimize the chance of a write to the device.

Examining a smart phone step-by-step

Using Paraben's Device Seizure product, the following steps illustrate the basic idea of how the process works when using mobile device forensic tools. The most difficult part is ensuring that the forensic software recognizes the device. Luckily for you, Paraben automates much of the guesswork!

1. **Isolate the device.**

   In the lab environment, the analysis room is effectively a shield from outside radio interference. Otherwise, contain the phone in a Faraday bag or at least turn off the phone by way of the Airplane mode switch (if it has one).

2. **Identify the device.**

   For example, if the phone is a smart phone that has been in the marketplace for several years and uses a USB port to synchronize to the computer, make a quick Internet search for information about the model. When you know which operating system it has, you have enough information to start.

3. **Connect the device.**

   If your device uses a USB port to connect to desktop computers, write-protect the USB before connecting the smart phone. The Paraben write-protection features are built-in, but write-protecting the USB port is a prudent step (see Chapter 6). If the computer forensic software has problems connecting due to the write block, you may have to enable the USB port and risk making a write to the device. As long as you can justify a possible write and document your procedures, however, the risk should be minimal.

   A wizard opens to help you acquire the data.

4. Choose the correct operating system from the list and click Next.

Figure 12-2 shows the list of devices you can choose from. For example, if the operating system is Windows Mobile version 5, you choose that one from the drop-down menu.

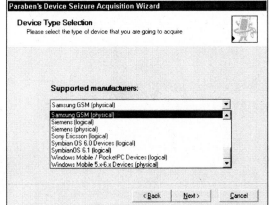

Figure 12-2:
Selecting
a Paraben
device type.

5. Choose to capture a physical image (see Figure 12-3) and then click Next.

You want to acquire a physical image rather than a logical image, so every memory register is part of the image, and not just the parts that the operating system can view. If you read through the tips and warnings of various mobile forensic software packages, you notice that they warn that a small file can be written to the device during a physical acquisition. Paraben is no exception, but it also clarifies or explains that the file is written to an area where no data is usually present.

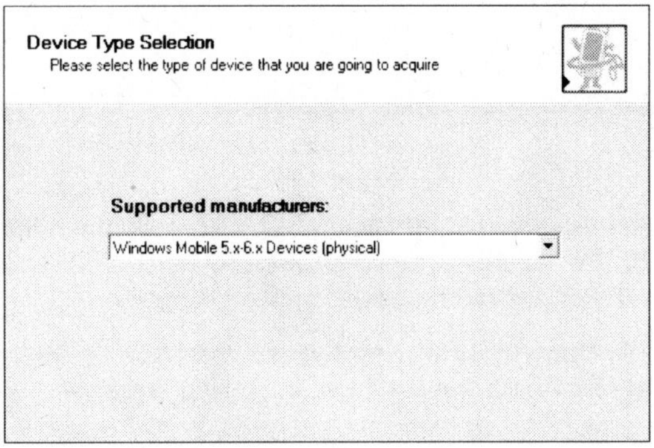

Figure 12-3:
Selecting
a Paraben
device
type for
Windows
Mobile.

Device Type Selection
Please select the type of device that you are going to acquire

Supported manufacturers:

Windows Mobile 5.x-6.x Devices (physical)

6. Select the model type of the device, as shown in Figure 12-4.

Paraben provides an auto-detect feature to automate the process for you. Essentially, the software queries the mobile device and recognizes the model, much like Windows does with its plug-and-play protocol.

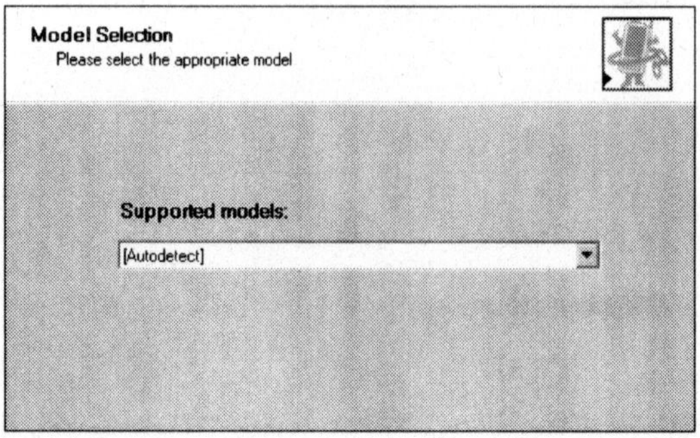

Model Selection
Please select the appropriate model

Supported models:

[Autodetect]

Figure 12-4:
Selecting
a mobile
device
model.

After the forensic software determines the device type and model, the software begins the forensic acquisition. In Figure 12-5, Paraben is reading the memory registers and creating an image.

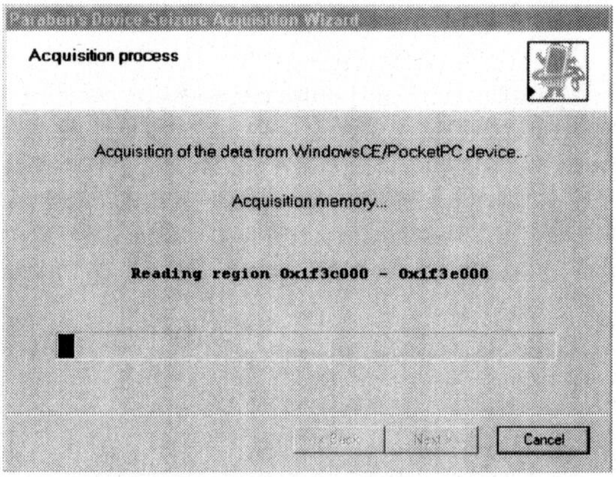

Paraben's Device Seizure Acquisition Wizard

Acquisition process

Acquisition of the data from WindowsCE/PocketPC device..

Acquisition memory...

Reading region 0x1f3c000 - 0x1f3e000

< Back   Next >   Cancel

Figure 12-5:
Acquiring
the image.

Depending on the device size and speed, the acquisition can take minutes or hours. In the case of smart phones, the acquisition usually takes much longer than it does on standard mobile phones.

Figure 12-6 shows the partitions and file structure of a smart phone after acquisition. You can begin the analysis and treat the case just like any other forensic case. Most phones are essentially just a small Windows computer with the same general file structure as a desktop computer.

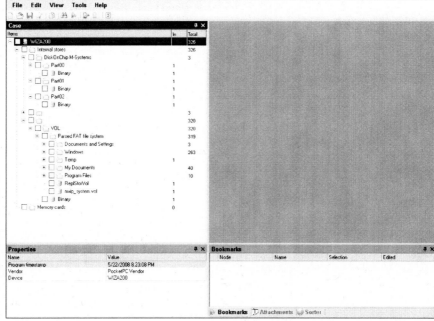

Figure 12-6:
This acquired image shows partitions and file structure.

7. **Prepare the mobile device data for case presentation.**

The data you find and extract that supports your case is treated in the same manner as any other computer forensic evidence. You must ensure that your report is accurate, concise, and unbiased and is documented from start to finish. Most, if not all, mobile forensic software tools have report functions built in to make it possible, and easy, to create reports for presentation in the courts.

Chapter 13

Network Forensics

*I*f computer forensics is a new field in the computer business, network forensics is in its infancy. Two changes have ignited the field of network forensics: Network forensics technology and its methods are now well understood by more than just hard-core network administrators, and storage device costs are affordable. Terabytes of data can now be stored on a network without breaking the storage bank.

Networks are high-volume traffic connections, which makes network forensic investigations challenging. Finding the right network forensic tool for your specific situation may be difficult, but it's not impossible if you have the right guidance. Working with network forensic tools is a complex process, but they make your job easy (or at least easier) by automating most data acquisition tasks. You still need to know, and the judge expects you to know, the general principles behind the use of these complex forensic tools.

Just as computer forensics has its roots in data recovery, network forensics is rooted in network security and intrusion detection. Network forensics deals with data that changes from millisecond to millisecond. Investigations of cyberattacks or intrusions are network forensic investigations. The major challenge you face is how to contain the intrusion while preserving the evidence for later study or use in court.

Mobilizing Network Forensic Power

Even though most systems (such as an IDS or IPS) can track and record network data, you should still take the extra step to add a forensic component to a network system. A forensic component to any system adds depth to your investigation; you can then use forensic tools, such as a timeline analysis, e-mail reconstruction, metadata analysis, packet/frame analysis, or a checksum (to show mathematically that no data has changed from the time it was captured).

The second and less-well-known area of network forensics is the subset of forensic software, which applies these concepts to a network by way of static forensic technology. In simple terms: You can conduct a computer forensic investigation over a network connection and not necessarily have physical access to the suspect computer. Essentially, you can make a forensic image of the suspect computer over a network connection and not even leave your computer forensic lab. The beauty of this situation is that you can investigate a computer in Dubai but be seated in Florida and not have to spend hours traveling in order to physically image the computer.

Although imaging a computer forensically is possible now from a technological point of view, make sure that your legal department allows you to image a computer based on where the suspect computer is physically located. Some countries have strict laws regarding how data is treated in their respective countries, and violating those laws can cause you anything from headaches to possible jail time.

Identifying Network Components

To understand how forensic systems work on networks, you need a thorough understanding of the way networks do their job and the types of equipment you find in a typical network. The good news is that network hardware has been standardized to a large degree, which makes understanding and investigating networks a whole lot simpler than it was in the past! This list describes the types of equipment you may find on a typical network:

✔ **Router:** A special-purpose computer that moves data across networks. Think of the router as the road or bridge between two cities.

A router primarily uses IP addresses to move data; you occasionally hear someone refer to a router as a Layer 3 switch, which refers to the layer in the Open Systems Interconnection Model (OSI) that routers primarily work in. At a networking level, you're dealing with the logical topology of a network, which is where you find the IP address design.

✔ **Switch:** A network component that uses the Media Access Control (MAC) identification of a host on a network to move traffic within a network. Think of a switch as the road or bridge within the city that connects the different parts of town.

People often refer to this type of switch as a Layer 2 switch, which is the OSI model layer in which it operates, or a multiport network bridge because the original use of Layer 2 devices was to bridge network segments. Switches can also consist of other types of network traffic management devices at other OSI layers and specific computer applications, but most networks use the Layer 2 switch as an accepted standard.

✔ **Hub:** The core piece of network equipment. Its only function is to repeat any signal received on any port and repeat the signal to all ports on the hub. A hub — simple device that it is — works at only Layer 1 of the OSI model because no addressing scheme exists at Layer 1.

Hubs aren't used as often in networks now because switches are much more efficient at moving data, but you occasionally find them. Just remember that hubs tend to increase traffic volume and slow down a network!

✔ **Network interface card (NIC):** A device that usually holds the MAC (Media Access Control) address of your computer that uniquely identifies your host or computer. The NIC is the physical bridge between the network and the host. If you see on the back of your computer a wire with an oversized phone jack and blinking lights, it's your NIC.

✔ **Host:** Any computing device, attached to a network, that has some form of addressing, whether it's an IP address or a MAC address. Because most hosts need to connect over a network, IP and MAC addressing can handle all addressing needs. Your computer is an obvious host, but network printers are also hosts; they usually have an IP address and a MAC address. Network copiers, laptops, PDAs, wireless access points (WAPs), network storage devices, network cameras, routers, switches, and even many mobile devices, such as a mobile phone or an iPod, also have identifying IP and MAC addresses.

✔ **Media:** An often overlooked part of a network that is the component that literally holds the network together. Media can take the form of copper-based wiring, fiber optic cables, or radio waves. You may need to connect your equipment to a network, and different media often have different protocols or services that are unique to them, which always helps when creating timelines or tying data to a suspect.

Looking at the Open Systems Interconnection Model (OSI)

The *Open Systems Interconnection Model (OSI)* is a network layer model designed to help people who are new to the inner workings of networks understand the different aspects of networks in a layered abstract form as well as being used as a reference by veterans in the field. Originally, the OSI model was released with an OSI protocol, but the protocol was abandoned in favor of the TCP/IP protocol. Although the model is somewhat dated and the protocol isn't used in real world networks, it's used as a training tool by technical schools and technology companies to help people who are new to the field to understand the complexities of networks in an organized and structured manner.

The layers of the OSI model are described in this list:

✔ **Application (Layer 7):** The top layer of the model contains services, such as file transfer protocol (FTP), HyperText Transfer Protocol (HTTP), and domain name system protocol (DNS), that support applications such as Web pages or e-mail. This layer contains not the applications but only the services or protocols that support the applications.

✔ **Presentation (Layer 6):** This layer works with the format and compatibility of data within the context of the operating system. It converts formats to accommodate the application-level services and protocols so that they can understand the file structure. This level also handles encryption and compression chores.

✔ **Session (Layer 5):** The session layer establishes and maintains the connections between two applications. This layer works in support of applications with protocols such as remote procedure calls (RPC), but doesn't regulate how the data flows across the network itself. This layer is considered the bottom of the application support area of the OSI model.

✔ **Transport (Layer 4):** This layer begins the process (from the application point of view) of connecting the hosts where each application resides. This layer allows two computers to communicate above the network level but below the application level. It typically handles error correction and flow control of data between the hosts. Think of this layer as a post office: The post office (transport layer) acts as the mechanism to ensure delivery of mail from one house (host) to another house (host).

✔ **Network (Layer 3):** The network layer is used primarily to route data on a network. This layer is where you find the logical address structures of networks, such as IP addresses. The router domains reside on this layer, and it's the primary means of moving data from one network to another.

Data link (Layer 2): The data link layer sends and receives data from a host by way of the network media. The addressing type used at this layer, the Media Access Control (MAC) address, is unique to every single host. Whereas the network layer handles network-to-network connections, the data link layer handles host-to-host or node-to-node connections by way of the MAC address. Protocols such as Ethernet and Token Ring work at this level.

Physical (Layer 1): The physical layer concerns itself with the raw data as it crosses a network. The data is essentially a set of electrical signals, light pulses, or radio frequency waves depending on whether the network is based on copper, fiber optic, or wireless technology. Because no addressing scheme exists at this level, all devices or equipment at this level move data without regard to protocols, services, or addresses. The highway system you use every day when you drive your car works on the same concept as Layer 1: The highway is designed to get you (the binary data) from one location to another as quickly and safely as possible without knowing exactly where you came from or where you are going.

Cooperating with secret agents and controlling servers

Although sometimes people associate the high-tech gadgets used in computer forensics as secret-agent tools designed to save the world from the latest bad guy who wants to take over the world, the truth is that the gadgets used by most computer forensic investigators more closely resemble the ones used by Geek Squad technicians than by Agent 007.

The basic structure of how a network forensic system works is based on the framework of a client/server network system. A client/server network works this way: One computer holds or has all the data (the server), and another computer is connected to the server to either send or receive data (the client).

In the case of network forensics, the client/server model is tweaked a bit. Rather than a client communicating with a server, an *agent* or *sensor* communicates with the server. Regardless of what these software programs are called, they relay information to the server to report on whatever task the programs are programmed to do. In the case of network forensic agents, the data that's sent back has additional safeguards to ensure that the data hasn't changed in transit and to determine whether the data is good data or labeled as suspect.

From a technical standpoint, *agents* are usually deployed within host systems, whereas *sensors* are deployed on network equipment, such as switches and routers.

Figure 13-1 shows the basic structure of how a network forensic framework is constructed.

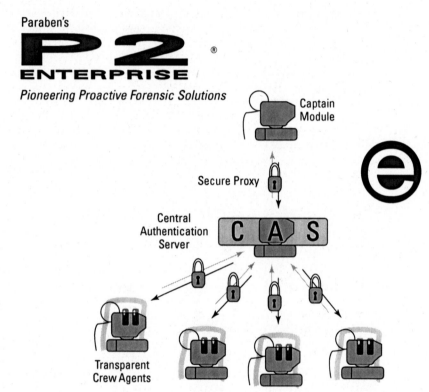

Figure 13-1:
Basic
structure of
a network
forensic
system
based on
Paraben's
Enterprise
system.

Using Paraben's diagram, the basic structure of network forensic tools is broken into three basic levels:

✔ **Command-and-control server:** The command-and-control server controls the operation of the network forensic apparatus. In most cases, this server has a GUI software package that lets you interface with all aspects of the forensic system and is the administrative authority of all aspects of the network forensic system. From this server, you can deploy software agents, set up acquisition parameters, acquire an image, and perform many other jobs in between. In the case of Paraben, the command-and-control server is the Captain module.

The connection between the command-and-control server and the other parts of the forensic network is completely encrypted and secured. Think of the command-and-control server as the conductor in an orchestra trying to keep everyone on the same sheet of music.

✔ **Storage:** The storage server is basically a data repository for all the data taken from all sources on the network. Data taken from agents or sensors is tested or authenticated forensically by using tools such as hash values or other types of data check values and then stored. In Paraben's system, the storage server is the central authentication server.

Because storing large amounts of data is no simple affair, the use of large databases such as Microsoft SQL is highly recommended because they're designed for large amounts of data. Later in this chapter, in the section "Figuring out where to store all those bytes," we discuss how much storage you need.

✔ **Agents:** The front lines of any network forensic system consist of the agents you deploy across the network. Most software agents are 200 kilobytes (K) or smaller and work in stealth mode, to avoid being seen by users and to capture all data, including some not normally seen by the operating system, such as the volume slack of a storage device. Paraben software agents are called crew agents.

Figure 13-2 shows the list of processes running on a typical computer. The forensic agent software can be disguised as any one of the programs listed, and the user has no idea that anything out of the ordinary is running on the system. The forensic software typically runs under the name svchost.exe, but as you can see, several instances of the file exist, and you have no way to tell which one is the forensic agent. Forensic agents typically send their data encrypted — maybe even randomized — to further disguise the data payloads as well as hide the data traffic from knowledgeable users.

Figure 13-2:
Typical
list of
processes
running on
a Windows
computer.

Image Name	User Name	CPU	Mem Usage
svchost.exe	SYSTEM	00	27,920 K
MsMpEng.exe	SYSTEM	00	35,512 K
iexplore.exe	Rey	00	8,596 K
svchost.exe	NETWORK SERVICE	00	4,480 K
svchost.exe	SYSTEM	00	4,716 K
lsass.exe	SYSTEM	00	1,296 K
services.exe	SYSTEM	00	3,388 K
WINWORD.EXE	Rey	00	19,668 K
winlogon.exe	SYSTEM	00	1,308 K
csrss.exe	SYSTEM	00	4,528 K
smss.exe	SYSTEM	00	384 K
GoogleUpdaterSe...	SYSTEM	00	144 K
BRSS01A.EXE	SYSTEM	00	2,084 K
spoolsv.exe	SYSTEM	00	6,232 K
BRSVC01A.EXE	SYSTEM	00	1,232 K
svchost.exe	LOCAL SERVICE	00	3,132 K
System	SYSTEM	02	264 K
System Idle Process	SYSTEM	82	16 K

If the data request is too large to go unnoticed, configure the forensic software to run at times when the network traffic is relatively slow, to keep network slowdowns to a minimum.

Saving Network Data

The majority of network devices are standardized to interoperate with other network devices without causing too many headaches for network administrators. But within each type of network device (such as a router, switch, or host), an infinite number of varieties, configurations, and capabilities exist that you have to contend with.

You may be wondering what type of information you can get from network components. You have to look at each type of network component or OSI layer it serves to find specific types of data.

Categorizing the data

The type of data you can find on a network forensic installation ranges from hard drive images to logs of the perimeter router. The type of data you collect is determined in large part by the focus of your unique needs — whether the system you put in place is designed to manage internal threats, such as industrial espionage or theft, to a system designed to track information from the network itself during an external threat or break-in.

You can collect data from these devices:

✔ **Host:** Regular computer forensic acquisitions, such as storage device images, RAM contents, and any static evidence physically located within reach of the agent, can be transmitted over the network to your forensic server. In addition to collecting standard forensic data (storage device images), you can usually have the agent collect real-time data that's picked up by the network interface card and archive the data stream for future study.

Hosts are not only workstations but also the servers on your network, such as e-mail, file, print, and database servers.

✔ **Router:** A router is designed primarily to move data between networks, so keeping track of data that may be used as evidence is somewhat low on the priority list of jobs for most routers. The type of information you can find on a router is related more to logs than to the storage of detailed network conversations. Router logs may contain errors that occur during a routing process, status details of router components, such as the interfaces, or even suspicious activity, depending on how the logs are configured. Routers also keep tables of IP and MAC addresses that resolve to other networks or hosts. Routers may act as firewalls, but in reality firewalls are usually treated as separate network components.

✔ **Firewall:** Firewalls keep detailed logs of activity that's occurring on its system. They keep logs on activity such as recognized attacks, dropped packets, applications that are allowed in or out, and sources of suspicious activity such as IPs, and they even tell you which protocols or services tried to break in.

✔ **Switch:** Information on network switches can be found in the content addressable memory (CAM), where the mapping of a MAC address to a specific port is located in addition to information about the virtual local area network (VLAN). Switches aren't designed to handle data logs because they have little in the way of extra processing capability or memory capacity, but they're useful platforms for adding network taps or mirrors in order to copy data streams in real-time.

✔ **Intrusion-detection system (IDS):** An IDS logs everything that's deemed even mildly suspicious. One purpose of an IDS is to log an event for further study in order to keep that event from happening again. Here's a list of items that an IDS may log:

- Port scans

- Traffic coming in on strange ports or protocols

- Recognized threats, such as worms or viruses attempting to enter the network

- Anonymous attempts at using FTP or other services on the network

- Originating IP addresses of attacks

- Bandwidth usage

IDSs are designed to be passive and are considered the burglar alarms of the computer world.

✔ **Intrusion-prevention system (IPS):** An IPS works to block or shut down any perceived threat on the network. An IPS logs many of the same events that an IDS does, but its main task is to analyze the data in the network in *real-time* to scan that data for threats. (An IPS not only calls the police but also barricades the door!)

✔ **Network printer:** Often overlooked as network devices with the capability to store information, printers often have logs showing print jobs with the associated metadata. Modern network printers use Linux and Mac OS X as operating systems, so you can put an agent on a network printer to capture its data.

✔ **Network copier:** Related to the network printer, network copiers also keep logs of what has been copied or printed.

✔ **Wireless access point (WAP):** A WAP logs everything a normal cabled router logs, with the addition of wireless-specific information, such as SSIDs and incoming connections.

Make sure that the network forensic package you use can read the log information of your particular network equipment. No standard methods exist for creating or maintaining logs that manufacturers follow. Each manufacturer creates its own method of how, what, where, and whether to log information that comes across the device. For example, the popular Snort IDS can interpret almost 1,000 different log types.

Figuring out where to store all those bytes

As you can probably imagine, the amount of data that crosses even a small network is substantial in terms of the storage space required in order to archive it and the amount of bandwidth required to transport the data to the storage media. From a logistical point of view, one limiting factor faced by security or forensic professionals is how much data can be stored. The answer to this question determines whether your system uses agents and sensors to analyze network data in real-time, and thus save only data deemed suspect, or your system archives every single bit for later in-depth analysis.

If your choice is limited by storage space, the option of real-time analysis to extract only suspect data saves you quite a bit of room because your data storage requirements are somewhat small. In this scenario, the agents or sensors alert you to suspicious activity and forward only that limited data, which reduces the storage load on your system.

If you have the ability to set up large storage areas, the storage options in the following sections are good options to consider.

Storage area network (SAN)

Storage area networks (SAN) are a separate network consisting of devices dedicated to data storage. The concept is rather simple, but the implementation of SAN systems is often complex because these systems can rival the size of the network, which can compromise the regular organizational network. SAN systems often have their own protocols and network operating system, to cope with the large amounts of data and the way the data is saved and accessed by other components of the network.

Most implementations of a SAN aren't done for security or forensic purposes at this point, but rather are implemented as a way to offload the storage of large amounts of data from servers to a centralized secure network. For example, a large organization such as the US government might use a SAN for its disaster recovery and database needs. The field of disaster recovery and regulations such as the Sarbanes-Oxley Act have accelerated the implementation of SAN architecture to the point where SAN manufacturers have standardized almost all components within a SAN environment. As an outgrowth of liability issues and regulations, in addition to Sarbanes-Oxley, organizations are looking at these networks not so much as costly investments but rather as liability-reducing mechanisms. It's only a matter of time until SANs are implemented solely for the purpose of security and forensic applications.

Figure 13-3 shows a typical SAN system like those that are centrally located in a server room. SAN systems can be located locally or, in the case of disaster recovery, hundreds or thousands of miles away, but are still seen as local storage devices.

Figure 13-3:
A typical SAN system usually located in a server room.

Network attached storage (NAS)

A network attached storage (NAS) system connects to the network with file level protocols such as NFS or Samba. You can strip a NAS system to be a server dedicated to nothing more than storage access, much like a normal file server but with even less general-purpose functionality. (In other words you can't play Solitaire on it.)

Because a NAS system works on existing file level protocols, its implementation is easier than a SAN architecture. Home users can even deploy a NAS system to handle all the storage issues associated with large multimedia files or other large files. It isn't uncommon to find a NAS system on the consumer market for the same price as a USB external drive. Figure 13-4 shows a prime example of a consumer-level NAS device that you plug into your home network.

Figure 13-4: A home- or consumer-rated NAS system.

Direct attached storage (DAS)

Unlike a SAN or NAS, a direct attached storage (DAS) system is nonnetworked storage. A DAS system connects to the server that's entering or extracting the data. It just extends the storage capability of the server by literally attaching another computer that's solely dedicated to storage. DAS systems are extremely fast because they have no network structure to contend with, but suffer from not being able to share storage space with other servers except for its directly connected host.

Small- to medium-size organizations usually start with a DAS system because it doesn't require massive amounts of network changes or structure and is usually enough to handle a typical data load of that size. In addition, the DAS can be physically located in the same room as the IDS or forensic computer, which makes it easier logistically to maintain the DAS.

Re-Creating an Event from Traffic

Most network forensic tools analyze and reconstruct data events for you with no problem, but you still must understand the basic concepts of what is occurring. You can always count on an attorney to ask you how the forensic system found and re-created the event in question. If you can answer that question in at the least the broadest sense, you're miles ahead of the poor expert witness who can only say he clicked the Run button.

Analyzing time stamps

The first step you should take in any network investigation is correlating the time stamps from all your network devices. If you cannot establish a baseline from which to compare your data time stamps, your case is hard to prove.

Establishing a time stamp can become complicated rather quickly. Fortunately for you, Dave Mills of the University of Delaware created a way to synchronize all devices on a network and eliminate the headaches of manually setting every network component's time function. We don't discuss the complex algorithms of how the Network Time Protocol (NTP) works, but the basic function of NTP is to keep all network components accurate within milliseconds of Coordinated Universal Time (UTC).

ITU or CUT? No, it's UTC

You probably noticed that the acronym for Coordinated Universal Time is UTC and not CUT. An international group of experts in the field of time management (not the expert group on managing your time to make you more efficient) working within the International Telecommunications Union (ITU) couldn't reach an agreement about using the English version, Coordinated Universal Time (CUT), or the French version Temps Universel Coordonné (TUC). After much discussion, a compromise was reached to shuffle the letters around to read UTC. So, Coordinated Universal Time or Temps Universel Coordonné — each one has the acronym UTC. *Vive la difference!*

UTC replaced Greenwich Mean Time (GMT) in 1972 as the standard to determine time in applications, such as computers or aviation, that required a clear-cut time stamp. The problem around the world with telling time is that so many time zones — and variations within time zones — exist, with factors such as daylight savings time, that differentiating local time zones can be confusing. Most airlines use local time stamps, and if you aren't paying attention, you can be completely confused when you land in a new time zone. Luckily, pilots use UTC (also called Zulu time) when they fly around the world, to eliminate any confusion.

In the case of network components, the UTC time stamp ensures that a network is accurate to within milliseconds of any other network component. This accuracy isn't necessary just because computer geeks like to be accurate, but rather because network communication relies on accurate time stamps to function correctly, such as in high-speed synchronous networks. (Other areas, such as financial software, business communication, military applications, and even broadcast television, now also require accurate computer network time stamps to function correctly.) Because networks are relatively accurate at keeping time, your job is much easier because a third-party verifies the data time stamps. Figures 13-5, 13-6, and 13-7 show the progression of time stamps on a small section of a larger data stream.

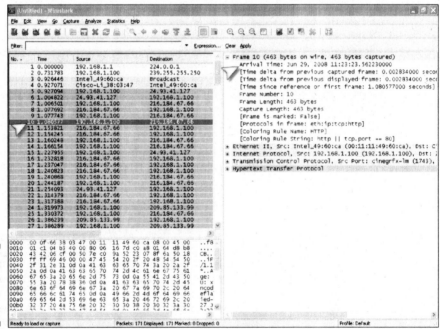

Figure 13-5:
Time stamp located in a packet.

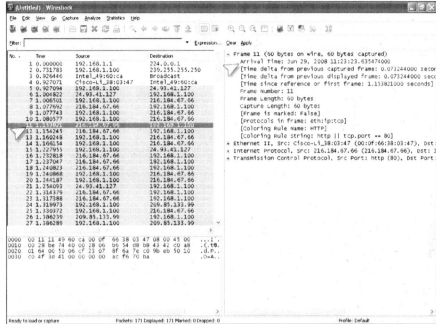

Figure 13-6:
Second packet in a data stream with a new time stamp.

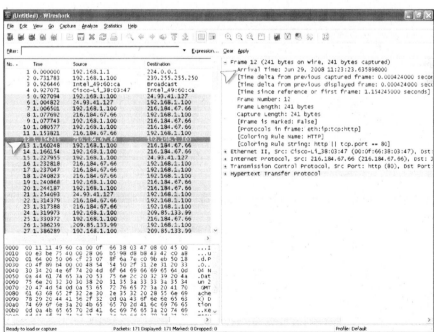

Figure 13-7:
Third packet in the sequence with a new time stamp.

Notice that the time stamps change in spans of only milliseconds, and if NTP or another synchronization method is working on your network, as shown in Figure 13-8, you know that the time stamps are accurate as checked by a third party. The time stamps aren't in UTC format because the operating system changed them to reflect the local time zone. If your computer is synchronized with a third-party system that uses local time stamps, the best solution is to document how many time zone offsets you are from UTC and use that number as a basis to establish your UTC. For example, the time synchronization stamp in Figure 13-8 shows the local time as 11:45 a.m. You know that the time zone is UTC-6 or US Central Time, so in order to convert this time to UTC, all you have to do is add six hours to the time to make it UTC. For local time cases, this may not be necessary, but for international cases, you must set up a timeline that makes sense.

Figure 13-8:
Network
time syn-
chronization
method
used by
Microsoft
Windows.

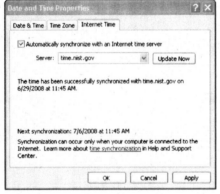

Putting together a data sequence

With billions of data packets traveling on a network, how does a network component keep track of that data? The simple answer is that network components only care about where the data is going and to a lesser extent where it came from. The hosts on the network are in charge of knowing what is contained within the data stream and how to make sense of all that data. Some network components dealing with security may analyze data to look for suspect data, but the bulk of the work — making sense of the data — is done by the hosts on the network.

Various protocols allow hosts to make sense of data streams, but the de facto standard is Transmission Control Protocol/ Internet Protocol (TCP/IP). It breaks up the data into pieces for transport over a network and then reassembles the pieces after traversing the network by the receiving host.

The magic behind this form of transport across a network is the use of sequence numbers and acknowledgment numbers. The network breaks the data into smaller pieces *(packets)* for easy transport, and the packets are then reassembled. But many packets often take different paths and arrive out of order to the destination host, so reassembling the data can be tricky. To work around this problem, TCP/IP has a numbering system based on sequence numbers that tell the receiving host the order of the packets.

Figure 13-9 shows an expanded view of the packet and the location of the sequence numbers. TCP/IP uses the acknowledgement numbers listed underneath the sequence numbers to let the sending host know that the receiving host received the packets. You can then rebuild entire network conversations with this information.

Figure 13-10 shows a data stream that has been pulled off the network wire. It was captured and assembled without needing to be at the receiving host's side. In Figure 13-10, you can even see time stamps in GMT (UTC) from the various servers that the data has originated from or passed through, giving you further clues to work with.

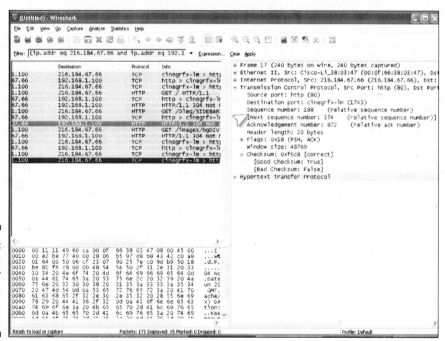

Figure 13-9:
Sequence number location in a typical data packet.

Figure 13-10:
Reassembled data stream based on protocols and sequence numbers.

Spotting different data streams

One way in which you can differentiate one data stream from another is to look at the protocol in which the data has been sent. The number of protocols in existence on networks is quite extensive, but most manufacturers and software companies use standard protocols to ensure compatibility among them. The basic idea is that protocols are similar to human languages in that each protocol is a language all its own. Imagine sitting on a street corner in New York City and listening to passers-by speaking dozens of foreign languages, and you get the idea of what it's like to listen to a network with dozens of protocols going by.

The following list describes some common protocols that you find on networks from an application standpoint:

- **Address resolution protocol (ARP):** Helps a host find a MAC address based on the IP address of another host.

- **Internet control message protocol (ICMP):** Sends error and informational messages through the Internet. Ping and trace route, for example, use this protocol to do their work.

- **Internet protocol security (IPSec):** A security protocol that encrypts or authenticates packets of data.

- **BitTorrent:** Used by a peer-to-peer network to move large amounts of data.

- **Domain name system (DNS):** Used by networks to translate IP addresses into human-readable names.

✔ **Dynamic host configuration protocol (DHCP):** Used by a host to acquire IP addresses on a network.

✔ **File transfer protocol (FTP):** Helps data traverse a network from one host to another.

✔ **HyperText Transfer Protocol (HTTP):** Transports data, such as Web pages, from one host to another.

✔ **Internet message access protocol (IMAP):** Used in e-mail systems.

✔ **Network time protocol (NTP):** Synchronizes network devices to UTC time.

✔ **Post office protocol version 3 (POP3):** An e-mail protocol that retrieves e-mail on a network.

✔ **Secure shell (SSH):** Creates a secure channel between hosts on a network.

✔ **Simple mail transfer protocol (SMTP):** E-mail protocol used to send e-mail on a network.

Looking at Network Forensic Tools

In addition to gathering data from network component logs, network tools exist that can either gather data from your existing network equipment or be installed in your network specifically to gather information directly off the wire.

The devices in the following sections record entire data streams, not just suspect data, directly from a network.

Test Access Port (TAP)

Network test access ports (TAPs) are essential in switched network environments because using network hubs isn't a good idea. Because network switches switch data only between ports that are actively communicating, rather than switch every port (such as a hub), the problem becomes how to view all traffic going into and out of a switch across all ports.

Network TAPs solve this problem by inserting themselves directly onto the network media; they can view all traffic headed to and from the switch. Computer network TAPs work in the same fashion as phone taps: You make a copy of the entire data flow while the flow of data continues to its original destination.

A network TAP is considered a high-speed, three-way hub in many ways:

✔ TAPs don't need addresses, such as IPs or MACs, because they're only copying information and aren't actually addressable network devices.

- ✔ TAPs copy everything from malformed data packets to VLAN information because the TAP copies everything at Layer 1 of the OSI model (essentially the bit level).

- ✔ Because a TAP is essentially a network splice, no major network topology or infrastructure changes need to be made, and you can install one in a matter of minutes.

TAPs are commonly used on copper-based networks, but other types of network media also have network TAPs designed for them. These other types include fiber optic and even wide-area network (WAN) equipment often used by the major telephone companies.

Another useful feature is its full duplex network — it allows you to copy both sides of the conversation on a network. In the old days, some networks worked in half duplex mode, where one computer transmitted and the other one waited until the first one finished. After the first computer finished transmitting, the second one responded. This system worked well with slow networks, but on superfast networks a half duplex system creates a huge bottleneck. Because network TAPs can see both sides of the conversation, they can record everything, whereas other types of network copying tend to see only half the conversation.

From a network security perspective, network TAPs are also useful because they're invisible to almost anyone on the network. The problem with firewalls and routers is that they require addresses of some sort to perform their network functions and are vulnerable to attack simply because you can see them. A network TAP is essentially invisible. If someone happened to notice the incredibly miniscule data delay, a physical device that has no address and runs on the power of the data network it is copying can't be attacked.

Here are two downside of TAPs:

- ✔ **They copy everything.**

  Unless you have a very good filter or massive amounts of storage space, your network forensic system or IDS gets full very quickly.

- ✔ **A TAP doubles the amount of traffic on your network if you use the same network infrastructure that you're monitoring.**

  Don't overlook this fact. The best solution is to create a separate network just for your IDS or forensic gathering activities to keep the traffic at reasonable levels if you plan to have a high number of TAPs. In the real world of budgets and departmental turf wars, this solution may not be practical, but it's always the best option.

Mirrors

Because network switches and routers have multiple ports, you need something that can copy the traffic from all ports to a single port where the IDS or forensic equipment is connected. The solution is port mirroring or port spanning. Mirroring simply copies data from multiple ports or a single port, depending on how the mirror is configured, to a port where your forensic or security equipment is connected.

Before you install mirrors, consider these limitations:

> ✔ **The way a switch or a router moves data from one port to another and how fast a switch can work limits the use of mirrors and spanners.**
>
>   On a high-speed network, the loss of data from collisions and dropped packets increases as the network traffic increases. To put this statement into perspective, if you mirror the entire switch to send all data to a single port, it's the same as putting all traffic from an 8-lane highway on a single-lane highway.
>
> ✔ **Switches operate at Layer 2 whereas routers work at Layers 2 and 3.**
>
>   These devices filter some of the data before sending it to a port. For most users, this situation isn't a problem, but for a security or forensic analyst who is re-creating events, the use of Layer 1 data streams or data that has errors can often yield useful clues.

You can install port mirroring and spanning relatively quickly, and if you use them within their speed limitations, they can be a helpful source of information. The most common use of a port mirror isn't to copy the entire contents of a network, but rather to copy the network traffic of a specific computer user or users. When used as a selective collection tool, port spanning fits right into the overall use of an IDS or forensic system.

A port mirror or span can be compromised by an attacker or even the suspect you're trying to monitor. The mirror or span can also be remotely accessed and configured, which can lead to being open to attack.

Promiscuous NIC

Not often used, but just as effective as a regular TAP, is a network interface card (NIC) known as a NIC TAP. Figure 13-11 shows a typical NIC of this type. The dual network connections make this NIC capable of sniffing network traffic. One advantage of having this type of TAP is that you have a computer and a storage device that filters and archives the data as it is flowing across the network directly connected to a network without the added problems of cabling the data back to a remote storage device. The negative side of this situation is that unless you have wheels on the personal computer, it isn't a mobile solution, and even then hooking up a desktop computer in a wiring closet is a chore because of all the wires you have to contend with.

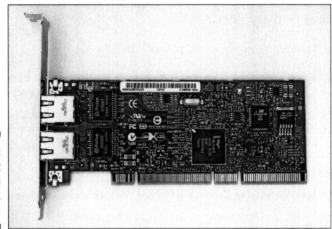

Figure 13-11:
Dual port
NIC used as
a network
TAP.

Wireless

Most people don't realize that you can copy and replay entire conversations between your wireless laptop and the local coffee shop network! On a copper or fiber optic based network, the network data is trapped inside the cable and you need a way to tap into those data pipes. In contrast, a wireless network transmits everything over the airwaves, and anyone with an antenna can just reach out and copy it.

As with regular network TAPs, a wireless TAP needs to be a passive system in order to hide its existence and not be vulnerable to an attack. From a hardware standpoint, you can use anything that's capable of receiving data on the proper frequency, such as a wireless NIC or any radio frequency receiver.

The important aspect of viewing wireless network traffic is what kind of software you use to view and analyze the data. A wireless laptop can record network traffic because it has the protocols in place to translate the wireless signals into a digital code that the operating system understands.

As more and more organizations deal with wireless technology, the ability to include a wireless component in their IDS and forensic systems is becoming a de facto necessity. Wireless system TAPs are still relatively new in the civilian world, but a helpful example of what can be done with a wireless sensor system is Kismet. Kismet works with your existing NIC and can work with various operating systems as well as generate logs that are compatible with almost all IDS and forensic systems.

One thing to keep in mind when dealing with wireless systems is that lower-level data is often dropped or stripped out by the time it makes it out into the wireless system. Essentially, you're dealing with packet-level data if you intercept the data after it becomes airborne. If you intercept the data *before or after* it hits a wireless access point, the encapsulation down to Layer 1 is often intact.

Discovering Network Forensic Vendors

Network forensic tools cover the spectrum of tools designed to extract data from a network, but they usually fall into two groups of forensic tools in the way they accomplish their tasks. The two distinct lineages of forensic software come from either the network security side or the computer forensic side. Depending on which side of the house they come from, network forensic tools work slightly differently.

The following list of network forensic manufacturers is by no means complete, but it does highlight the top group of forensic tool manufacturers in the industry.

- ✔ **Guidance Software:** Considered by many investigators to be the gold standard in the computer forensic world, Guidance Software (see www.guidancesoftware.com) has gone to great lengths to make inroads into the network forensic world. With its EnCase Enterprise Edition network forensic solution, Guidance can disburse agents across a network to perform a multitude of forensic-related jobs, from running a baseline scan of a host to finding suspicious processes running on a host.

- ✔ **Paraben:** A relatively new kid on the block in the network forensic field, Paraben's P2 Enterprise Edition (see www.paraben.com) accomplishes the standard disc forensic jobs in addition to monitoring network activity in real time by way of forensic agents.

- ✔ **Niksun:** Having come up through the security side of the network forensic family, Niksun (see www.niksun.com) has an appliance- or physical-based forensic solution. Highly regarded — it uses a different approach from agent-based systems — Niksun can monitor the network and, more importantly, record everything.

- ✔ **Sandstorm:** The NetIntercept security-side device from Sandstorm (see www.sandstorm.net) has been upgraded to the point that it can be considered a forensic tool that gathers and monitors a multitude of network-related data.

Chapter 14

Investigating X-Files: eXotic Forensics

*Y*ou probably don't realize just how much computers have changed the way you live. Few activities you perform during the course of your day do not have some form of electronic footprint somehow associated with them. Unless you shun electronic devices and electricity in general, chances are good that a generous portion of your activities can be re-created by someone who has the right equipment and motivation.

Your digital alarm clock and electricity meter indicate exactly when you wake up, your computer logs the information you look up and when, and your home security system records when you leave or enter your house. Your car indicates how fast you drive, how many miles per gallon your car reaches, how far you can go until you run out of gas, and your GPS location. A computer cash register logs your debit card transaction, as does your bank's computer. Cameras located on the roadway record the time you pass by; if you use a toll road, your wireless toll card dutifully deducts the correct amount from your account.

In this chapter, we take a look at all the places you can extract forensic evidence.

Taking a Closer Look at Answering Machines

The days of using a tape cassette for answering machines have mostly gone the way of the dodo bird (a few people still use them). To analyze a digital answering machines with no tape cassette, you had to access the storage microchips or recording audio from the speakers or by way of replay. Both extraction methods left something to be desired.

A modern-day answering machine is nothing more than a digital audio recorder connected to a phone line with telephone functionality.

These modern-day answering machines are shipped with USB connections so that your computer can access the storage area of the answering machine to store or retrieve messages.

Because the typical USB-enabled answering machine is considered a storage device by your desktop computer, the use of an answering machine to hide data isn't so far-fetched. As the forensic examiner, you can now use the FTK or EnCase forensic tool to acquire and image the answering machine just like you would with a regular computer storage device. One key marker to look for on the desktop computer is one or more link files that point to another storage device. If you see link files on the suspect computer and notice an answering machine sitting close by, it may be time to examine that answering machine a bit closer. Link files are covered in much more detail in Chapter 11.

Examining Video Surveillance Systems

Home entertainment digital video recorder (DVR) equipment can track the programs you watch, but the real reason to examine DVR equipment is that it can store files as an external hard drive to your desktop computer.

DVR technology isn't used only in convenience stores but also in camera systems on roadways, hotels, restaurants, airports, railway stations, bridges, supermarkets, schools, and just about any other place where people visit or congregate.

Most camera storage devices are now digital, and you can extract data from them. Figure 14-1 shows a standard DVR device that is essentially a computer dedicated to video recording. The video is saved in a readable format by the DVR, which allows the user to save and play back the video recordings.

Most DVR devices use a storage device to save the video files, and you can image the storage devices in the same way you image regular desktop computer storage devices.

Figure 14-1:
Standard
DVR device.

You can extract information from a DVR in two ways:

✔ **If you're lucky:** The video formats are fairly standard (such as AVI or MPEG) and you can play the video on any standard video player.

✔ **If you aren't so lucky:** If you're working with a proprietary format, the best option is to clone the original storage device and use the cloned storage device to use the device's own player or similar model to view the videos without risking damage to the original storage device.

Always check with the manufacturer to see what action it recommends. It might even have software to help you view or extract the video.

The newest version of EnCase can now interpret TiVo file systems 1 and 2.

Cracking Home Security Systems

Most home security systems rely on a small computer system with a minimal operating system and few hardware resources (similar to a mobile phone). These systems use storage spaces to store logs, security codes, and configuration settings. If the system is capable, the logging function can show activation and deactivation of the system and indicate which code was used. If each person uses a separate code, you can easily figure out who accessed the alarm system.

Home security systems can also be programmed to remotely perform a number of tasks, such as activate and deactivate at certain time intervals, create new codes, and even shut down certain zones while leaving others on. You can see these types of activity if you view the logs, but you have to know to look there. When you run across a crime scene that indicates no forced entry or tripping of the alarm, one of your first stops must be the alarm system logs to see what happened. The results may answer a few questions or, at worst, create more! Figure 14-2 shows some typical information that can be extracted from alarm system logs. Most alarm panels have a menu system from which you can view events on the system panel and other, more sophisticated alarm panels can download the information to your computer. Check with the alarm manufacturer to see whether the alarm panel you're working with can download log data.

	A	B	C	D	E
1					
2	Date	Time	Event	User	Zone
3	8-Jul-08	11:24:00 PM	Authorized Disarm	Fred	
4	9-Jul-08	12:31 AM	Authorized Arm	Fred	All
5	9-Jul-08	6:08 AM	Perimeter Violation		1 Front Door
6	9-Jul-08	6:35 AM	Authorized Disarm	Janie	
7	9-Jul-08	8:03 PM	Authorized Arm	Sam	
8	12-Jul-08	7:30 AM	Authorized Disarm	Janie	
9	13-Jul-08	7:33 PM	Authorized Arm	Sam	
10	14-Jul-08	7:20 AM	Authorized Disarm	Janie	
11	15-Jul-08	8:13 PM	Authorized Arm	Sam	
12	16-Jul-08	7:32 AM	Authorized Disarm	Janie	
13	17-Jul-08	8:37 PM	Authorized Arm	Sam	
14	18-Jul-08	7:30 AM	Authorized Disarm	Janie	
15	19-Jul-08	6:43 PM	Authorized Arm	Sam	
16	20-Jul-08	7:23 AM	Authorized Disarm	Janie	
17	21-Jul-08	7:15 PM	Authorized Arm	Sam	

Figure 14-2:
Typical alarm panel log data.

If the security system is monitored or connected to a central alarm company, the possibility of your finding data increases dramatically because the security system is connected to systems with logging and recording capability. Additionally, some alarm systems have built-in speakers and microphones so that the operators can communicate with you, which means that they can listen and record whatever information is transmitted over that microphone, especially if the alarm has been tripped.

Tracking Automobiles

With the advent of GPS technology, tracking a vehicle has never been easier. In case after case, law enforcement has used GPS technology to catch people who aren't exactly telling the truth. The conversation goes something like this:

Police officer: Where were you on the night of July 5, 2008 at 9 p.m.?

Suspect: I was at Leo's Bar on 5th Street.

Police officer: That's funny because your car was parked outside City National Bank on the other side of town while the bank was being robbed at that time.

GPS technology is rather simple in concept: A receiver uses satellite signals to establish a car's position to within several meters. The implementation becomes a bit more complex, though when you add satellites, atmospheric interference, and *multipath effects* (radio waves essentially bouncing off big objects and throwing off the GPS calculations). The system relies on a group of 24 orbiting satellites.

This capability ensures that a trusted third party can verify, with reasonable accuracy, exactly where that receiver was and at what time. You can find out exactly where a particular car was at a particular time.

GPS devices are available in two different forms:

- **Handheld or dashboard-mounted unit:** Can be purchased at your local shopping mall or sporting goods store. The most popular consumer GPS brand is now Garmin, shown in Figure 14-3. This device is usually the size of a paperback book or mobile phone.

- **Original equipment manufacturer (OEM) unit:** Usually embedded in vehicles, truck fleets, aircraft, and many other applications by the manufacturer. An OEM-type GPS receiver is shown in Figure 14-4. This device is typically about the size of a large mailing stamp.

Figure 14-3:
Handheld
GPS
receiver.

Figure 14-4:
OEM GPS
receiver.

If the times and locations on the GPS receiver don't comprise enough information to satisfy an investigator, the newest GPS devices are capable of data storage, have MP3 players built in, and interface or pair with mobile phones by way of Bluetooth or direct connection.

With all this information on the GPS device and the ability to connect by way of USB or Bluetooth, you can forensically acquire and image GPS devices quite easily to extract useful data. Because desktop computers consider the devices to be storage devices, the forensic process works the same way as imaging a desktop computer or mobile phone. If you're dealing with a GPS device paired with a mobile phone, the type of information passed to the GPS can include call lists, text messages, and even phone book data, which links the GPS with the user of the mobile phone and vice versa.

Extracting Information from Radio Frequency Identification (RFID)

In radio frequency identification (RFID), very small and very low-power transmitters are used to interface with a type of receiver or interrogator to identify a person or an object. In its simplest form, the RFID transmitter sends a radio frequency signal encoded with an identification number that is then received by the RFID reader or receiver. After the reader receives the encoded signal, the reader converts the signal to digital and passes it along to whichever process or device it's connected to.

Most people have heard of RFID technology in the context of supermarket inventory control; however, RFID technology is finding its way into many other areas, such as

- **Fuel stations:** Just drive right up, wave your RFID card at the pump, and start pumping fuel.

- **Vending machines:** Using your RFID debit card or key fob, you can pluck a snack or a drink from a vending machine and it deducts the cost directly from your bank account.

- **Supermarket checkout lines:** After the cost of all your groceries is totaled, you just tap the RFID card on the reader and your transaction is complete.

- **Your pets:** Implant RFID technology into Fluffy or Rover, and easily identify the pet if later it gets lost or stolen. People with high-value animals are literally flocking (no pun intended) to this technology because it makes identifying stolen or lost animals so easy.

- **Casinos:** RFID in betting chips lets casinos track them on the floor and study customer betting habits.

- **Identification systems:** RFID tags are being inserted into all forms of identification systems, such as employee badges, passports, student badges, and even human beings.

Collecting information from a MVEDR

Installed in most modern vehicles for "data analysis" purposes are Motor Vehicle Event Data Recorders (MVEDR), or "vehicle black boxes." The primary purpose of the MVEDR in its original formation was to record data before and after an accident. The system usually activated and recorded the information when it sensed high G forces resulting from an accident or even a near accident. Elements such as speed, seat belt use, brake use, and more than 40 other factors are now recorded by the MVEDR, but the amount of data logged by the MVEDR is expected to increase every year as more vehicle components becoming computerized. Ford and General Motors (GM) have used the information to analyze their vehicles in accidents, and the MVEDR system contacts GM in real time to transmit data regarding incidents. Some states, such as California, are considering using

this type of data to track drivers' mileage and tax people for having low miles per gallon. That plan is somewhat far-fetched at this point, but you can see what kind of data can be retrieved from MVEDRs!

If you need to collect information from an MVEDR, the best source of information is the vehicle manufacturer. OnStar (from GM) claims to keep its data for more than a year after an event. The National Highway Traffic Safety Administration (NHTSA) has mandated standards to be implemented in 2011, but for now, setting standards is left to individual vehicle manufacturers.

Other vehicle manufacturers, such as Volvo, BMW, and Mercedes-Benz, also have systems similar to OnStar, and Toyota and Honda are developing their own systems.

In every case of RFID, the technology is designed to leave a digital trail. From the forensic point of view, you can re-create the movements and actions of a person by simply extracting this information from the RFID reader or interrogator. For example, a casino using RFID chips can literally track a chip's movement *and* track whoever is carrying that chip from table to table to re-create that journey based on the data that's stored. Another example often touted by security firms is the ability to watch security guards make their rounds in real time as the RFID tags sequentially check in at predetermined points!

Because the RFID system involves the use of radio frequency waves, anyone with the right type of receiver can intercept RFID signals. Also, RFID cloning devices already exist, so just because the data shows that the RFID device was nearby at that time, you should always find a way corroborate that evidence.

Not to be left out, mobile phone manufacturers are beginning to produce RFID-capable mobile phones that will more than likely become electronic wallets or billfolds. The classic example that mobile phone companies use to promote RFID is that you only have to put your phone next to a Broadway show advertisement and confirm the number of tickets you want to purchase, and the RFID system (plus the mobile phone wireless connection) handle the transaction. This situation may not happen tomorrow or next week, but the future is arriving fast. (Just remember not to lean on a glass display and accidentally order a dozen tickets to a show!)

Examining Copiers

The modern-day copier in your office is a wonder of office technology. Figure 14-5 shows a model. It can not only make copies but also act as a network printer, network storage device, and fax — it can even archive every single copy ever made on it.

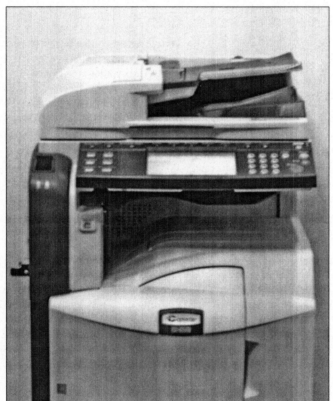

Figure 14-5:
Typical newer-model copier.

This capability is due in large part to the transition from analog to digital technology. In short, a copier is essentially a low-end computer with a scanner attached to its top. The key to extracting the information in a copier is its storage device, which is often a hard drive.

From the forensic point of view, you have access to the data stored within the copier via any access point, which might be a network port, a USB port, or a wireless access point (WAP), depending on the forensic tool you use. The most direct method of extracting data from the storage device is to simply take apart the copier and physically extract the storage device. Any computer forensic software now on the market can do an extraction and then image the contents. The problem becomes how to read the data.

Some copier manufacturers use proprietary methods to save their data; the file systems they use may not be recognized by any forensic tools. Network copiers tend to use file systems that are recognizable to the network, such as FAT or NTFS, and some still use MS-DOS. You might have to look at the data found on the storage device in a different way than you normally would — simply clicking buttons in your forensic software manner doesn't work. You might even have to use a hex editor (gasp!) to view file headers to figure out exactly which type of file you have. (Chapter 11 covers file headers in much more detail.) The problem with nonstandard file systems is that you have to dig through raw data to make sense of how the company organized its file system for its copier. Contacting the manufacturer is always a good idea at this point because it can help you immeasurably in technical expertise and in saving time.

If a copier uses a proprietary system to archive copies, your best option is to contact the copier manufacturer for advice, and possibly the software manufacturer to extract the copier images. We can't stress enough how useful a copier examination can be for finding evidence. Beyond the scope of this book, but within the realm of computer security forensics, copiers are becoming a frequent place for hackers to plant rootkits and "back doors" into networks because most copiers aren't as well protected as desktop computers.

Taking a Look On the Horizon

The next hurdle for forensic scientists to conquer is the issue of extremely large storage devices, on the order of terabytes, or TB (1000 gigabytes), and petabytes (1000 terabytes). With storage devices measuring 500 gigabytes (GB) on store shelves now, the possibility of working with terabytes of information isn't as remote as it might seem. The problem that forensic scientists need to resolve is how to acquire and analyze extremely large storage areas in a timely fashion. The question becomes "How do you find a digital needle in a 2TB database haystack without the process taking weeks or months?

The trend in computing power is for devices to become smaller while also becoming more portable. Almost any device you can think of now will eventually have some form of computing and storage ability. For example, some refrigerators made by Frigidaire are equipped with a flat-screen monitor and computer. Home entertainment systems can correlate what you watch and even recommend shows that fit your tastes! These trends, plus lots of other anecdotal evidence, appear to show that computer forensic investigators will have plenty of data to parse when looking for evidence of who, what, when, where, why, and how. The trick will be to keep computer forensic tools — and computer forensic analysts' training — up-to-date.

Part IV
Succeeding in Court

The 5th Wave — By Rich Tennant

"I've been an expert computer witness for over 20 years. I've testified about fraudulent whatnots, failed doohickies, missing thingys, you name it."

In this part . . .

The term *forensics* means "to bring to the court." From the start, the case and e-evidence collected by you and your team are headed toward court — unless a resolution is reached before that destiny takes place.

Losing an otherwise winnable case happens, probably a lot. The chapters in this part help you understand what you need to know and do to win.

Winning means more than bringing evidence to court, which only gets you to the door, so to speak. You still face the court's triathlon. In place of swimming, cycling, and running, however, your three hurdles are getting yourself qualified as an expert and getting your work admitted into evidence (see Chapter 15); making the judge and jury understand the relevance of the e-evidence, and surviving cross examination (see Chapter 16). You're the party trying to get the e-evidence admitted, so you have to show that you truly are qualified to testify. Your testimony must relate closely to facts that matter in the case and defend against (survive) attempts to discredit your you and your work. Bare speculation doesn't get you far, which is what your testimony will sound like unless you prepare, rehearse, and then prepare some more. Find out how to win your case and build your career in Chapter 17).

It usually takes more than three weeks to prepare a good impromptu speech.

— Mark Twain

Chapter 15

Holding Up Your End at Pretrial

Trials can be dreadfully time-consuming and expensive. Hurdles, by way of federal rules (as covered in Chapter 2), are in place to resolve civil and criminal cases in a "just, speedy, and inexpensive way." (We're speculating that writers of these rules didn't foresee the age of digital trails, or else they had a weird sense of humor.) If most cases went to trial, the justice system would suffer the equivalent of a denial-of-service (DoS) attack. A *DoS* attack occurs when a Web site receives so many requests for service that it grinds to a halt. Preventing a court-system DoS attack comprises the *pretrial phase*. In this busy period — the period before trial — every legal, technical, and constitutional issue can be scrutinized to try to resolve the case.

You interact frequently with retaining and opposing lawyers during this stage.

Depending on where you stand, a pretrial is a good idea because it offers another chance to bring an end to a case before it reaches trial. Pretrial events help identify and weed out nontrial cases to spare public and private costs. The three pretrial procedures used by either side in criminal or civil cases are

▶ Motions

▶ Pretrial hearings

▶ Depositions

Pretrial procedures are part of the legal system. Whether a party is motivated to cut and run, take a plea, or proceed to trial usually depends on the reliability of the evidence, investigative methods, and witnesses. This chapter explains the key pretrial issues and the ability of e-evidence, computer forensics methods, and reports to withstand pretrial attempts to bar them. You see how loopholes can bring a quick end to a case.

Pretrial Motions

A *motion* is a formal request to a judge to make a legal ruling. Both parties try to maneuver into a better position by using motions.

In civil cases, after the plaintiff files a complaint, the defendant has two options:

✔ File an answer.

✔ File a *motion,* which is a response to the complaint but doesn't constitute an answer to the complaint.

Lawyers do the filing, but may need the help of a computer forensics expert to respond.

In criminal cases, the prosecution and defense may file any number of motions with the court. If a defendant wants to file a motion, it must be done five days before the trial and must be in writing.

Each motion must be accompanied by the legal reasons to grant the request. Legal reasons tend to be based on the reliability of the evidence, violations of constitutional rights, or violations of rules of evidence.

When e-evidence plays a role in a motion, so do computer forensics experts.

Motions can be viewed as tools by either side in an effort to define the boundaries of the case. Parties can be extremely aggressive with motions.

The legal system uses *pretrial motions* and *motions for pretrial hearings* — and uses many of them. In the following sections, we discuss the following three types of common pretrial motions that are relevant to computer forensics in civil or criminal cases:

✔ Motion to suppress evidence (applies to criminal cases)

✔ Motion in limine (applies to civil cases)

✔ Motion to dismiss

We discuss one type of motion in Chapter 2: the Rule 16 motion to discover. It's the request for discovery or e-discovery. This motion controls the exchange of evidence between the opposing lawyers during discovery.

Motion to suppress evidence

A *motion to suppress evidence* asks the court to exclude evidence from the trial, such as a motion to suppress a defendant's prior convictions. It's the only motion that applies only to criminal cases. The legal basis in criminal trials is usually that evidence was collected in violation of the defendant's constitutional rights. For example, if a defendant is arrested illegally and his computer is searched after the arrest, the e-evidence found during that search may be inadmissible.

In civil cases, evidence is *excluded* — rather than *suppressed.* A motion to exclude evidence is commonly termed a motion in limine.

Motion in limine

A motion *in limine* (pronounced "in lim-in-ay" and means "at the threshold") asks the court to limit the evidence at trial or to rule that certain evidence cannot be used. For example, in a discrimination case, this motion can be used to prevent the introduction of inflammatory evidence or evidence about past cases because it would show a pattern. Or, the prosecutor may want to introduce evidence that cannot properly be linked to the defendant or the alleged crime because of the way in which it was collected.

Motion to dismiss

A *motion to dismiss* is an attempt to have the charges dismissed. The basis for this motion is that the case doesn't have a sound legal basis, even if all alleged facts are proven to be true.

Either side can bring a motion to dismiss. If the prosecutor handling a criminal case determines that there's not sufficient evidence to obtain a conviction, he may file a motion asking the judge to dismiss the case. This motion is made after the case has been completely investigated, and after the police have exhausted all avenues for obtaining additional evidence. The judge may grant the motion to dismiss if she is satisfied that the case cannot be proven in a trial.

Other motions

A variety of other motions may be filed before trial that pertain to you or your work, including the ones described in this list:

✔ **Forensics:** Motions challenging computer forensics reports will be filed, so plan for them. Motions may be filed by defense lawyers seeking independent testing or review of the e-evidence.

Beginning in the 1990s, the U.S. Supreme Court imposed greater scientific rigor on forensic testimony. In a defining 1993 decision, *Daubert vs. Merrell Dow Pharmaceuticals*, the court demanded that such testimony not simply meet the existing standard of "general acceptance" in its field but also address some of the hallmarks of scientific inquiry — testing, peer review, and rates of error. (See Chapter 5 for more information about *Daubert*.)

✔ **Depositions:** Motions may be filed seeking to interview under oath — called *taking a deposition* — other witnesses, including expert witnesses, or to block their depositions.

✔ **Production of evidence:** Defense attorneys almost always file a motion seeking *Brady material,* which is exculpatory evidence that could possibly indicate that the defendant isn't guilty.

Such exculpatory material is named after the Supreme Court case *Brady v. U.S.* Defendants are entitled to receive, before trial begins, prosecution evidence that includes police and lab reports, statements made by defendants, names of expert witnesses, photographs, financial records, evidence of wiretapping and other surveillance, and any evidence that might help the accused demonstrate his innocence. Withholding such evidence by a prosecutor can be grounds for a new trial.

Handling Pretrial Hearings

Pretrial hearings are an opportunity for negotiation in good faith between the parties. Judges can also hear evidence to determine whether the parties involved in the case followed the law and the United States Constitution and that the evidence was collected legally.

Pretrial hearings are critical because they determine what jurors will hear or learn from the evidence and witnesses.

All the e-evidence you examine can be examined also by the opposing side's computer forensics expert. Requests may be made at a pretrial hearing for tests of your e-evidence methods. Plan to respond to this request for an explanation of what you did to arrive at your conclusions.

E-evidence, as well as your tools, techniques, and methodologies used in an examination, is subject to being challenged in a court of law or in other formal proceedings. If you don't have proper documentation, including chain of custody, you have a problem.

Defense lawyers may attempt to stop prosecutors from presenting certain e-evidence. They might argue that it was illegally obtained or should be barred as irrelevant. Prosecutors may do the same. You may be asked for your opinion about the strength of the e-evidence. This is not the time to be overly optimistic or to exaggerate.

Suppose that an emergency situation occurs with a high probability that e-evidence might be compromised or destroyed, so you seize the computer without a warrant. At pretrial, the opposing side may claim that no emergency situation existed, so the warrantless search was illegal and the e-evidence was obtained illegally. You may be slapped with that type of accusation; and not answering to the satisfaction of the judge isn't an option. Your chain of custody documentation is critical when you find yourself in this spot, which you read in Chapter 2.

If the primary incriminating evidence is suppressed at a pretrial hearing, there may be nothing left of the case. You might think "This can't be the end!" The judge's decision to toss your e-evidence can be appealed, but a discussion of the court of appeals and appellate processes is way beyond the scope of this chapter.

Giving a Deposition

Your work as an expert witness may begin with giving a deposition before trial. A *deposition* (or *depo*) is your testimony given under oath to tell the truth.

Up to this point, you worked as an investigator. Now you're an expert giving factual and accurate testimony about the e-evidence and your methods. You're allowed as an expert witness to offer an opinion as testimony in court without having been a witness to any occurrence relating to the lawsuit or the crime. (See the section "Swearing to tell truthful opinions.") You're speaking on behalf of a computer or digital device, which you may find to be a bizarre experience.

The party seeking discovery has the right to depose any experts, including you. What's different about depositions as compared to trials is that direct examination is conducted by the opposing attorney. If a cross-examination takes place, it's done by the attorney who retained the expert. (Chapter 16 covers direct and cross-examination). No one asks you to be deposed. You're notified that you will give a deposition.

Basically, depositions are sworn question-and-answer conversations. You're asked questions by the opposing attorney, and the questions and your answers are recorded by an official court reporter. No judge or jury is present, but otherwise your testimony is similar to the way it is in the courtroom. Depositions have these three purposes, to

Being completely honest

A company suspected that a former employee had, just before leaving the company for a competitor, stolen confidential technical files by copying them to an external device and then deleting them from the laptop and company's server. Management gave the laptop to its IT department to search for and locate the missing files. The IT staff searched the laptop directly.

Three weeks later, management decided to send the laptop to a computer forensics company for forensics imaging. The investigator imaged the hard drive using EnCase, which is software recognized by the courts, and reported the results honestly. The forensic investigator's report was extremely well prepared, fully documented, and truthful with respect to when the work was performed and the lack of chain of custody.

Still, to people who weren't experts in computer forensics, the evidence looked convincing and damaging. The defendant's computer forensics expert pointed out the serious flaws pertaining to the chain of custody during pretrial and ended the case.

 ✔ Obtain relevant information

 ✔ Avoid surprises at trial

 ✔ Motivate a settlement before trial

Before you give a deposition, the lawyer on the case will want to prepare you. Agree to it! Any preparation helps you be a more competent and convincing witness. Good opinions can go bad quickly without proper preparation.

The persuasive power of e-evidence and your qualifications and testimony during pretrial have a direct effect on which e-evidence becomes admissible — and can affect the result of the case.

Swearing to tell truthful opinions

At the deposition, you're testifying out of court and under oath, so you have to tell the truth and remain ethical. Everything you say — and we mean *every* word you say — is recorded by the court reporter. Actually, everyone involved in the deposition is recorded. Make sure that you form and express your opinions so that they reflect the truth. When you're presenting your opinions, you should

 ✔ **Give your opinion the weight it deserves.**

 Do not try to make your opinion more important than you know it is by overstating it.

✔ **Know the meaning of every acronym you use.**

Even if you would never refer to DOS as disk operating system, your job is to know what all acronyms mean. For example, if you refer to an MD5 hash, you must be able to answer the question, "What does MD5 stand for?"

✔ **Prepare convincing opinions based on a thorough analysis to the best of your ability.**

When you agree to the terms and scope of your work for the case (see Chapter 5), you create a responsibility. When giving an opinion about an issue that you didn't analyze in order to save money, you can't avoid blame by saying "I didn't get paid enough to do that."

✔ **Prepare to explain your review of the opinions of the opposing side's computer forensics expert and reasons why you disagree with them.**

You have to explain why your opinions are correct *and* why the opposing side's opinions aren't correct, or are less correct. You have a double role to fulfill regarding opinions. For example, when asked why you disagree with the other expert's opinion, you need convincing reasons to show that you considered other possibilities. You want your opinion to look thorough, knowledgeable, and respectful of all opinions regardless of how off-the-planet they are.

✔ **Know the weakness of each opinion.**

Every opinion is based on an assumption or interpretation. Opinions aren't facts — they're only based on facts (see Chapter 7). You have to *fess up* to the weakness of your opinion and then provide a reasonable explanation of how or why that weakness doesn't change the opinion. A *reasonable explanation* is one that's more likely than not to be correct. You keep the testimony under control by knowing your strengths and weaknesses and being prepared with answers. No one said that testifying as a computer forensics expert was easy — but we think that it's always interesting.

✔ **Be concise.**

When you're not well prepared, you probably talk too much or act evasive. Unless it's a riveting, media-crazed case, no one wants useless details. Rambling on is a sign that you're talking around the issues because you can't zero in.

Court reporters play a critical role in legal proceedings where spoken words must be preserved as a written transcript. The reporters are responsible for ensuring a complete, accurate, and secure legal record.

Answering questions truthfully may not be easy. You should let the opposing lawyer know that you need clarification or a different wording of the question in these types of situations:

✔ **You need a question reworded.**

The opposing lawyer may not be wording things exactly right, in your opinion. He may be doing it deliberately to trick you, or unintentionally out of limited knowledge. Either way, don't answer until the question is reworded. To dramatize the difference, suppose that he's used to Latin phrases and you're used to hexadecimal. In response to a question that you can't answer as asked, you might say something simple but blunt, such as "I'm not able to answer your question as worded. Would you rephrase it?"

If you're inclined to help others, don't do so at deposition. Good witnesses stick to doing their job, which is only to answer questions and not to offer or volunteer any additional information.

✔ **You need a question stated more precisely.**

The opposing lawyer's wording of the question may not be as precise as you need for it to be in order to give an answer. You may want to answer the question, but feel that you first have to correctly formulate the question for the lawyer. Asking questions isn't your job. You're the computer forensics expert witness, not the lawyer. Don't ask what the lawyer meant to ask. Respond by asking for clarification about the vague or misleading part of the question.

✔ **You didn't hear the question.**

You may not have heard or understood each of the words in the question. Despite sharing the same currency, people in Brooklyn, Boston, and Biloxi with their respective accents don't seem to share the same version of English. Ask for the question to be repeated to be sure that you heard it correctly.

Surviving a deposition

Depositions can be the most painful and mentally exhausting activity you perform during the case.

The questioning lawyer (the *deposing lawyer*) has a lot of leeway in the types and scope of questions to ask, unlike at trial. It can make a deposition sort of a scavenger hunt. The deposing attorneys can ask you questions that are leading, vague, hypothetical, or beyond your competence. Your lawyer can object for the record, but you're still stuck answering the question. As always, there are exceptions, but your lawyer will know about them and stop you from answering.

Your job is not to win the case. If your goal were to win, you would be a hired (biased) expert. You present your opinions and let the chips fall where they may.

You're also being sized up by the opposing lawyer during the deposition. You're the enemy, so to speak. The lawyer is looking for ways to disqualify or discredit you by checking out how you react, how prepared and confident you are, and how the jury will react to you.

Bulletproofing your opinions

During the deposition, remember these five things not to do:

- **Don't make assumptions about what the question means or the lawyer's motivation for asking it.**

  Ask for rephrasing if you're unsure of the question. Say "I don't understand your question. Please repeat it or clarify it or rephrase it."

- **Don't argue or get defensive.**

  You're being sized up for court. Your strength as an expert witness is also being rated by the opposing lawyer. If that person sees that you can be made to look erratic or unprofessional in court by provoking you to argue or look defensive, that becomes a weakness in your side's case.

- **Don't allow your answer to get cut off.**

  Always finish your answer because the ending may be critical to the truth. If you're cut off, wait until it's your turn to speak, and then politely *ask* whether you can finish your answer. Wait for the answer. Then turn to the jury and give your answer from the beginning. Being polite is a good weapon because it makes it much tougher for opposing counsel to discredit you.

- **Don't act like you're trying to win a marathon.**

  When you're tired, ask to take a break, which you have the right to do. You can't be on top of your game if you're exhausted. (You're also more likely to be ornery.)

- **Don't talk when someone else is talking.**

  The court reporter must record every word and who said it. It's impossible to record more than one person's words.

During the deposition, remember these five dos:

- **Be simple, clear, concise, complete, and jargon free.**
- **Wait until the lawyer has finished asking the question so that you know you heard the entire question.**
- **Allow yourself a moment to think before you answer.**
- **Say "I don't recall" when you truthfully don't recall or remember.**
- **Say "I don't know" when you truthfully don't know.**

Checking your statements

When your deposition is done, the lawyer advises you of your right to review and sign the transcript. You probably don't want to read the transcript thoroughly and critically or make any corrections to it. You've invested many hours (yes, hours!) of your life in the deposition. Don't quit now.

Don't waive your right to review or to sign. And, never sign the transcript if you haven't read it carefully.

You need to review and correct your testimony in your deposition because

- ✔ It may be entered as testimony.
- ✔ If your mistakes are found and pointed out in front of the jury, your credibility tanks.

Fighting stage fright

As lawsuits and criminal cases become more complicated, lawyers may turn to video depositions. Imagine the worst home video you've seen. Now stop imagining that video before you stress out. That short exercise should make you recognize the importance of being well prepared to testify with all your reports and papers organized and labeled. Of course, you should be prepared regardless of whether you're starring in a video.

What you say, how you sound, and how you appear when testifying influence the jury, and thus, the case.

You sound your best if you understand what to expect and how to respond so that you're not surprised or stressed out. As in many careers, you need to practice to be good at your sport, art, music, craft, or testimony. For example, you can attend conferences that teach you how to testify. Practice giving opinions and testimony about each case too. Ask the lawyer who retained you for a rehearsal to prepare you, but don't memorize your testimony. Then rehearse on your own as part of your preparation work before giving a deposition or appearing in court.

Anything that adds stress isn't good for you or the case. When you feel relaxed and confident, it shows.

Chapter 16

Winning a Case Before You Go to Court

*Y*our ability to be responsive, adaptive, and resourceful is an invaluable asset because surprising things tend to happen that help or harm the case. For example, as e-evidence is found revealing more of the truth, the charges may change, defendants may countersue, or plaintiffs may lose their ability to think rationally. (If you doubt the last item, search YouTube for incriminating videos.)

In addition, clients may have no clue as to why something's important or not from a forensics point of view. Perhaps a reality show about e-evidence would help. . . . Putting reality into perspective for them is part of the job. Plaintiffs who crave punishing e-evidence, for example, need help seeing the potentially high cost of their line of attack — no *CSI* script-writers can ensure the outcomes they want. Doing certain tasks discussed in this chapter is beneficial to you and the case in court.

This chapter helps you understand how to move the scales of justice (along with your career) in the direction of a win. We describe how to deal — or duel — with opposing expert witnesses. Topics covered relate mostly to private or smaller cases where you work for either the plaintiff or the defense. Huge cases (international industrial espionage or fraud, for example) are beyond the scope of this chapter, but who knows — you may catapult into this type of case later in your career.

Working Around Wrong Moves

By the time you're engaged as an investigator or expert witness to provide testify, it may already be too late to authenticate some of the evidence if do-it-yourselfers (DIYs) went to work on it. Convincing a client to wait for a computer forensics investigator who can testify about the methodology and any positive findings on a target computer or device may be impossible for a lawyer to do. Contamination probably happened before the call to a lawyer. When victimized people or companies decide to fight back against harm, the first step they take is usually the wrong one. But e-evidence might reside in other locations that DIYs had not thought about so it may still be uncontaminated. All messages have at least one sender and one receiver and files are backed up. Get everyone with knowledge of the people or technology involved together to identify alternative sources. Talking to them individually takes more time, but do it if you can't arrange a brainstorming session.

Litigants may want you to overlook their DIY work ("We just looked around but didn't change anything") and pretend that it hasn't happened. Be prepared with a clear answer so that you don't commit perjury. You can also add these tasks to your list of don'ts: installing spyware, wiretapping, and other illegal tactics to capture or grab messages or files.

Being resourceful comes in handy when handling less-than-pristine e-evidence. This is a very tricky point to make regarding imperfect e-evidence. If perfect procedure has not been followed, it doesn't necessarily mean the e-evidence is useless. Depending on the case, lack of perfect e-evidence handling may only reduce the weight of that evidence. For example, in a criminal case, if prosecution has made some mistake with the evidence, it may reduce the sentence, but it doesn't get the entire case tossed out. The jury may still hear the evidence, and with help from an expert witness, decide how much value to attach to it. That value might be influential enough when it's corroborated by other evidence or used to corroborate. Of course, if the imperfect e-evidence is the sole piece of exculpatory evidence, then its weight is zero.

Special handling is needed when using imperfect e-evidence. You must admit to it upfront and put a positive spin on it. That is, show why or how the e-evidence is still material. You want to get out in front of that issue or you give the opposing side a sledgehammer to bring down on you for trying to sneak one past the jury. Getting caught in court can make you want to slither out of the witness box.

If the case involves responding to e-discovery requests and producing materials, be familiar with the issues covered in Chapter 2.

Responding to Opposing Experts

You most likely have a counterpart — the opposing computer forensics investigator and expert witness. In criminal cases, your counterpart works for the DA's office or law enforcement. You may need to interact with the person face-to-face at a forensics lab, over the phone, or in court. These other experts tend to be quite helpful and accommodating. In civil cases, you're less likely to have contact outside the courtroom, if the case moves that far along. Relationships with experts on civil cases tend to be more competitive.

Dealing with counterparts

Follow these guidelines when you interact with an opposing expert:

✔ **Be cordial.**

Nothing can be gained by antagonizing or bullying your opponent. You're both working for the justice system and are bound by rules of ethics. At the same time, your opponent is attempting to weaken the value of your work and opinions — but you're doing the same to him.

✔ **Remember that you're not perfect, at least not all the time.**

The downside of all types of evidence is that it can implicate the wrong person or indicate a crime that didn't happen, particularly if e-evidence has been planted to frame someone. The risk always exists that your interpretation is wrong.

✔ **Don't reject the expert's opinion or set out to demolish it.**

Examine and research it just like you research your own. You have to justify your opinion of the other expert's opinion. Be prepared to respond intelligently.

Responding to an expert's report is a methodical process. Read the charges to refresh your memory before tackling the report.

Formatting your response

As part of your examination and review of materials and documents provided by the opposing side, you prepare responses to statements made in affidavits. Responding to each material statement, charge, or allegation is necessary. Ignoring any critical issue makes you look like you're avoiding e-evidence that harms your case. And you know the risks of loopholes from Chapter 5.

Structure your report with these sections. Each statement, or *item,* is numbered for easy reference in the report — and later still in court. Here's the scenario: You represent the defendant, Rog Rabbit, who's charged by his former employer, A1 Company, with stealing confidential or intellectual proprietary (IP) files before leaving to work at a competitor. Rog's new employer is also named in the lawsuit, but they have their own legal team.

Everything you write, you may need to defend in court.

✔ **Section A: Introduction.**

Outline the key issues of the case. You usually take this information from the affidavit.

- *State the plaintiff's theory of the case:* You want to include what the plaintiff, A1 Company, believes happened. A theory is that the defendant stole proprietary files from the company by copying them from the company laptop to CDs to use at a competitor. Then those files were deleted from the server to try to hide the theft.

- *State the basis for plaintiff's theory:* Explain why the evidence supports the plaintiff's theory. For example, evidence was found indicating that files had been copied from the server, and company files couldn't be found there.

- *State your purpose in one or two sentences.* For example: The purpose of my investigation is to determine if there is evidence to indicate that [*list the plaintiff's charge*].

✔ **Section B: Materials Available for Review**.

List the materials given to you for review as well as the materials you referenced to form your opinion. Include any Web sites you visited, software products listed in the affidavit, and technical reviews of software. Include the full URL and the date you accessed it. If you reviewed reference books or manuals, list them in full, including the publisher and date.

✔ **Section C: Background.**

Explain the facts of the case straight from the affidavit. For example, you would include the date the defendant stopped working at the company. Then the company retained Computer Forensics R Us who created a forensics image.

✔ **Section D: Analysis.**

List each material provided to you and that you reviewed from the list in Section B. List each material reviewed as a heading. (Responses to Statements Contained in the Affidavit of Person-Z). Under the heading, write your statements in a numbered list.

You're laying a foundation for your interpretations and conclusions, just like a bricklayer does — one brick at a time. Respond with precision, facts, and legitimate or respected references. Don't use wikis or blogs as legitimate references unless you can defend their recognized authority in court.

✔ **Section E: Findings.**

Start this section with a statement that has some flexibility followed by your conclusions, which you would number.

> *Within the bounds of reasonable computer forensics certainty and subject to change if additional information becomes available, it is my professional opinion that:*

You build your defense with the following

- *State defense's theory of the case:* Counteract the plaintiff's theory with your own. For example, suggest that the defendant was performing his standard job responsibilities by backing up the files as he had done for the past four years. Also suggest that the plaintiff cannot find its own files and is blaming a former employee and his new employer.

- *State the basis for defendant's theory:* Back up your theory with your reasoning. For example, the defendant could have copied the files while backing up the files to another location — in this case, the server. Not being able to find files doesn't mean that the files were deleted.

- *List the key e-evidentiary issues:* Outline the key points you're making in your report. For example, the defendant's laptop had been investigated in-house for two weeks to look for the missing files. Afterward, the laptop was imaged by a professional forensic imaging company's expert.

✔ **Section F: Attachments.**

If you have any attachments, list them here. Don't forget to actually include them with the report.

At the end the end of your response, remember to sign your name.

When responding, don't "blast" anyone, especially the opposing expert, even when the expert knew that, for evidentiary purposes, the forensics image was a dud. You would just look unprofessional.

Responding to affidavits

We show you sample responses to statements made in an affidavit. The affidavit is of Ken Kanine, who is A1 Company's director of information technology (IT).

Items listed in the affidavit that you're responding to are:

- ✔ Item 3: Each team has its own network drive space that can be password-protected to limit access of that space to members of that team. Thus, for example, only members of the "Big Dogs" team can access documents in the "Big Dogs" directory.

- ✔ Item 7: A1 Company doesn't have an electronic document management program. A1 Company relies on its employees to backup, preserve, and maintain copies of the electronic documents they create.

- ✔ Item 8: When A1 Company provided Rog Rabbit with a laptop, the company specifically directed him to backup files on a weekly basis to his personal drive space.

- ✔ Item 10: Rog Rabbit submitted his resignation on May 1, 2008 and left the company on May 3, 2008.

- ✔ Item 11: On May 3, 2008, the company took possession of Rog Rabbit's laptop, and A1 Company's IT department made backup copies of his laptop and his e-mail.

- ✔ Item 12: On May 17, 2008, IT personnel began to examine his laptop.

- ✔ Item 15: Documents that Mr. Rabbit copied to CDs contain A1 Company's confidential and proprietary data. A competitor can use that data to compete against A1 and profit from its value.

- ✔ Item 19: The IT staff tried to recover the deleted files from Mr. Rabbit's laptop using a program called "Recover-Software version 5.5," which identified about 1,800 files as having been deleted from the laptop, and that the IT personnel weren't able to recover any of those files with "Recover-Software version 5.5."

You might respond to each of these statement from the affidavit of Ken Kanine in this way:

1. In Item 3, Ken Kanine states that each member of a team has his own network drive space that is password-protected to limit access to the members of a specific team, such as the Big Dogs. This item indicates that passwords were shared by everyone on the team and are not confidential.

2. In Item 7, Ken Kanine states that A1 Company did not have an electronic records-management program. Instead, A1 Company relied on employees to preserve and maintain copies of the electronic documents they created. This item indicates that employees were expected to save copies of their documents.

3. In Item 8, Ken Kanine states that Rog Rabbit had been specifically instructed to regularly back up all his files to his personal network drive space. This item indicates that one would expect him to have copied files as part of his job responsibility.

4. In Item 11, Ken Kanine states that IT staff took possession of Rog Rabbit's laptop computer on May 3, 2008. This item does not indicate that the laptop was secured against use by others.

5. In Item 12, Ken Kanine states that on May 17, 2008, IT personnel began examining Mr. Rabbit's laptop. This item indicates that others besides the defendant had used the laptop. This item does not state the IT personnel were qualified to perform a forensics investigation.

6. In Item 15, Ken Kanine states that Rog Rabbit had copied to CD some files that contained confidential and proprietary information. Now the response is different because this is an allegation against the defendant.

Offer alternative interpretations of what the item indicates, such as

- The copying of files may indicate that backup copies of A1 Company's files were created, in accordance with A1 Company's requirement that employees and managers with company laptops save copies of their documents.

- It is reasonable that at least some of the A1 Company files that were saved as backup copies would contain confidential and proprietary information.

7. In Item 19, Ken Kanine states that IT personnel used "Recover-Software version 5.5," which identified about 1,800 files as having been deleted from the laptop, and that the IT personnel weren't able to recover any of those files with "Recover-Software version 5.5."

Here's how to respond to the claim in this allegation:

According to the independent test results of the recovery effectiveness <insert URL of technical review> of "Recover-Software version 5.5":

- "Recover-Software version 5.5" software cannot recover files over a network.

- Copies of files were saved on the network, so the files would have been found using this software.

Don't chastise or make snide remarks, because you want the focus to be on your evaluation. Putting down other people to make your report look better makes *you* look juvenile or desperate.

Hardening your testimony

Your report prepares your testimony for trial, if the case isn't settled beforehand. In your report, avoid exposing yourself to any of the following risks, which would surface during a trial:

- ✔ **Relying on ignorance:** Don't expect an attorney or opposing expert not to know enough to challenge the validity of e-evidence you present.

- ✔ **Overqualifying yourself or your expertise:** It may not occur to you that it's dangerous to describe yourself as an expert in a general way. Saying that you're a computer expert exposes you to questions later in court that may be beyond the scope of your knowledge or expertise. Faced with a computer question that you can't answer gives the opposing lawyer the chance to ridicule your abilities and toss doubt on your credibility. Stay "inside the box" by describing yourself, for example, as an expert in the collection, preservation, and examination of electronic evidence from computers and certain types of handheld devices.

- ✔ **Failing to understand key legal and forensic words:** Be prepared to give definitions of terms such as *IP address* and *forensic image*. You need to use and be able to explain every word in your report, including what's reasonable. (*Reasonable* means "more likely than not.") A reasonable conclusion, for example, is more likely than not to be valid or true. If you're asked why you think your conclusion is reasonable, that phrase needs to be in your response.

Chapter 17

Standing Your Ground in Court

. . . .

In This Chapter

▶ Delivering value to the case

▶ Finding order in the court, and disorder in the court

▶ Exhibiting e-evidence

▶ Speaking to the judge and jury

. . . .

*I*n this chapter, we focus on you in the courtroom. In court, you have two influential roles — present e-evidence and testify as an expert witness. What you have to do depends on whether you're working for the prosecution, plaintiff, or defense or acting as an officer of the court as a neutral expert.

The party that has the burden of proof — and that party's computer forensics expert — tends to have the most work to do. Why? Because the justice system says "He who asserts must prove." That's legal language for "Put up or shut up." The court system puts the burden on the prosecutor or plaintiff to present sufficiently persuasive evidence and testimony to support the material facts. If that hurdle isn't met, the defendant's motion for a dismissal of the case may be granted. Evidence puts heinous criminals in jail, but wrongly used evidence can put an innocent person inside instead.

A huge number of cases end up in court. Yet they represent 5 percent or fewer of the total number of cases that are filed, because most cases are resolved by pretrial (see Chapter 15). For cases that reach trial, you need to be armed and prepared for the court's "barroom brawls."

In this chapter, we start with what is expected from you. (***Hint:*** It's not a forensics image.) We explain court procedures regarding rounds of testimony. You find out the don'ts and do's of presenting persuasive proof and surviving tactics under rapid-fire questioning from opposing counsel.

Making Good on Deliverables

Why is an investigator part of the team? Think about why you were retained as a computer forensics investigator. If your reasons are listed on the left side of Figure 17-1, you bring those skills to the job, although they don't do you much good in court. Lawyers want you to help prove their cases or defend their clients. In a word, they want *deliverables*, things produced as a result of the investigation that they can use. Deliverables are listed on the right side of Figure 17-1.

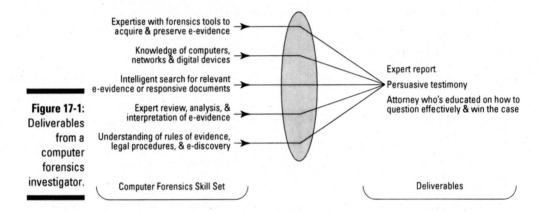

Figure 17-1:
Deliverables
from a
computer
forensics
investigator.

Expertise with forensics tools to acquire & preserve e-evidence

Knowledge of computers, networks & digital devices

Intelligent search for relevant e-evidence or responsive documents

Expert review, analysis, & interpretation of e-evidence

Understanding of rules of evidence, legal procedures, & e-discovery

Computer Forensics Skill Set

Expert report
Persuasive testimony
Attorney who's educated on how to question effectively & win the case

Deliverables

You're brought into a case for your reports and testimony to persuade a judge and jury toward a particular way of thinking. If a defense lawyer needs you to shoot down a time- and location-based alibi that the accused gave in a deposition, that's what you bring to the trial. For example, your testimony might include these elements:

- ✔ Cellphone records identifying precise times, numbers, duration of outgoing and incoming calls, text messages, and even calls to voice mail (VM).

- ✔ Lists of *name on phone* for each telephone number listed as incoming or outgoing.

- ✔ Transcripts of text messages sent and received and images found on the smart phone.

- ✔ E-mail records and transcripts of messages.

- ✔ Printouts of pages from online accounts showing the full transcripts of all messages sent and received — with names, images, dates, subjects, and incriminating content in an easy-to-read format.

Another deliverable is the ability to educate the lawyers about which questions to ask so that they know how to question — or corner — others effectively to best represent their clients. E-evidence is good at catching someone in a lie.

You help prepare the catch and turn it into a story for the jury. Juries remember stories more than sterile facts. Every computer and handheld device has in it a story of someone who is a suspect. You bring that story to the courtroom.

Understanding Barroom Brawls in the Courtroom

In this section, you see how the adversarial court system works with and against expert witnesses, and you see the challenges of courtroom procedure and its drama. The system is highly structured. According to the Constitution, suspects are presumed innocent until the judge or jury decides that the evidence says that they're not. Then an appeal process takes place if the jury finds someone guilty.

Trial scheduling isn't precise. To be as efficient as possible, and recognizing that many cases are settled on the courthouse steps, courts schedule many different trials on the same date. If too many cases remain, some are rescheduled to a new date.

Managing challenging issues

The courtroom can be the setting for rather interesting or mind-bending legal disputes. Issues that don't seem worth arguing about can involve the justices of the Supreme Court. Other issues about evidence can be resolved by simply having each side *stipulate* (agree not to disagree) that something is a fact. The court may have to agree on the stipulation — for example, the prosecution might get the defense to stipulate that a piece of evidence is admissible. Don't expect to understand why issues are or are not argued.

For issues that aren't resolved before trial, here are three reasons for disputes (only the last two involve the investigator's work):

- ✔ **Legal issues:** Legal *loopholes,* or novel situations for which no case law or precedent exists. Basically, legal issues are about whether a crime has been committed. Consider this mind-twisting instance: If an adult in a private chat room performs a lewd act in front of a Webcam in view of someone whom the adult believes is a minor but who is in reality another adult, is this action a crime? Does it violate a law against public obscenity or harming a minor or someone else? This situation raises legal issues, not evidentiary ones (at least not until the legal issues are straightened out). Legal issues might concern whether the chat room qualifies as a public place or whether a minor child was in view of the computer.

The responsibility for resolving such issues rests with the courts, thankfully. A case you're working on might involve unique legal issues because the Internet and wireless technologies enable situations not well defined in the law.

Judges decide questions of law.

✔ **Evidentiary issues:** Disagreements over the e-evidence, such as its authenticity or interpretation. See the following sidebar "Disputing e-mail admissibility" for an example of an evidentiary issue in a fraud case. Expect to be knee deep in this type of issue given the many rules of evidence that can lead to disagreements over what's allowed and what's not.

Evidence that's presented as scientific by expert witnesses may seem subjective to the jury when it's challenged as an interpretive art by defense lawyers or their experts. Being too smug or complacent makes you less sharp.

Never overestimate the strength of your e-evidence.

✔ **Technique or procedural issues:** Lapses in the chain of custody, poorly documented e-evidence collection techniques, or an investigator's lack of credibility. Advanced law enforcement procedures for handling e-evidence, following the chain of custody, and performing proper forensics imaging make these issues rare. To verify, check the RCFL Lab Web site at www.rcfl.gov and review its ongoing investigations at www.rcfl.gov/index.cfm?fuseAction=Public.N_investigations.

Determining what the e-evidence proves is a job for the jurors. Your job is to persuade jury members by making sure that they understand what the e-evidence does or doesn't mean, what your inferences and opinions are, how you derived them, which possible flaws exist, and why those flaws are of no consequence.

Sitting on the stand

You don't get to sit on the stand to give testimony about your investigation and findings and then stand down. After you take the stand, you're in play (so to speak) for several rounds with both lawyers. Keep this perspective in mind — your testimony gives the opposing lawyer an ice pick to poke away at you, your work, and your conclusions. Supposedly, badgering witnesses isn't allowed, but lawyers get away with it unless the judge decides to stop it. (There's a reason that those cruel-but-true lawyer jokes are passed around.) You don't get to object to any question or claim foul play. Only the lawyers have that kind of power.

Disputing e-mail admissibility

In *United States v Siddiqui (2000)*, the defendant was convicted of fraud, making false statements, and obstructing a federal investigation. To receive a National Science Foundation (NSF) award that included a $500,000 research grant, Mohamed Siddiqui had sent bogus letters of recommendation in the names of two individuals and then urged them to support his scheme. Both individuals refused and later served as witnesses for the prosecution when the case went to trial.

E-mail messages between Siddiqui and the two individuals were recovered and used as e-evidence. Siddiqui appealed the guilty verdict. He challenged evidentiary rulings including the admission of e-mails from him to the two witnesses in the case. He argued that because the e-mails had not been properly authenticated, they were inadmissible hearsay.

Under Fed. R. Evid. 901(a), documents must be properly authenticated to be admissible. A document may be authenticated by "[a]ppearance, contents, substance, internal patterns, or other distinctive characteristics, taken in conjunction with circumstances." Siddiqui lost on appeal. The Court of Appeals gave the following reasons for accepting the authenticity of the e-mail messages:

✔ The e-mail messages reflected an e-mail address that included a variation of the defendant's name and the URL of the defendant's employer.

✔ The e-mail address in the messages was consistent with the address in an e-mail that the defendant had introduced into evidence.

✔ The messages' contents indicated that the authors knew the details of the defendant's conduct in trying to get the NSF award.

✔ The e-mail messages referred to the sender by the nickname Mo, which both recipients recognized.

✔ The e-mail messages were sent during the same period in which the recipients spoke to the defendant by telephone and had conversations consistent in content with the e-mail messages.

For details of the issues and how the court responded, see `http://bulk.resource.org/courts.gov/c/F3/235/235.F3d.1318.98-6994.html`.

The *United States v Siddiqui* case provides two big lessons:

✔ **The issue of style can be critical if e-mail has been planted or forged.** Less clever e-mail forgers may not be aware of distinctive writing styles and may use their own style.

✔ **Keep a little "flex room" in your wording.** Notice that the Court of Appeals' reasons for determining the authenticity of e-mails aren't worded in dry, absolute terms. The terms that are used — *reflected, was consistent,* and *indicated* — cut some slack and, ironically, are harder to attack. Proving something absolutely is an extremely tough standard to defend. Using absolute terms is asking for trouble. When you ease the wording, you can reduce the burden of proof on circumstantial e-evidence.

Courts have a procedure for everything, including giving testimony. Not knowing those procedures or how to position your testimony for what's coming at you every step of the way puts you at a big disadvantage.

The timeframe for when you take the stand and testify depends on which team you represent. The following example outlines the process for giving testimony on the witness stand (*plaintiff* refers to the prosecuting, or plaintiff, lawyer):

1. **Direct examination (also called *direct*) by plaintiff**

   The plaintiff calls its first witness (P-Witness #1) to introduce evidence supporting the allegations. Assume that's you. You're sworn to tell the truth, and then you answer the lawyers' questions from the witness stand. Because you're on the same team, you're treated well because it's presumed that you're giving favorable testimony. You should be prepared for this line of questioning. Here's an example of a direct question:

   Q: *Which personal accounting software did you find, if any, on the defendant's laptop computer?*

2. **Cross-examination (also called *cross*) by the defense**

   You're still P-Witness #1, but you're now questioned by the defense. Questions on cross are limited to the subject matter introduced during direct, which is generally a good thing. What's different is that the defense lawyer (who probably doesn't like your testimony) can ask you leading questions. *Leading* questions are in a form that suggests the answer to the witness.

   Here's an example based on the question posed in direct examination if you had answered Yes:

   Q: *Is it true that you found QuickBooks accounting software on the defendant's laptop computer?*

   If you had answered No, the leading question could sound like this:

   Q: *Is it true that you did not find QuickBooks accounting software on the defendant's laptop computer?*

   Courts permit leading questions on cross, on the assumption that the cross-examiner needs to suggest answers to the witness in order to explore adequately the reliability of the direct examination and the credibility of the witness. During cross, the lawyer tries to undermine or impeach your credibility or attempts to show that you're not reliable, to create doubt about you in the minds of the jury members.

   Never underestimate how high the stakes are during cross. Everyone familiar with the courts has seen cases won almost entirely because of the skillful use of cross or essentially lost because of a bungling or overconfident cross-examiner.

   A leading question can be tricky when the lawyer deliberately tangles it up with a misstatement, such as this one:

Q: *You told this jury this morning that, in your opinion, the images found on the defendant's laptop computer hard drive could have been downloaded to that hard drive by anyone who had access to the laptop, didn't you?*

When faced with a misstated leading question on cross, you should

1. Deny the misstatement.

2. Restate what you had said.

Assuming that you had not made such a statement to the jury, your answer might be, "I did not say that. What I did say was that the laptop computer was password protected. The person who downloaded the images would have had to know the password or have been given access to the laptop by someone who knew the password."

The defense may decide not to cross-examine you after you give your direct testimony. That's usually a good sign because the cross mantra is "When in doubt, don't cross-examine." If you're not cross-examined, you're spared from having to experience Steps 3 and 4.

If you haven't seriously harmed the defense's case or if the defense doubts that your testimony can be impeached successfully, cross doesn't take place. The defense doesn't risk damaging its case.

3. **Redirect examination (also called *redirect*) by plaintiff**

   You're questioned again by the plaintiff about issues that were uncovered or that didn't go well during cross. You're back in friendly territory, so don't expect that someone will try to trick you.

4. **Re-cross-examination (also called *recross*) by defense**

   Recross gives both sides an equal number of times to ask you questions. You face questioning again by the opposing lawyer if a redirect raises an issue that's leaving a bad impression with the jury. The defense has the chance to try to clean it up.

   Steps 1 through 4 are repeated for any witnesses in addition to you until all the plaintiff's witnesses have testified.

5. **Case rested by plaintiff**

   In this defining moment, the court is informed that the plaintiff rests its case. No more witnesses can be called to the stand or evidence introduced by the plaintiff.

6. **(Optional) Directed verdict of acquittal**

   If the plaintiff hasn't proved its case, the defense may make a motion for a directed verdict from the judge. (The jury doesn't get to vote here.) If the judge agrees that the evidence is too weak, the trial is over. This verdict from the judge saves time and money because there's no reason to continue the trial if the case has already been lost. If the judge doesn't agree, the defense is entitled to present evidence, but isn't required to do so. Expect that the defense will continue.

7. **Direct examination by the defense**

   The defense begins its direct examination with its own witnesses and evidence, with the roles reversed, until all defense witnesses have testified. If you're working for the defense, this step is where you first take the stand.

8. **Cross by plaintiff**

   As in Step 2, cross-examination might not take place. If it does, you can expect the tactics discussed in Step 2 to take place. If not, Steps 9 and 10 don't take place, either.

9. **Redirect by defense**

10. **Recross by plaintiff**

11. **Defense rests**

    All testimony ends. You're done, as are all witnesses.

12. **Closing or final arguments**

    It's last call for the lawyers to influence the jury in this case. Your testimony might be mentioned here. No matter what's said about what you said, you remain silent.

13. **Jury instructions**

    The judge gives instructions and charges to the jury, explaining the appropriate law and the steps they must take to reach a verdict. Your testimony may be brought up in these instructions. See the later section "Instructing jurors about expert testimony."

14. **Jury deliberation and verdict**

    Jurors consider the evidence and reach a verdict of guilty or not guilty. In some cases, the jury doesn't reach a verdict.

15. **Appeal**

    Either party can appeal the verdict.

You may face examination as many as four times in court and under oath to tell the truth. You must tell the truth, no matter how damaging it might be to the case. Vigorous or harsh cross-examination, the presentation of contrary e-evidence, and careful instruction about the burdens of proof are the traditional and appropriate means of attacking shaky but admissible evidence. You find out how to give effective testimony in the later section "Presenting E-Evidence to Persuade."

 In 2008, John B. Torkelsen became a former expert witness after pleading guilty to perjury, a charge that carries up to five years in prison, for lying in court. Torkelson served as an expert witness for plaintiffs in hundreds of class action suits and shareholder actions against major companies, such as AT&T and Microsoft, that were litigated in U.S. federal and state courts. The law firms that hired Torkelsen told the courts he was an independent expert.

Therefore, the law firms that hired him were precluded by rules of professional responsibility from paying him on a *contingent* basis — they couldn't
pay Torkelson based on the outcome of a case. But several law firms secretly
paid Torkelsen on a contingent basis and concealed the payment arrangement
from the courts and defendants. He had made tens of millions of dollars as an
expert witness in hundreds of lawsuits. "It is simply unacceptable for anyone
involved in litigation to lie to the courts. Torkelson has compromised the
pursuit of justice," according to Thomas P. O'Brien, the U.S Attorney in Los
Angeles. For details, visit the US Department of Justice site at www.usdoj.
gov/usao/cac/pressroom/pr2008/020.html.

Instructing jurors about expert testimony

The judge may instruct the jury specifically about your testimony. Here's
an adaptation of the jury instructions from a New York court — you can
download the PDF file from www.nycourts.gov/cji/1-General/CJI2d.
Expert.pdf:

> You might recall that [expert witness's name] testified about certain com-
> puter forensic and electronic evidence matters and gave an opinion on
> such matters. Ordinarily, a witness is limited to testifying about facts and
> isn't permitted to give an opinion. Where, however, scientific, medical,
> technical, or other specialized knowledge helps the jury understand the
> evidence or determine a fact in issue, a witness with expertise in a spe-
> cialized field may render opinions about such matters.
>
> You should evaluate the testimony of any such witness just as you would
> evaluate the testimony of any other witness. You may accept or reject
> such testimony, in whole or in part, just as you may with respect to the
> testimony of any other witness. In deciding whether to accept such testi-
> mony, you should consider these factors:
>
> - Qualifications and witness believability
>
> - Facts and other circumstances on which the witness's opinion was
>   based
>
> - Accuracy or inaccuracy of any assumed or hypothetical fact on
>   which the opinion was based
>
> - Reasons given for the witness's opinion
>
> - Whether the witness's opinion is consistent or inconsistent with
>   other evidence in the case

All along the way and right into the jury room, you are personally and professionally scrutinized.

Presenting E-Evidence to Persuade

Think back to your high school science or math class. After a topic became too complicated or drawn out, all you might have heard was a voice in the distance as your mind drifted away. Imagine a teacher explaining Newton's theory of gravity or geometry using formulas — without pictures or diagrams. Could you have assessed the truth of those lessons? If not, then you understand why you may need to use visuals in your testimony. Human attention is limited and tough to hold on to.

The jury isn't sitting in its box by choice. Jurors may be committed to their civic responsibility, but there are limits to what they can absorb and remember. Help them out: Plan, prepare, and present visual aids to make it easier to grasp, believe, and remember your e-evidence. The best way to represent a complex topic is with simplicity. Simple illustrations work best because they create fewer distractions for viewers. Although too many possibilities exist to consider for the design of your presentations, you can avoid certain risks when you use technology to present e-evidence.

Staging a disaster

Relying on computer technology, wireless connections, or electronics to work precisely the way you need them to at the moment you need them to is outright dumb. You can minimize disastrous moments by following these guidelines:

- **No surprises:** Don't surprise the judge or your opponent. Get permission before trial for your demonstrations or presentations and the equipment you need for them.

- **No live events:** Don't rely on anything live, such as a live Internet connection, Web site, or chat room. Use screen captures and label everything so that you don't have to rely on your (live) memory.

- **No ad libs:** Don't expect things to work unless you've rehearsed and tested them yourself. If someone prepares a slide presentation for you, test it. Verify that none of the slides was accidentally hidden. Slides with swooshing sounds, poorly picked colors (no yellow, pink, vibrant turquoise or magenta because those colors can be extremely difficult to read and may look horrible if they're paired with other colors incorrectly!), or sideways or illegible text are tough for anyone to endure. Know how to use the software or device. You don't want to look like you don't know how to use computer equipment.

- **No epics:** Consider the attention span of jurors. Too much detail can mess up the major points you need to make. Keep it simple.

✔ **No gaps:** Connect the dots for the jury. If you're presenting a series of events, walk the jury through them. Create time maps that explain (lay out) events that are linked, such as showing the timeline of files that were downloaded and then copied to another media and then deleted.

✔ **No-tech backup:** Expect problems and plan alternative displays as backups.

✔ **No forgetting all items you need.** Think out every possible "oops" and find a solution for it. Similar to showing up at a crime scene to collect and capture e-evidence, you need equipment to display your e-evidence to the jury, and someone's budget determines what that equipment is. Bring extension cords or power strips. If you need to use a whiteboard, buy brand-new dry erase markers of the appropriate thickness.

Before any exhibit is admitted into evidence, the defense has the opportunity to challenge it. Prepare hard copy (printout) binders containing all exhibits to show to whoever needs to see them for review or approval.

Exhibiting like an expert

Design your exhibits as simply as possible. If you need professional help with the design and creation of exhibits because you're artistically tone-deaf, find the help. You need to inform, not impress, but there's no excuse for low-quality or sketchy work. Consider these other tips:

✔ **Use terms that nontechnical types can understand, unless precision is necessary.**

You don't want to call a *forensic image* a "copy of the hard drive."

✔ **Use analogies to explain complex technical material.**

IP addresses may be tough for nontechnical types to understand, for example, until you explain that they work similarly to phone numbers. Explaining e-mail headers and delivery by relating them to physical mail is a simple but effective analogy.

✔ **Be prepared to explain and define technical material.**

If the opposition tries to show that you're not such a helpful expert, you'll be ready.

✔ **If you're allowed to, stand up and point to elements on the exhibit to ensure that everyone is looking at the right spot as you describe it.**

If you can't point, have someone on your team do it. As an element of the exhibit is being pointed out, describe what it is or its specific location so that the court stenographer can capture it in the transcript.

> ✔ **Don't forget that your attention belongs on the jury and not on your displays.**
>
> Ask jurors whether they have any trouble reading exhibits and give them enough time to read. If one of them has a problem, fix it.
>
> ✔ **Never testify beyond your expertise.**
>
> Exhibits must fall within your area of expertise.

"Every contact leaves a trace." This statement is the basis of Locard's principle. In the early 20th century, forensic science became a specialized profession. Experts working in labs tried to link suspects to crime or crime scenes definitively. The scientist Locard recognized that "physical evidence cannot be wrong, it cannot perjure itself, it cannot be wholly absent. Only human failure to find it, study and understand it, can diminish its value." Because of Locard, the statement "Every criminal leaves a trace" became a cornerstone of police investigations.

Communicating to the Court

Good testimony feels natural and flows well. When your testimony is being ground up by opposing counsel, you feel that too. The best expert witnesses persuade the jury by artfully and simply communicating the facts through reports, exhibits, and testimonies.

After being hired as an expert, all your materials or work product — analysis, notes, reports, correspondence, opinions, research — are subject to discovery. Be very careful with your work product practices to avoid creating misleading materials that can be used against you during testimony.

Giving testimony about the case

Beyond technical skills, lawyers need experts who testify well and are credible and likable to juries. Your opinion may be perfect but worthless if you can't persuade anyone to believe or understand that opinion.

Giving oral testimony is much less tricky if you know the rules. The following tactics and techniques can help you perform well during direct and redirect, and make you resistant to cross and recross attacks:

> ✔ **Compose a logical and focused testimony outline of the facts in the case.**
>
> Make sure that this outline is relevant to the opinions and is easily understood.

✔ **Prepare testimony that the judge and jury will believe.**

If you don't believe it, don't try to sell it.

✔ **Establish rapport with the judge and jury by making eye contact with them.**

Think of yourself having a conversation with the judge and jury when explaining methods and opinions.

✔ **Don't spar with the lawyers.**

Be pleasant and patient no matter how hard it is. Juries react to you more favorably if you remain calm, answer matter-of-factly, and avoid clenching your teeth.

✔ **Be as natural and relaxed as you can be.**

Don't look rehearsed or mechanical because it hurts your credibility. If you're stressed over not being well prepared, at least look relaxed.

✔ **Be aware of your body language, facial expressions, eye movement, and good posture.**

Death-ray stares at the person causing you pain will be seen by the jury. Be prepared for a sneeze or cough.

✔ **Watch the jurors to determine their level of understanding.**

If they look bewildered, change your pace or use more analogies or recap, if possible. Connect the dots with simple explanations of each step or e-evidence item.

✔ **Focus on the right thing.**

Focus on the question that's being asked rather than on wondering what the lawyer is up to or where the questioning is headed.

✔ **Don't get misled.**

If you're asked a hypothetical question, first consider whether answering it is smart or risky. If it's too complex or strange, respond with "I would rather not speculate."

The objective of giving testimony should never be based solely on winning the case.

Answering about yourself

Your credibility and qualifications are on trial too. Qualifications are skills and knowledge from education or experience.

You may be asked to discuss your earlier testimonies, state how much you were paid or charged, describe how you keep your expertise up-to-date, or explain other issues unrelated to the case being tried. Juries pay attention to your answers.

Avoid these mistakes:

- ✔ Not being familiar with the facts of the case.
- ✔ Not being prepared to defend your methodology and aware of its limitations.
- ✔ Billing for work you weren't authorized to perform by the lawyer or client.
- ✔ Charging too much or too little.
- ✔ Not getting paid until after you testify or being paid based on the outcome. Payment issues are more serious than you might expect. See the later section "Getting paid without conflict."
- ✔ Having a conflict of interest. Before accepting a case, you must verify that you have no conflict of interest (a situation where you can't be unbiased for any reason). The penalty for acting as an expert in a conflict of interest includes being disqualified from testifying, which could destroy the case.
- ✔ Being inconsistent or giving a report or testimony that contradicts earlier reports or testimonies — in effect, fitting testimony to the theory of the case or to favor the side you represent.
- ✔ Not identifying all the time spent examining the e-evidence. Your bill shows the amount of time you spent examining the e-evidence. If that length of time is significantly shorter than the time the opposing side's expert spends, it may lead to a charge that your opinion lacks sufficient basis. The opposite can be an issue too.
- ✔ Stretching the truth.
- ✔ Speaking to or on the media about a case, which can indicate that you're on the case for fame or other personal gain.

If you create an invoice for your services using a spreadsheet, such as Microsoft Excel, check your work. Dates, hours worked, and services performed must be accurate. If you format hours worked as currency or dates are changed because you copied them to another location, you create mistakes. Formulas or functions used in calculations must include the correct range of cells. How would you explain charging for services on the wrong dates or a total bill showing that you overcharged because of the wrong cell range? If you send multiple invoices, be sure not to double-charge.

Getting paid without conflict

A federal rule allows lawyers to pay a fee for the professional services of an expert witness. Having such a rule may seem ridiculous, but the history of the rule isn't important — only the rule is. The process of getting paid isn't written into the rule.

All parties need to be careful and precise with this payment issue because

✔ The lawyer needs to avoid any action or expense that can lead to disputes between himself and the client over fees.

✔ The lawyer and the client need to avoid disputes with the expert witness.

✔ The expert witness wants to maintain an unblemished reputation by not "stiffing" the lawyer or client.

Suppose that an expert witness is retained by the lawyer, who intends to pass along the expert's bill to the client for payment. The expert is paid based on an hourly rate. This type of arrangement needs to be written into some sort of signed agreement. Why? Assume that later, after work has been performed, the client decides that the fee for the expert's services is too high — and shouldn't get any higher. Then what? The dispute over fees or payment could turn into potentially damaging testimony if it's not resolved before trial. Everyone could get harmed as a result.

Here are some common-sense recommendations for minimizing conflicts and disputes:

✔ **Use a detailed written fee agreement with the expert together with an engagement letter.**

Having a fee agreement ensures that all parties clearly understand the arrangements — who and when — under which the expert is paid.

✔ **Discuss specific provisions for the withdrawal of the expert before the agreement is signed.**

Include provisions in the engagement letter or fee agreement.

You cannot have an agreement with an expert that requires payment of a fee only for testifying in a certain way or only if the outcome of the case is favorable to the client.

Part V
The Part of Tens

The 5th Wave — By Rich Tennant

"I have everything ready for you to start filling out your final report. Writing materials, the evidence, a morphine drip..."

In this part . . .

This part of the book gives you quick tips on how to get qualified, dangerous, and equipped. At this time, no universally accepted qualifications are required of a computer forensic investigator, so you need to build your own. In Chapter 18, we list ten certifications to consider and an extra ten journals and higher-education programs to put you, or keep you, on the leading edge. Chapter 19 lists the tactics of a computer forensic superhero — who is bulletproof and irrefutable and fights for justice. What's a superhero without superpowered equipment? Chapter 20 lists the items you need to have to perform your forensic feats, in the lab and as a road warrior.

In the field of computer forensics, digital devices collide with legal gavels. You're exposed to a lot of techno- and legal-speak, not to mention those riveting rules of evidence and courtroom procedures. You need a glossary, which you find at the end of this part.

Once a new technology rolls over you, if you're not part of the steamroller, you're part of the road.

— Stewart Brand, publisher of *The Whole Earth Catalog,* 1968

Chapter 18

Ten Ways to Get Qualified and Prepped for Success

In This Chapter

▶ Getting certified in person or online

▶ Staying current in computer forensics

*A*fter you're certified, you should keep your hard-earned certifications in force. Renewing them requires keeping current by reading articles, participating in events, and attending seminars. You might even be interested in a university certificate or degree programs.

In this chapter, we "pull a double" and borrow from the world of sports by offering a front ten and then a back ten.

The Front Ten: Certifications

You can obtain various types of certifications. Some are from vendors that offer product-specific training in using their software tools, and other certifications verify a broad foundation in computer networks or forensics methods.

Here are ten certifications for you to consider, presented in alphabetical order. Other certifications may also be available now and in the future.

ACE: AccessData

```
www.accessdata.com/Training/TrainAceOver.aspx
```

Training and certificates are provided by AccessData, at `http://accessdata.com`, the vendor offering Forensic Toolkit (FTK). AccessData Certified Examiner (ACE) certification requires that you demonstrate skill, knowledge, and ability in using AccessData imaging and analysis technology, FTK, Password Recovery Toolkit (PRTK), and Registry Viewer.

CCE: Certified Computer Examiner

```
www.certified-computer-examiner.com/index.html
```

This vendor-neutral certification is open to anyone. A possible advantage to you is that you can take the exam over the Internet. The certificate is sponsored by the International Society of Forensic Computer Examiners `www.isfce.com` (ISFCE).

CFCE: Certified Forensic Computer Examiner

```
www.cops.org/cfce
```

The Certified Forensic Computer Examiner (CFCE) course is provided by International Association of Computer Investigative Specialists (IACIS), the international, volunteer, nonprofit corporation of law enforcement dedicated to education in the field of forensic computer science. To earn the CFCE certification, you must successfully complete the two-week training course and solve correspondence proficiency problems. This certification is only for law enforcement professionals.

CEECS: Certified Electronic Evidence Collection Specialist

```
www.cops.org/ceecs
```

CEECS training courses teach best practices in seizing computers and digital media. It's only for law enforcement professionals.

Cisco: Various certifications

```
www.cisco.com/web/learning/le3/learning_certification_
            overview.html
```

Cisco offers a variety of excellent network and information security training programs and certificates. Training for the Cisco Certified Design Associate (CCDA) certification provides basic knowledge of network design. Training for the more advanced Cisco Certified Network Associate (CCNA) certification teaches how to install, configure, operate, and troubleshoot medium-size routed and switched networks. The certifications verify that the person possesses the respective abilities and expertise.

CISSP: Certified Information Systems Security Professional

```
https://www.isc2.org/cgi-bin/content.cgi?category=539
```

To become a certified information systems security professional (CISSP), you must successfully complete two separate processes: examination and certification. The eligibility requirements to sit for the CISSP examination are completely separate from the eligibility requirements necessary to be certified. Experience is needed in order to obtain the certificate. Check out *CISSP For Dummies,* by Lawrence H. Miller and Peter H. Gregory (Wiley Publishing).

CompTia: Various certifications

```
www.comptia.org
http://certification.comptia.org
```

CompTIA certifications are well known and respected as one of the best ways to break into the information technology field and build a solid career. Certifications valuable to a computer forensics career are CompTIA Network+, CompTIA Security, and CompTIA A+.

EnCE: Guidance Software

```
www.guidancesoftware.com/training/EnCE_certification.aspx
```

The EnCase Certified Examiner (EnCE) certificate is available to public- and private-sector professionals in the use of Guidance Software's EnCase computer forensic software.

Paraben training

```
www.paraben-training.com
```

Paraben offers a wide range of forensics training, for cellphone, PDA, network, and mobile forensics. Although you don't become certified, the certificates of completion are worthwhile to own.

SANS and GCFA: GIAC Certified Forensics Analyst

www.giac.org/certifications/security/gcfa.php
www.sans.org/sans2008

Getting the GIAC Certified Forensic Analysts (GCFAs) certification means that you have the knowledge, skills, and abilities to handle advanced incident-handling scenarios, conduct formal incident investigations, and carry out forensic investigation of networks and hosts.

The Back Ten: Journals and Education

We added a "back ten" to this chapter because we want to keep you up-to-date. Research journals and degree programs dedicated to computer forensics continue to emerge. To keep up with advances and events, be sure to bookmark at least a few of these — and check this book's Web site for more links to cutting-edge computer forensics and e-evidence issues:

Journals and research

✔ *International Journal of Digital Evidence:* Supported by the Economic Crime Institute (ECI) at Utica College and the Computer Forensics Research and Development Center (CFRDC). Find it at www.ijde.org.

✔ *Journal of Digital Forensics, Security and Law:* A publication of the Association of Digital Forensics, Security and Law (ADFSL). Check it out at www.jdfsl.org.

✔ *National Institute of Justice Journal:* Find it at www.ojp.usdoj.gov/nij/journals/254/digital_evidence.html.

✔ *Small Scale Digital Device Forensics Journal:* Check out this site at www.ssddfj.org.

✔ SANS' Information Security Reading Room: Find this site at www.sans.org/reading_room/index.php.

Education and research centers

✔ Champlain College computer and digital forensics (CDF) degree program: www.champlain.edu/majors/digitalforensics

✔ Purdue University Cyber Forensics Lab master's area of specialization: cyberforensics.purdue.edu

- Rochester Institute of Technology (RIT) degree in information security and forensics (ISF): `nssa.rit.edu/~nssa/nssa/undergrad/isfBS.maml`
- University of Central Florida (UCF) degrees and certificate: `www.ncfs.org/home.html`
- Utica College, cybercrime investigations and forensics specialization: `www.onlineuticacollege.com/online-cyber-security-degree.asp`

Chapter 19

Ten Tactics of an Excellent Investigator and a Dangerous Expert Witness

In This Chapter

▶ Enhancing your computer forensics career

▶ Knowing how to withstand tricky tactics

▶ Getting your message to the judge and jury

A lot is riding on your being a determined and ethical investigator and an expert witness: the justice system; your career success; someone's quality of life or liberty, such as defendants, victims (if any), and their families. Many professional careers have ended abruptly and painfully as a result of how the media handled their personal e-mail or exposed the digital trails of their activities. The same thing happens in the courtroom, so you should read about and apply these tactics to be prepared to perform convincingly and fairly. Don't get tricked or trapped by opposing counsel!

Life in your forensic lab doesn't resemble life in the courtroom. You don't have the home team advantage. Plus, the court's way of operating may be bizarre. The practice of law is loaded with theory. Lawyers argue, expound, and pontificate about the legal and evidentiary issues and how they want the jury to interpret the facts of the case. In contrast, you, as an expert witness, generally work with hard facts and only with evidentiary issues. In a legal duel with opposing lawyers, defending your interpretation about what those facts mean or what they represent may not be easy. This chapter presents ten other warnings and words of advice.

Stick to Finding and Telling the Truth

You've heard your job description many times on TV and in the movies: ". . . to tell the truth, the whole truth, and nothing but the truth." Witness testimony must be relied on as being truthful. The truth starts at the same time as the investigation and continues throughout your testimony in court. Misrepresenting the truth or getting caught in a lie destroys your credibility and may also destroy the case. An expert with a credibility problem is a problem (to future clients). Your obligation isn't to support a lawyer's theory unless the e-evidence supports it.

Lying under oath is perjury. Perjury is the *big lie* — the lie that has an effect on material issues. Charges of perjury rely on at least these three issues:

✔ Whether the question was clearly worded

✔ Whether the answer was unequivocal

✔ Whether the witness knew that the answer was false

Don't Fall for Counsel's Tricks in Court

In court or deposition, if you don't know the answer to a question, don't try to bluff your way through an answer. Admit that you don't know before someone points it out. Imagine that during a brutal cross-examination, opposing counsel asks whether you understand the theory of *GET SMART*. You don't have a clue, but are afraid to admit it, so you say Yes, desperately hoping that the next question gives you a hint. Bam! Counsel destroys you by saying that no such theory even exists. You won't recover from that mistake.

Bluffing or stretching the truth is ammunition that can and will be used against you. You may have your client's best interests at heart, but intentions don't count.

If you cannot answer a question for any of the following reasons, don't. Be respectful in your response by stating why you cannot respond:

✔ **The question is too vague.**

   If you have to help construct the question to answer it, you're working for the wrong side. Respond instead with, "The question you asked is too vague."

✔ **The question doesn't make sense as asked.**

   Either out of ignorance or purposely, the lawyer may word a question in such a way that it doesn't make sense to you — or to other computer forensic examiners.

> ✔ **The question is beyond the scope of your expertise.**
>
> For example, you cannot give an opinion about why someone did something. Don't testify "outside the lines" (outside the boundaries of your expertise).

Be Irrefutable

Whenever you introduce and explain e-evidence in court, as an expert, you can safely assume that someone will try to pick you apart bit by bit. (Yes, it's a pun, but it's true.) The good news is that if you have command of the facts and can brilliantly explain the basis for every opinion in your report, there's no way you can be picked apart successfully in the eyes of the jury. The jury may think that you're being treated unfairly, which is a good thing for you.

Being irrefutable also involves confirming that the chain of custody was maintained at all times. An incomplete or broken chain is similar to a broken mirror: It cannot be undone. So, from the start, handle all data and devices of every case as evidence.

Submit a Descriptive, Complete Bill

Your invoice is a form of documentation. Your client is interested in how you bill for your services, of course, but your bill may also be examined in court. Keep a detailed log of your work so that you can submit a detailed invoice. Dates and descriptions must be consistent with your testimony.

For several reasons, expect questions stemming from or about your bill for expert service. Opposing counsel looks at dates, descriptions of services, and hourly rates, and notes who is paying the bill. Be sure to check your invoice for accuracy. You can too easily make a mistake that may seem trivial to you but becomes magnified out of proportion in court. For example, if the dates you record don't match dates in your report, how do you explain your sloppiness?

You also have to consider the issue of how much you charge. If your hourly rate is unusually high, you look like a hired gun. If your rate is too low, you look unprofessional.

Prepare a Clear, Complete Report

Expect to refer to your written report during testimony, for example, to refer to all the work you performed, how and when you performed it, and which inferences you made. Working backward to the time when you're writing the report, keep in mind that you're writing it as your own memory aid as well as for others. The report helps jog your memory when you most need it.

If the opposing side also has an expert witness who was deposed or who submitted a report that you disagree with, you report should explain your disagreements with that expert's opinions. Refuting another person's expert opinion can be fun in a wacky sort of way, so don't dread doing it. As always, you need to be polite and respectful of the other person's opinions. It may help to explain how that person may have made mistakes, but don't push the issue. If the other expert's opinion seems like it was bought and paid for, don't try to justify or rationalize it. Then use that opportunity to reinforce your correct procedures, analysis, interpretations, or whatever relevant information you have.

Avoid the urge to give an "I don't remember" response about an important issue during cross-examination. The theory is that it's your work, so you ought to know it. If your report isn't complete or organized, you may give off negative nonverbal cues.

Understand Nonverbal Cues

Nonverbal communication establishes rapport with jury members so that they're more likely to be receptive of your verbal communication. Your non-verbal behaviors may win the trust and confidence of jurors by projecting a sense of authority, integrity, alertness, and other positive characteristics.

Appearing relaxed and confident is much easier to do when you truly feel that way. If you're nervous, trembling, or hyperventilating, those aren't good signs. Of course, if you look comatose, you're taking the relaxed look too far.

The perfect persona is relaxed excellence.

Another nonverbal cue is your response rate to questions. Wait until the lawyer has stopped talking, think for a moment, and then start to answer. Don't jump in. Interruptions play havoc with the court stenographer, who has to record everything that's said, and you look argumentative to the jury.

Look 'Em Straight in the Eye

You're a performer on the witness stand. You're probably going to explain complex technical issues in nontechnical terms or by using analogies. Worse, you may be doing so after lunch, when the jury's attention and interest aren't at their highest level. No matter what the conditions are, you should maintain eye contact with the person questioning you or the jury. Don't look down, up, or away.

If you need to read your report or other documents, resume the straight-in-the-eye look as soon as you finish.

Eye contact doesn't mean staring someone down or trying to burn them with your relentless gaze, no matter how strong your desire to do so. You have to stay in control and avoid showing weakness or hesitancy, and never roll your eyes, no matter how stupid the question.

Dress for Your Role As a Professional

Dress for success in front of a judge and jury. You may not like it, but you can't change it. Lieutenant Columbo was an excellent detective. James Bond achieved his missions. Neither of these infallible guys, however, should be your role model for courtroom wear. Avoid extremes in your clothes, shoes, hair, and, if applicable, jewelry, manicure, and makeup. You don't want to startle anyone. And, as the judge warned Joe Pesci in the movie *My Cousin Vinny*, wear something made out of cloth. That movie may have dramatized that an improper way of dressing insults the judge and the integrity of the court, but that drama is real.

You want to look well dressed, but not flashy or vain. You can safely assume that silver-tipped alligator boots and Birkenstock sandals aren't appropriate footwear. Closed-toe shoes work best.

The key principle is moderation. You don't want the way you look to interfere with what you're saying to persuade the jury to accept your expert testimony.

Stay Certified and Up-to-Date

It happens. Some professionals become retired on active duty (RAD). Your credentials are your credibility. In addition to getting certified (see Chapter 18), you should attend seminars, webinars, courses, and similar events to maintain your certification and stay current in your profession. You should also check out our blog for up-to-date information.

Several computer forensic and e-discovery journals and other blogs that you can visit are a helpful part of your routine. See Chapter 18.

As with everything else you do, your résumé may be reviewed in court, or you may be asked to verify how you keep yourself informed. Have something credible to report.

Know When to Say No

Getting a call for your expert services isn't like taking an order for a pepperoni pizza with a 30-minute delivery guarantee. Turn down cases that discourage thoroughness or that have you on an impossibly tight budget. If you accept a case under such conditions, no one will care or consider that you did the best you could under the circumstances.

There are no superheroes in court. Justice may be blind, but it can still see things your way if you're right for the investigation.

Chapter 20

Ten Cool Tools for Computer Forensics

*E*very computer forensic gumshoe needs a set of good, solid tools to undertake a proper investigation, and the tools you use vary according to the type of investigation you're working on. The list of tools in this chapter isn't all-inclusive — and you may have your own favorites — but the ones we describe are the basic ones you should use.

Computer Forensic Software Tools

The days of hard-core computer geeks knowing every square digital inch of an operating system are years behind us. Although computer forensic professionals can now do the drudge work of scanning for evidence using nothing more than a keyboard and a hex editor, that person has access to tools that automate the work in order to use their time more effectively. In fact, modern computer forensic software can find evidence in only minutes, whereas in the "old days" the process took hours or even days! You still have to know your way around a computer, but these tools are true time-savers. Just remember that a tool is only as good as the person who uses it.

EnCase

EnCase, the gold standard, is used by countless organizations for almost any computer forensic investigation. The power of this must-have item for your computer forensic toolbox, and your ability to customize it for unique searches, set it apart from most competitors.

EnCase comes built-in with many forensic features, such as keyword searches, e-mail searches, and Web page carving. The numerous versions of its forensic software range from mobile device acquisitions to full-blown network forensic-analysis tools. Two other cool features are its

- ✓ **Scripting language:** You can customize searches.
- ✓ **Fully automated report function:** It builds reports for you quickly.

EnCase is sold by Guidance Software on its Web site, and by its sales force, at www.guideancesoftware.com. Support for EnCase is rock solid, and the technical support staff knows how to solve problems fairly quickly in addition to providing multilanguage support.

Forensic ToolKit (FTK)

AccessData has created a forensic software tool that's fairly easy to operate because of its one-touch-button interface, and it's also relatively inexpensive. The new version of FTK is even easier to use, and AccessData has started a forensic certification, ACE, based on its software.

FTK has automated, to a high degree, the hard, behind-the-scenes work of setting up searches. Press the Email button and out pop the e-mails. The FTK report generator does the hard work of putting a useful report into the automated hands of the forensic software while still allowing the investigator control over the report, if needed.

FTK is sold on the AcessData Web site at www.accessdata.com. Everything you need to order the software and training is on the site. Even the certification process is available for you to peruse.

Device Seizure

The Paraben forensic tools compete with the top two computer forensic software makers EnCase and FTK (described earlier in this chapter), but the company truly shines in the mobile forensic arena. Using Paraben's Device Seizure product, you can look at most mobile devices on the market. With more cases going mobile, Device Seizure is a must-have tool.

You can use Device Seizure to access and download almost all information contained in a mobile device, such as text messages or user data, and in a way that's forensically acceptable in court.

Device Seizure and all the extras that can go with it are at www.paraben.com along with other useful forensic tools.

Computer Forensic Hardware

In contrast to computer forensic software designed to extract data or evidence in a timely manner and from a logical point of view, forensic hardware is primarily used to connect the physical parts of the computer to help extract the data for use with the forensic software. The basic idea behind forensic hardware is to facilitate the forensic transfer of digital evidence from one device to another as quickly as possible.

FRED

The Forensic Recovery of Evidence Device (FRED) forensic workstation from Digital Intelligence has an interface for all occasions — and then some. In addition to the laboratory version, FRED comes in mobile versions that facilitate the acquisition of evidence in the field for quick analysis.

FRED combines just about every available interface into one convenient workstation so that you don't have to connect and disconnect a toolbox full of interfaces. Another helpful FRED feature is the collection of software packages that's loaded on it if you request it: EnCase, FTK, Paraben's P2, and many others.

Digital Intelligence, at www.digitalintelligence.com, has all the information you could ever want about the FRED systems. The company also offers training in the use of its systems and provides helpful technical support.

WiebeTech Forensic Field Kit

When you need a small footprint and useful equipment for field use, the WiebeTech field kit is hard to beat, figuratively and literally. Even with its small footprint, this field kit has the most popular interfaces available, and you can even customize it for your unique needs.

Using the WiebeTech field kit, you can carry the most essential pieces of your forensic toolkit. The heart of this field kit consists of the write protect devices that WiebeTech manufactures in-house. The kits also contain interfaces for EIDE, SATA, and laptop hard drives.

You can find WiebeTech field kits at www.wiebetech.com, and they're also listed at some third-party Web sites.

Logicube

Logicube offers some of the fastest disk-to-disk and disk-to-image transfer equipment now on the market. As storage devices grow larger, transferring 4 gigabytes per minute can save quite a bit of time over other methods of field data acquisition.

The Logicube data capture equipment captures data from a target media and transfers it to another disk or an image while at the same time performing an integrity check to ensure a forensic copy. The devices have various interfaces and usually come in a field kit configuration.

The Logicube Web site at www.logicube.com has information about the devices and how to order them. The company also offers other forensic products and has an in-house research-and-development team.

Computer Forensic Laboratories

Every good computer forensic scientist or investigator needs a place to do their work. In the ideal location to conduct an investigation, you have absolute control of security, tools, and even the physical environment. Ideally, we're describing your computer forensic laboratory! As in any field of science, computer forensics requires its own set of laboratory tools to get the job done.

Computer forensic data server

Any computer forensic investigative unit of any size rapidly runs into the problem of where to store cases that are in progress or that need to be archived for possible later use. A centralized data storage solution is the best and most secure solution.

A forensic data server allows you to keep forensic images in a centralized, secure, and organized manner that lets you focus more on analyzing cases than on looking for them. A server needs to have large data capacity, the ability to authenticate users for security purposes, with the capacity to perform backups of all data in case the storage devices fail.

You can find commercial-grade servers at any of the larger computer vendors, such as Dell and HP, and at forensic companies, such as Digital Intelligence.

Forensic write blockers

One basic piece of equipment that a computer forensic laboratory needs is the simple but effective write blocker. Although most software tools have built-in software write blockers, you also need an assortment of physical write blockers to cover as many situations or devices as possible.

A write blocker is used to keep an operating system from making any changes to the original or suspect media to keep from erasing or damaging potential evidence. Software write blockers work at the operating system level and are specific to the operating system. In other words, a software write blocker works on only the operating system in which it is installed. A physical write blocker works at the hardware level and can work with any operating system because, at the physical level, the write blocker is intercepting (or, in many cases, blocking) electrical signals to the storage device and has no concern about which operating system is in place.

The technology used by computers to read and write to storage devices is well understood and fairly straightforward — you can find dozens of manufacturers of write-protect devices. For reliability and support, stick with these name brands in the industry:

✔ **Digital Intelligence:** The UltraKit write-block product (see www.digital intelligence.com) follows the everything-but-the-kitchen-sink model. All standard storage device formats, such as IDE, SCSI, SATA, and USB, are supported. In addition, the cables and power supplies are furnished, to make this kit one of the most complete in the industry.

✔ **Paraben:** Paraben has taken the idea of a Faraday box and added silver-lined gloves to allow an investigator to work on a wireless device located inside the box. The Wireless Stronghold Box (see www.paraben.com) is a must-see for any computer forensic laboratory working with wireless devices. This box, a Faraday cage, isolates any enclosed wireless device, thus making it a wireless write blocker. For added protection, all connections leading into the box are filtered.

✔ **Wiebetech :** These write-protect devices run the spectrum from field kits to RAID systems. Wiebetech products (see www.wiebetch.com) are also sold by the major forensic software makers, which adds to their credibility.

Media wiping equipment

Whether you complete one case per year or one case per day, you need to wipe the media you work with before you even start your case, to ensure that no cross contamination between your cases occurs.

Forensic data wipers ensure that no data from a previous case is still present on the media. Most data wipers don't erase existing data per se, but instead overwrite the data with either random binary strings or a repeating pattern of bits. You need, in addition to this capability, a report when the device is finished to prove that you wiped the drive beforehand. In a lab environment, you usually should have a dedicated device just for wiping your media so that you don't use up valuable forensic tool resources spent wiping drives rather than analyzing evidence.

All the major computer forensic software and hardware manufacturers carry data wiping equipment. Chances are good that, wherever you bought your computer forensic software, you can also purchase a dedicated data wiping unit. Just be wary of third-party data wiping tools that don't have a way to verify the data wipe and don't have a data wipe report function.

Recording equipment

Human perceptions being what they are, having an unbiased way to record events and objects is essential to computer forensic investigators. The choice of which device or devices you ultimately choose is based on your needs, but you must use some form of unbiased documentation method.

Using video or audio equipment to record important aspects of a case is a useful way to permanently record an unbiased view of your case. Using a video camera, you can repeatedly visit a crime scene to look for that single clue you missed. You can document your methods directly by recording your work or even record the output of a computer screen in a pinch. Recording your thoughts in a simple manner is often best accomplished by using a simple digital recorder that essentially acts as your personal note taker!

You can find digital video cameras and audio recorders in any good retail electronics store, such as Best Buy or Radio Shack, and at Internet retailers. The basic models now available are more than enough to document all your case needs, as long as you carry extra batteries and data storage capacity.

Find a digital video camera with low light capabilities, in case you end up on scene in less-than-ideal, camera-ready circumstances.

Glossary

.e01: A proprietary file format that stores the physical bitstream of an acquired hard drive. When evidence is acquired, the MD5 hash value, or MD5, is calculated on the acquired bitstream image and not on the `.e01` file; the bitstream image and MD5 are stored in the .e01 file with the MD5 at the end of the file.

802.11: A set of standards for wireless networks.

acquisition: The creation of an exact physical duplicate of the original. The creation is the forensic copy.

active file: A file that's accessible from normal use of the operating system.

Adam Walsh Child Protection and Safety Act: Legislation that states that in any criminal proceeding, any property or material that constitutes child pornography shall remain in the care, custody, and control of the government or court.

admissible evidence: Relevant evidence presented at trial and allowed by the judge. It's your goal!

alternate data streams (ADS): An uncommon data storage concept that was developed to fix problems with operating system incompatibilities. A clever user can hide nefarious files in ADS because the files don't show up using a `DIR` (directory) command, nor do they appear in Windows Explorer. An ADS scanner is needed to find them.

authenticate: To provide sufficient proof that something is what it claims to be.

authentication: Ensures that the forensic image and the original computer media are identical.

Best Evidence rule: A rule specifying that a party seeking to admit a writing or recording or other content type must submit the original in order to prove its content. For electronic content, any printout or other output that's readable by sight, and shown to reflect the data accurately, is an original.

bit (or *binary digit*): The smallest unit of computer data. A bit consists of either 0 or 1. Eight bits equals 1 byte.

bitstream image: An exact duplicate of the entire hard drive using non-invasive procedures. This read-only evidence file is also called a *sector-by-sector image*.

Bluetooth: A set of standards for short-range wireless connectivity from fixed or mobile devices.

boot sector: The first sector on a hard drive; holds the codes to boot up the computer. It contains the partition table, which describes how the hard drive is organized. Also called *master boot record* or *MBR*.

brute force: A password-cracking technique that tries possible combinations until the right password is found.

cache: (Pronounced "cash") A "closet" that your computer or handheld device uses for storing recent data and passwords that a user has the computer remember in order to avoid having to type them repeatedly. Because the size of cache is capped, individual temporary Internet files are usually created and then discarded on a first-in-first-out basis.

CAM: Abbreviation for create, access, modify; a timestamp of when a file was created, accessed, or modified that helps to track a document and determine a timeline of events. CAM metadata is often part of the circumstantial evidence that helps support other aspects of a case.

case journal: A running list of the analysis you've completed and the results of this analysis.

chain of custody: The care, control, and accountability of evidence at every step of an investigation to verify the integrity of the evidence. The process of validating how the e-evidence was gathered, tracked, and protected on its way to a court of law. If you don't have a chain of custody, you don't have evidence.

chat log: Computer files, usually stored on an individual's computer, that contain the content from online chat sessions. These logs can include the dates and times of communications, file transfers, and the text of the communication.

checksum: The primary method used by all major forensic software packages to perform an integrity check of the acquired e-evidence.

circumstantial evidence: A type of evidence without a witness; can be stronger and more convincing than direct evidence. The evidence shows surrounding circumstances that logically lead to a conclusion of fact about what happened. (E-evidence is circumstantial.) Also called *indirect evidence*. See also ***direct evidence***.

cluster: A group of sectors on a hard drive that represents the smallest amount of data that can be allocated in a file system. Because sectors are at the hardware level and clusters are at the operating system level, techies often refer to sectors as physical address space and to clusters as logical address space. See also *sector*.

compression: A content-altering algorithm applied to data or a message to shrink the size of the file. The result is a file that's unrecognizable from its original form. Compression adds a layer of complexity to forensics, but compressed files aren't themselves suspicious.

computer forensics: A branch of science that deals with circumstantial *(indirect)* evidence found on computers or other digital memory devices.

contraband: Property that's illegal to possess, produce, or distribute.

cookie: A simple text file that collects and stores data about you on the hard drive of your own computer, such as which Web pages you visited.

CRC (Cyclic Redundancy Check): The bitstream image is continually verified by both a CRC value for every 32k block of data and an MD5 hash calculated for all data contained in the image file. Used to check data integrity.

cryptography: The science of writing in secret codes. Encryption is one type of cryptography where readable plain text (data, message, or any type of file) is scrambled by applying an algorithm (the cipher) to it to convert it into unreadable ciphertext.

Daubert test: Primarily a question of relevance or fit of the evidence. In order for testimony to be used, it must be sufficiently tied to the facts of the case to help judges and juries understand the disputed issues.

defendant: The person or party who's accused. The defendant is listed on the right side of the *v.*, as in *Plaintiff v. Defendant.*

defense: The producing party in e-discovery.

delete: To hide a file or its filename. Deleted files are recoverable because a computer system never truly deletes (gets rid of) files.

demonstrative evidence: A type of evidence that's offered to explain or summarize other evidence, but that's not usually admitted into evidence or considered by the jury. Examples are charts and maps and other types of computer-generated evidence.

deposition (or depo): Testimony given under oath in the presence of a court reporter before the trial begins, but not in court. A deposition can be the most painful and mentally exhausting activity you perform during the case.

destination address: The IP address of the destination or recipient's computer. See also *Internet Protocol (IP) address.*

dictionary attack: A trial-and-error password-cracking technique that works remarkably often because of weak passwords. A dictionary of passwords or hashes is compared to the hash value stored on the suspect's password file to look for a match.

direct evidence: Evidence from a witness based on one of the five senses. For example, someone may have seen a person get shot, heard a scream, smelled smoke, or tasted or felt something. See also *circumstantial evidence.*

directory structure: An organization of directories (or folders) and files on a hard drive. The main directory is the *root directory.*

discovery: The pretrial process during which each party has the right to learn about, or discover, as much as possible about the opponent's case.

discovery request: An official request for access to information that may be used as evidence. Also called *production request.*

disk duplicator: A hardware device, such as the Logicube Forensic Talon, that duplicates storage media quickly and forensically at the rate of about 4 gigabytes per minute.

disk partition: A hard drive containing a set of consecutive cylinders. Before files are stored on a disk partition, it must be formatted to create a logical volume. See also *extended partition.*

DIY: *Do-it-yourself.* A DIY-er is an amateur who tinkers around in a computer and damages e-evidence.

DNS (domain name server): A way to translate domain names into IP addresses. Internet traffic depends on the functioning of the DNSs.

document: An original version or a copy of words or information generated by printing, typing, longhand writing, electronic recording, or other process, regardless of the form. Examples include published materials, reports, e-mails, records, memoranda, notices, notes, marginal notations, minutes, diagrams, drawings, maps, surveys, plans, charts, graphs, data, computer files, PDA appointment books, invoices, and performance evaluations.

drive imaging: The forensic capturing of everything on a disk drive.

driver: The program that controls various devices, such as your keyboard or mouse.

e-discovery: A part of the legal system that allows parties involved in a lawsuit to request electronic documents from the opposing party in preparation for trial.

e-discovery extortion: The process of threatening a party with expensive e-discovery to force that party to settle a winnable lawsuit or case.

e-mail: A digital message sent by way of a network. It's the richest source of electronic evidence because a message is typically candid, casual, or careless.

electronic discovery: See **e-discovery**.

electronic evidence (or e-evidence): Evidence in digital or electronic form, such as e-mail, computer files, instant messages, PDA calendars, and Blackberry phone lists. (It's like a vampire lurking out of sight that can neither be destroyed nor intimidated.)

electronically stored information (ESI): Digital content; a term used by the 2006 amendments to the Federal Rules of Civil Procedure.

encryption: The process of scrambling readable plain text (data, a message, or file) by applying an algorithm (the cipher) to it to convert it into unreadable ciphertext. Encrypted files are easy to spot because they usually have common file structures or extensions.

evidence: Proof of a fact about what did or did not happen; material used to persuade the judge or jury of the truth or falsity of a disputed fact. See also *circumstantial evidence* and *direct evidence.*

evidence law: A long list of rules about evidence that have exclusions that have exceptions. *Rules* state which evidence is admissible. See also *exception, exclusion.*

exception: A rule that contradicts exclusions and makes evidence admissible. See also *evidence law, exclusion.*

exclusion: A rule that makes evidence inadmissible. See also *exception.*

exculpatory: A type of evidence which tends to show that a criminal defendant isn't guilty of the charges against him.

extended partition: The fifth or higher-level partition on a hard drive that's divided into more than four partitions. See also *disk partition.*

Facebook: A social network where you might sometimes learn about people (suspects) if they have an account.

FAT (File Allocation Table): A system of keeping track of where files are stored on a hard drive. The FAT system is used by the operating system to locate files within the computer by pointing to the starting cluster of the file. This is the original (and ancient) file system developed by Microsoft to organize data on a storage medium.

Federal Rules of Civil Procedure (Fed. R. Civ. P.): The rules that federal courts use to determine proper procedure for civil cases, including what material is subject to discovery or e-discovery.

Federal Rules of Criminal Procedure: Rules that control the conduct of all criminal proceedings brought in federal courts to ensure that a defendant's rights are protected.

Federal Rules of Evidence (Fed. R. Evid.): The rules that federal courts use to determine what evidence is relevant in civil or criminal cases.

file header: A sequence of characters at the beginning of a file that signifies what type of file it is.

file slack: The space between the logical end of the file and the end of the cluster. See also *slack space.*

fixed storage device: Any device that stores data and is permanently attached to a computer.

forensic copy: A technical term for the end-product of a forensics acquisition of a computer's hard drive or other storage device. See also *bitstream image.*

forensic tool: A type of program that applies computer science operations to establish facts in accordance with legal evidentiary standards.

GIF (Graphic Image File): One of the two most common file formats for graphical images. See also *JPG.*

gigabyte (GB): One thousand megabytes.

hash: A computer-based mathematical process of calculating a unique ID for the target drive to authenticate e-evidence. A *hash value* is calculated for a hard drive at the time it's copied from a computer system. The hash assists in subsequently ensuring that data hasn't been altered or tampered with.

hash algorithm: A way of analyzing a computer drive or file and calculating a unique identifying number for it, called a *hash value.*

hash value: The unique number of a computer file used to detect any manipulation of the data. Also known as the *condensed representation* or *message digest (MD)* of the original.

hashing: The process of using a mathematical algorithm against data to produce a numeric value that's representative of that data. Hashing generates a unique alphanumeric value to identify the combination of bytes that make up a particular computer file, a group of files, or an entire hard drive.

header: Part of the data packet; contains transparent information about the file or the transmission. A file header is a region at the beginning of a file where bookkeeping information is kept; for example, the date the file was created, the date it was last updated, and file size. The header can be accessed only by the operating system or specialized programs.

hearsay: Secondhand evidence. Sometimes it's considered unreliable unless a rule of evidence says that it's reliable. See also *hearsay rule.*

hearsay rule: The rule specifying that hearsay evidence is inadmissible. Thirty exceptions to the rule, however, specify that certain types of hearsay evidence are admissible. Electronic business records are an exception to the hearsay rule, so it may be admissible.

hex editor: A software tool for digging into the structure of file systems and their files. Power users use these tools for deeper analysis, but require a fair amount of knowledge of file structures.

HFS (hierarchical file system): An operating system developed by Apple in the mid-1980s and used until Apple switched its operating system to Mac OS X.

hidden file: A file that's marked as hidden but can still be viewed by selecting the Show Hidden Files and Folders option. Hidden files are no more hidden than deleted files are deleted.

hidden share: A shared area on a network where files are stored but shares are hidden. Tech-savvy criminals can use hidden shares on remote computers rather than risk using their own machines. Finding hidden shares is more difficult than finding hidden files, but if you have the proper software, the process is straightforward.

hive: A logical group of keys, subkeys, and values in a computer's Registry. Also called a *registry hive.*

host: Any computing device attached to a network that has some form of addressing, such as an IP address or a MAC address.

human nature: A concept which stipulates that people usually behave a certain way regardless of the consequences. As it relates to computer forensics, few people use different passwords for all the files or accounts they want to protect; and many people make incriminating statements in e-mail messages. Human nature is important to understand in order to perform well as a computer forensics investigator.

image: A short term for *bitstream image* or *forensic image*. The evidence file created by using forensic software that contains all files from the hard drive or other storage medium.

IMAP (Internet Message Access Protocol): An e-mail system that downloads messages to the local destination without deleting them from the e-mail server until the user deletes them purposely.

index.dat file: A file used by Internet Explorer to create a database of cookies, Web sites visited, and other Web browsing details.

infrared: An older method of wireless communication between mobile devices using the infrared part of the light spectrum.

intake form: An inventory list showing which evidence and equipment was entered into your possession.

Internet Protocol (IP) address: A computer's private number that enables it to communicate with a network. It uniquely identifies a host computer connected to the Internet or another network.

interrogatory: A type of question used to prepare for key witness depositions or to discover facts about an opposing party's case. Interrogatories are part of the pretrial discovery stage of a lawsuit and must be answered. See also *e-discovery.*

intrusion detection system (IDS): Logs every event that's even mildly suspicious on a network for further study to prevent that event from happening again.

intrusion prevention system (IPS): Detects, blocks, and shuts down any perceived threat on the network by analyzing events in *real-time* (as it's happening).

JPG: Stands for Joint Photographic Experts Group, one of the two most common file formats for graphical images. See also *GIF.*

keystroke logger: Software installed manually or by way of a Trojan on a computer to capture passwords or any other content by recording the keys that are pressed. This password-cracking technique resorts to sleuthing — when it's legal to do so, of course.

legal sufficiency: The consideration of evidence in the light most favorable to the prosecution such that any rational fact-finder could have found all essential elements beyond a reasonable doubt. See also *preponderance of the evidence.*

link file: A pointer that's created whenever a file is stored or copied so that the operating system knows where the file is located. The link file is used to establish a trail (or link) from one computing device to another and can show the connection between where the e-evidence was found in relation to where it resided earlier.

Linux/Unix: An operating system that is gaining in popularity and whose smallest unit of storage space is a block.

log: A type of text file that doubles as an audit trail; contains IP addresses and information in the cache.

logical level search: A search of a hard drive that looks at the directory structure on the computer itself; for example, the way that you would search a filing cabinet. An average user can see files in the directory structures and open and view them by clicking on the filename.

magnetic disk drive: a basic digital storage medium.

MAPI (Messaging Application Programming Interface): A proprietary e-mail protocol used by Microsoft to power Microsoft Outlook.

master boot record (MBR): A sector, located in front of the first partition, that contains bootstrap information and unique storage device identifiers. This information can often be used to track USB drives that have been attached to the computer system..

MD5 hash (or MD5 hash value): A way to verify data integrity; a 128-bit number that (like a fingerprint) uniquely identifies the forensics image (evidence file). An MD hash value, for example:

578BCBD1845342C10D9BBD1C23294425

is assigned to the evidence file by the software during acquisition of the hard drive. This verification process prevents the possibility of evidence tampering and provides for a very high degree of data and evidence integrity. It's supposedly computationally infeasible to produce two messages having the same MD5. See also *SHA*.

megabyte (MB): One thousand bytes.

memory card: A digital storage (memory) device. To read this type of memory device, you often have to use a multimedia card reader.

memory storage area: A storage area on a mobile device that exists only as long as the device has power.

metadata: Data describing a file or its properties, such as creation date, author, or last access date. Invisible information that programs such as Microsoft Word, Excel, and Outlook attach to each file or e-mail. A good source of e-evidence about who created a file and when — just in case someone is trying to hide the truth. Even hidden files have metadata.

motion: A formal request to a judge to make a legal ruling. This tool is used by either side in an effort to define the boundaries of the case.

motion in limine: A request that the court limit the evidence at trial or rule that certain evidence cannot be used.

Motor Vehicle Event Data Recorder (MVEDR): A vehicle's black box that records data before and after an accident.

network interface card (NIC): A device that holds a computer's MAC (Media Access Control) address, which uniquely identifies it to a network. It's similar to a computer's phone number.

NTFS (New Technology File System): A more sophisticated operating system than FAT, created by Microsoft in 1993.

operating system (OS): A master control program that runs a computer; provides an interface between hardware and software. Examples are Windows, DOS, MacOS, Unix, and Linux.

original: For data stored in a computer or similar device, any printout or other output that's readable by sight, shown to reflect the data accurately.

partition: A logical division (or a logical volume) of a physical storage device that acts as a file organization method.

payload: The data or message in a packet.

perjury: The crime of lying under oath.

permission: What you always need to obtain from the owner or person in authority before investigating.

petabyte (PT): One thousand terabytes.

PGP (Pretty Good Privacy): A heavily armored encryption algorithm.

physical-level search: A type of search performed by a software program to find and recover remnants of files that were overwritten or deleted from the hard drive. The program searches everything on the drive rather than simply search the computer's directories (folders).

plaintiff: The party bringing the charge; the requesting party in e-discovery. See also *defendant.*

POP (Post Office Protocol): The language an e-mail system uses to retrieve messages from an e-mail server. After POP retrieves a message, it deletes the original message from the server and downloads a copy to the destination computer.

portable storage device: Any device that stores data and can be carried, such as a flash drive, an iPod, an MP3 player, or a mobile phone.

preponderance of the evidence: The standard of proof that must be established to win a civil case. This standard is met when a party's evidence indicates that it's "more likely than not" that the fact is as the party alleges it to be. See also *legal sufficiency.*

preservation: Protection from destruction and alteration.

pretrial: The extremely busy period before trial begins — when every legal, technical, and constitutional issue can get scrutinized to try to get the case resolved.

privilege: Material or electronic communications protected from being used as evidence.

probable cause: The reasonable basis to believe that a defendant has committed a wrong or is guilty of the crime charged. Prevents fishing expeditions for evidence.

probative value: A standard by which evidence is judged. It's a characteristic of evidence that's sufficiently useful to prove something worthwhile in a trial.

rainbow table: A password-cracking technique that uses huge hash databases of possibilities. They're typically stored on the Internet because of their large size.

RAM (random access memory): A computer's short-term memory. Provides memory space for the computer to work with data. Information stored in RAM is lost when the computer is turned off.

RCFL (regional computer forensics lab): The FBI's full-service forensics laboratory and training center for examination of digital evidence in support of criminal investigations. At least 14 RCFLs exist across the United States.

Registry: A Microsoft Windows database in which applications and system components store and retrieve configuration data. Data stored in the Registry varies according to the version of Windows. The Registry has evolved over the course of 20 years into a complex database that tracks almost everything that's done on the computer and keeps all configuration settings up-to-date.

RFID (radio frequency identification): A tracking technology designed to leave a digital trail.

router: A special-purpose computer that uses IP addresses to move data across networks.

Rule 16 pretrial conference: Requires opposing parties to meet and discuss a discovery plan and evaluate the protection and production of electronically submitted information. See also *electronically stored information (ESI).*

Rule 26: Each company has the duty to preserve documents that may be relevant in a case.

Rule 26(a): The initial disclosure of sources of discoverable information. Parties must identify all sources of ESI that may be relevant by category and location.

Rule 34: E-records and communications are subject to subpoena and discovery for use in legal proceedings.

Rule 702: The Federal Rule of Evidence governs the admissibility of expert testimony. The witness must be qualified as an expert in order to be allowed to provide testimony.

rules of evidence: Rules that control which material the judge and jury can consider (what's in) and cannot consider (what's out).

sector: A group of bytes on any given track of a hard drive's platters. It's the smallest unit of storage on a storage medium and, therefore, the smallest area of information that can be accessed on the drive. See also *cluster.*

SHA (secure hash algorithm): An algorithm for computing a condensed representation of a message or data file. The condensed representation is of fixed length and is known as a message digest (MD) or fingerprint. It's similar to a human fingerprint in that it uniquely identifies the forensics image (evidence file). Either SHA or MD5 is used to verify the evidence file. If the hash values of the forensic image and the original match, there's no way the that data could have been modified through the normal course of your investigation. See also *MD5 hash.*

SIM (Subscriber Identity Module) card: A portable memory chip, used in some cellular telephone models, that holds the user's identity information, cell number, phone book, text messages, and other data.

slack space (or file slack): Unused space on a cluster that exists when the logical file space is less than the physical file space. May hold the content of files that previously occupied this space.

SMTP (Simple Mail Transfer Protocol): The language used in an e-mail system to send messages to an e-mail server. SMTP pushes (delivers) the messages to e-mail servers.

snooper: A type of software that logs not only keystrokes but also almost any activity that occurs on the computer, including screen shots, printouts, chat sessions, e-mails, and even the number of times the computer was turned on.

source address: IP address of the originating or sender's computer, unless that IP address has been disguised. See also *Internet Protocol (IP) address.*

spoliation: The destruction of evidence. It's a crime because it's an obstruction of justice.

steganography (or stego): A system of hiding files within other files using one of many algorithms, which require stego-detecting software to extract (if the extraction is possible). Stego refers to covered writing, such as invisible ink. In the digital world, this technique involves hiding a message inside an innocuous image, music file, or video that's posted on a Web site, e-mailed, or stored on a hard drive.

subpoena: A writ commanding a person designated in it to appear in court or face a penalty for not showing up.

subpoena ad testificandum: A writ commanding a person to appear in court to testify as a witness.

subpoena duces tecum: A writ commanding a person to produce in court certain designated documents or evidence.

subscriber identifier: Information used by the mobile phone network to authenticate the user to the network and verify the services tied to the account.

swap file: An operating system function that acts like RAM but uses the hard drive or storage device rather than memory microchips. If an application needs the data, the operating system retrieves it from the swap file and deletes the data from the storage device. Because the swap file is written and then deleted, the information is still physically on the storage device and can be retrieved.

switch: A network component that uses the Media Access Control (MAC) identification of a host computer on a network to move traffic within a network.

temporary file (or temp file): A file type, commonly created by Internet browsers, that is stored for only temporary use. Temp files store information about Web sites a user visited. Forensic techniques can be used to track the history of a computer's Internet usage through the examination of temporary files.

terabyte (TB): One thousand gigabytes.

triers of fact: Judges and juries.

unallocated space: The space created when a file is deleted that can be reused to store new information. Until unallocated space is used for new data storage, in most instances, the old data remains and can be retrieved by using forensic techniques.

virtual memory: A type of memory in which a file of adjustable size temporarily stores "imaginary" memory. The file can be written and deleted like any other file on an operating system.

volume: A specific amount of storage space on hard drives, CDs, and disks. In some instances, computer media may contain more than one volume, whereas in other cases, one volume may be contained on more than one disk.

weakest link: Typically, the human link.

wiping software: Software used on storage media to ensure that no cross contamination of cases or evidence occurs. Failing to wipe all storage media, including brand-new media, dooms the investigation and your credibility.

write blocker (protector): Hardware or software that protects the original evidence while creating a forensics copy. Devices such as the Weibetech Forensic Ultradock keep you from accidentally writing to storage devices during a preview or acquisition from a suspect's media. Don't copy without it. Also called a *write protector.*

write protection: An operation that allows data to be written onto a disk or other storage device just one time. After that, the data is permanent and can be read any number of times.

Index

• D •

• E •

● *F* ●

• S •

• Y •

• Z •

BUSINESS, CAREERS & PERSONAL FINANCE

Accounting For Dummies, 4th Edition*
978-0-470-24600-9

Bookkeeping Workbook For Dummies†
978-0-470-16983-4

Commodities For Dummies
978-0-470-04928-0

Doing Business in China For Dummies
978-0-470-04929-7

E-Mail Marketing For Dummies
978-0-470-19087-6

Job Interviews For Dummies, 3rd Edition*†
978-0-470-17748-8

Personal Finance Workbook For Dummies*†
978-0-470-09933-9

Real Estate License Exams For Dummies
978-0-7645-7623-2

Six Sigma For Dummies
978-0-7645-6798-8

Small Business Kit For Dummies, 2nd Edition*†
978-0-7645-5984-6

Telephone Sales For Dummies
978-0-470-16836-3

BUSINESS PRODUCTIVITY & MICROSOFT OFFICE

Access 2007 For Dummies
978-0-470-03649-5

Excel 2007 For Dummies
978-0-470-03737-9

Office 2007 For Dummies
978-0-470-00923-9

Outlook 2007 For Dummies
978-0-470-03830-7

PowerPoint 2007 For Dummies
978-0-470-04059-1

Project 2007 For Dummies
978-0-470-03651-8

QuickBooks 2008 For Dummies
978-0-470-18470-7

Quicken 2008 For Dummies
978-0-470-17473-9

Salesforce.com For Dummies, 2nd Edition
978-0-470-04893-1

Word 2007 For Dummies
978-0-470-03658-7

EDUCATION, HISTORY, REFERENCE & TEST PREPARATION

African American History For Dummies
978-0-7645-5469-8

Algebra For Dummies
978-0-7645-5325-7

Algebra Workbook For Dummies
978-0-7645-8467-1

Art History For Dummies
978-0-470-09910-0

ASVAB For Dummies, 2nd Edition
978-0-470-10671-6

British Military History For Dummies
978-0-470-03213-8

Calculus For Dummies
978-0-7645-2498-1

Canadian History For Dummies, 2nd Edition
978-0-470-83656-9

Geometry Workbook For Dummies
978-0-471-79940-5

The SAT I For Dummies, 6th Edition
978-0-7645-7193-0

Series 7 Exam For Dummies
978-0-470-09932-2

World History For Dummies
978-0-7645-5242-7

FOOD, GARDEN, HOBBIES & HOME

Bridge For Dummies, 2nd Edition
978-0-471-92426-5

Coin Collecting For Dummies, 2nd Edition
978-0-470-22275-1

Cooking Basics For Dummies, 3rd Edition
978-0-7645-7206-7

Drawing For Dummies
978-0-7645-5476-6

Etiquette For Dummies, 2nd Edition
978-0-470-10672-3

Gardening Basics For Dummies*†
978-0-470-03749-2

Knitting Patterns For Dummies
978-0-470-04556-5

Living Gluten-Free For Dummies†
978-0-471-77383-2

Painting Do-It-Yourself For Dummies
978-0-470-17533-0

HEALTH, SELF HELP, PARENTING & PETS

Anger Management For Dummies
978-0-470-03715-7

Anxiety & Depression Workbook For Dummies
978-0-7645-9793-0

Dieting For Dummies, 2nd Edition
978-0-7645-4149-0

Dog Training For Dummies, 2nd Edition
978-0-7645-8418-3

Horseback Riding For Dummies
978-0-470-09719-9

Infertility For Dummies†
978-0-470-11518-3

Meditation For Dummies with CD-ROM, 2nd Edition
978-0-471-77774-8

Post-Traumatic Stress Disorder For Dummies
978-0-470-04922-8

Puppies For Dummies, 2nd Edition
978-0-470-03717-1

Thyroid For Dummies, 2nd Edition†
978-0-471-78755-6

Type 1 Diabetes For Dummies*†
978-0-470-17811-9

---

* Separate Canadian edition also available
† Separate U.K. edition also available

Available wherever books are sold. For more information or to order direct: U.S. customers visit www.dummies.com or call 1-877-762-2974.
U.K. customers visit www.wileyeurope.com or call (0)1243 843291. Canadian customers visit www.wiley.ca or call 1-800-567-4797.

INTERNET & DIGITAL MEDIA

AdWords For Dummies
978-0-470-15252-2

Blogging For Dummies, 2nd Edition
978-0-470-23017-6

**Digital Photography All-in-One
Desk Reference For Dummies, 3rd Edition**
978-0-470-03743-0

Digital Photography For Dummies, 5th Edition
978-0-7645-9802-9

**Digital SLR Cameras & Photography
For Dummies, 2nd Edition**
978-0-470-14927-0

**eBay Business All-in-One Desk Reference
For Dummies**
978-0-7645-8438-1

eBay For Dummies, 5th Edition*
978-0-470-04529-9

eBay Listings That Sell For Dummies
978-0-471-78912-3

Facebook For Dummies
978-0-470-26273-3

The Internet For Dummies, 11th Edition
978-0-470-12174-0

Investing Online For Dummies, 5th Edition
978-0-7645-8456-5

iPod & iTunes For Dummies, 5th Edition
978-0-470-17474-6

MySpace For Dummies
978-0-470-09529-4

Podcasting For Dummies
978-0-471-74898-4

**Search Engine Optimization
For Dummies, 2nd Edition**
978-0-471-97998-2

Second Life For Dummies
978-0-470-18025-9

**Starting an eBay Business For Dummies,
3rd Edition†**
978-0-470-14924-9

GRAPHICS, DESIGN & WEB DEVELOPMENT

**Adobe Creative Suite 3 Design Premium
All-in-One Desk Reference For Dummies**
978-0-470-11724-8

**Adobe Web Suite CS3 All-in-One Desk
Reference For Dummies**
978-0-470-12099-6

AutoCAD 2008 For Dummies
978-0-470-11650-0

**Building a Web Site For Dummies,
3rd Edition**
978-0-470-14928-7

**Creating Web Pages All-in-One Desk
Reference For Dummies, 3rd Edition**
978-0-470-09629-1

**Creating Web Pages For Dummies,
8th Edition**
978-0-470-08030-6

Dreamweaver CS3 For Dummies
978-0-470-11490-2

Flash CS3 For Dummies
978-0-470-12100-9

Google SketchUp For Dummies
978-0-470-13744-4

InDesign CS3 For Dummies
978-0-470-11865-8

**Photoshop CS3 All-in-One
Desk Reference For Dummies**
978-0-470-11195-6

Photoshop CS3 For Dummies
978-0-470-11193-2

Photoshop Elements 5 For Dummies
978-0-470-09810-3

SolidWorks For Dummies
978-0-7645-9555-4

Visio 2007 For Dummies
978-0-470-08983-5

Web Design For Dummies, 2nd Edition
978-0-471-78117-2

Web Sites Do-It-Yourself For Dummies
978-0-470-16903-2

Web Stores Do-It-Yourself For Dummies
978-0-470-17443-2

LANGUAGES, RELIGION & SPIRITUALITY

Arabic For Dummies
978-0-471-77270-5

Chinese For Dummies, Audio Set
978-0-470-12766-7

French For Dummies
978-0-7645-5193-2

German For Dummies
978-0-7645-5195-6

Hebrew For Dummies
978-0-7645-5489-6

Ingles Para Dummies
978-0-7645-5427-8

Italian For Dummies, Audio Set
978-0-470-09586-7

Italian Verbs For Dummies
978-0-471-77389-4

Japanese For Dummies
978-0-7645-5429-2

Latin For Dummies
978-0-7645-5431-5

Portuguese For Dummies
978-0-471-78738-9

Russian For Dummies
978-0-471-78001-4

Spanish Phrases For Dummies
978-0-7645-7204-3

Spanish For Dummies
978-0-7645-5194-9

Spanish For Dummies, Audio Set
978-0-470-09585-0

The Bible For Dummies
978-0-7645-5296-0

Catholicism For Dummies
978-0-7645-5391-2

The Historical Jesus For Dummies
978-0-470-16785-4

Islam For Dummies
978-0-7645-5503-9

**Spirituality For Dummies,
2nd Edition**
978-0-470-19142-2

NETWORKING AND PROGRAMMING

ASP.NET 3.5 For Dummies
978-0-470-19592-5

C# 2008 For Dummies
978-0-470-19109-5

Hacking For Dummies, 2nd Edition
978-0-470-05235-8

Home Networking For Dummies, 4th Edition
978-0-470-11806-1

Java For Dummies, 4th Edition
978-0-470-08716-9

**Microsoft® SQL Server™ 2008 All-in-One
Desk Reference For Dummies**
978-0-470-17954-3

**Networking All-in-One Desk Reference
For Dummies, 2nd Edition**
978-0-7645-9939-2

**Networking For Dummies,
8th Edition**
978-0-470-05620-2

SharePoint 2007 For Dummies
978-0-470-09941-4

**Wireless Home Networking
For Dummies, 2nd Edition**
978-0-471-74940-0

OPERATING SYSTEMS & COMPUTER BASICS

iMac For Dummies, 5th Edition
978-0-7645-8458-9

Laptops For Dummies, 2nd Edition
978-0-470-05432-1

Linux For Dummies, 8th Edition
978-0-470-11649-4

MacBook For Dummies
978-0-470-04859-7

Mac OS X Leopard All-in-One Desk Reference For Dummies
978-0-470-05434-5

Mac OS X Leopard For Dummies
978-0-470-05433-8

Macs For Dummies, 9th Edition
978-0-470-04849-8

PCs For Dummies, 11th Edition
978-0-470-13728-4

Windows® Home Server For Dummies
978-0-470-18592-6

Windows Server 2008 For Dummies
978-0-470-18043-3

Windows Vista All-in-One Desk Reference For Dummies
978-0-471-74941-7

Windows Vista For Dummies
978-0-471-75421-3

Windows Vista Security For Dummies
978-0-470-11805-4

SPORTS, FITNESS & MUSIC

Coaching Hockey For Dummies
978-0-470-83685-9

Coaching Soccer For Dummies
978-0-471-77381-8

Fitness For Dummies, 3rd Edition
978-0-7645-7851-9

Football For Dummies, 3rd Edition
978-0-470-12536-6

GarageBand For Dummies
978-0-7645-7323-1

Golf For Dummies, 3rd Edition
978-0-471-76871-5

Guitar For Dummies, 2nd Edition
978-0-7645-9904-0

Home Recording For Musicians For Dummies, 2nd Edition
978-0-7645-8884-6

iPod & iTunes For Dummies, 5th Edition
978-0-470-17474-6

Music Theory For Dummies
978-0-7645-7838-0

Stretching For Dummies
978-0-470-06741-3

Get smart @ dummies.com®

- **Find a full list of Dummies titles**
- **Look into loads of FREE on-site articles**
- **Sign up for FREE eTips e-mailed to you weekly**
- **See what other products carry the Dummies name**
- **Shop directly from the Dummies bookstore**
- **Enter to win new prizes every month!**

* Separate Canadian edition also available

† Separate U.K. edition also available

Available wherever books are sold. For more information or to order direct: U.S. customers visit www.dummies.com or call 1-877-762-2974.
U.K. customers visit www.wileyeurope.com or call (0) 1243 843291. Canadian customers visit www.wiley.ca or call 1-800-567-4797.